Donated ✓

P9-CLP-956

27,030

BR
1720
.P26
P38
1983

Patrick

DATE DUE

DE 9 '96			

Patrick: sixteen centuries with Ireland
BR1720.P26P38 19   27030

Proudfoot, Alice-Boyd
VRJC/WRIGHT LIBRARY

*Donated
by*

Mrs. C. L. Henderson

Vernon Regional
Junior College Library

PATRICK

★ Prehistoric sites and find-places

● Early Christian sites and find-places

CARNDONAGH

FAHAN MURA

BROIGHTER

DERRY

MOYLARG

ANTRIM

WOODLANDS

DOOEY

DONEGAL

CASTLEDERG

TYRONE

BELFAST

KILLYLEAGH

BOA ISLAND

ARMAGH

NAVAN FORT

TEDAVNET

DOWN

FERMANAGH

ARMAGH

DRUMCLIFF

SLIGO

CARROWNANTY

CULLARD

LEITRIM

CAVAN

CLONES

MONAGHAN

LOUTH

MOYLOUGH

RATHTINAUN

KESHCARRIGAN

CORLECK

CLOONLARA

ROSCOMMON

DRIMNAGH

RALAGHAN

KILLARY

MONASTERBOICE

MAYO

CASTLEREA

LONGFORD

KELLS

BETTYSTOWN

DULEEK

BALLINCHALLA

ARDAKILLIN

LOUGHCREW

NEWGRANGE

CONG

CASTLESTRANGE

CLOONBRIN

WESTMEATH

NAVAN

FOURKNOCKS

ST.JOHN'S

ROSS

TARA

CASTLEKELLY

MULLINGAR

LAGORE

GALWAY

ATTYMON

ATHLONE

BALLINDERRY

MEATH

DUBLIN

SOMERSET

DURROW

KILMAINHAM

GREENHILLS

TUROE

CLONMACNOISE

ARAN ISLANDS

CLONFERT

OFFALY

KILDARE

GLENINSHEEN

DERRINBOY

LAOIS

WICKLOW

MOONE

GLENDALOUGH

DYSERT O'DEA

SHINRONE

ROSCREA

CASTLEDERMOT

GORTEENREAGH

CLARE

AGHABOE

MAGANEY

DERREEN

MOOGHAUN

TIPPERARY

KILKENNY

CARLOW

BALLYCONNELL

BAGENALSTOWN

HOLYCROSS

ARDAGH

LOUGH GUR

KILLAMERY

KILREE

LIMERICK

CASHEL

WEXFORD

KILGULBIN

AHENNY

TULLYLEASE

WATERFORD

GALLARUS

AGLISH

LISMORE

KILMALKEDAR

BALLYNACOURTY

KERRY

ARDMORE

CORK

SKELLIG

CLOYNE

PATRICK

*Sixteen Centuries with
Ireland's Patron Saint*

COMPILED AND EDITED BY
ALICE-BOYD PROUDFOOT

MACMILLAN PUBLISHING CO., INC., New York
COLLIER MACMILLAN PUBLISHERS, London

VERNON REGIONAL
JUNIOR COLLEGE LIBRARY

Copyright © 1983 by Alice-Boyd Proudfoot

All rights reserved. No part of this book may be reproduced or transmitted in any form or by any means, electronic or mechanical, including photocopying, recording or by any information storage and retrieval system, without permission in writing from the Publisher.

Macmillan Publishing Co., Inc.
866 Third Avenue, New York, N.Y. 10022
Collier Macmillan Canada, Inc.

Library of Congress Cataloging in Publication Data
Main entry under title:
Patrick: sixteen centuries with Ireland's patron saint.
Bibliography: p.
1. Patrick, Saint, 373?–463? 2. Christian
saints—Ireland—Biography.   3. Patrick, Saint,
373?–463?—Cult.   I. Proudfoot, Alice-Boyd.
BR1720.P26P38   1983   270.2′092′4 [B]   82–16189
ISBN 0–02–599280–5

10 9 8 7 6 5 4 3 2 1

Text design by Antler & Baldwin, Inc.

PRINTED IN THE UNITED STATES OF AMERICA

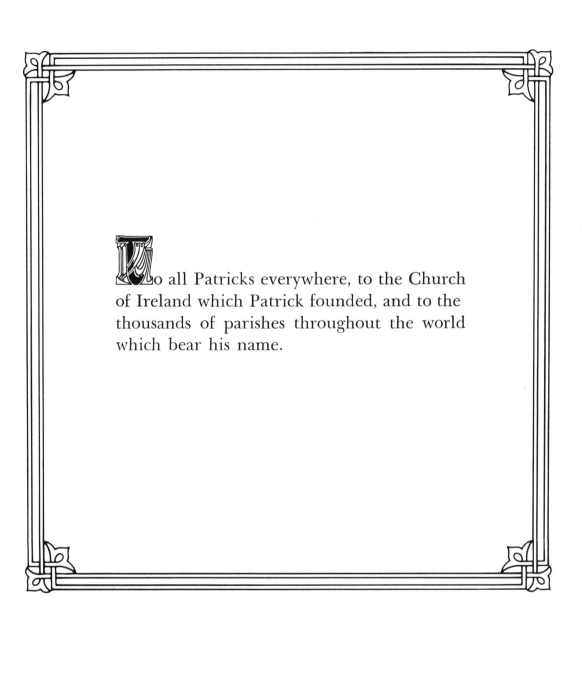

To all Patricks everywhere, to the Church of Ireland which Patrick founded, and to the thousands of parishes throughout the world which bear his name.

CONTENTS

Chapter 10   THE PROLIFERATION OF PATRICK   156

Chapter 11   PATRICK IN MODERN IRELAND   170

Chapter 12   THE AMERICANIZATION OF PATRICK   186

EPILOGUE   201

PREFACE

IF God were to make a list of his best salesmen, Patrick might well take top honors for aggressiveness and effectiveness. March 17—Saint Patrick's Day—brings out the Irish in everybody, even those without a drop of Irish blood in their veins!

There is probably no other saint whose feast day is so widely observed, often to extremes, as Saint Patrick's. Why is there not a Saint Francis Day Parade? A Saint Christopher's Day Parade? Why a Saint Patrick's Day Parade? What is there about Patrick that has not only endured but has proliferated for almost sixteen hundred years?

It is as if Ireland were *waiting* for him when he arrived in 432 to begin his passionate mission of converting pagans to Christianity. As a result of his remorseless energy and spiritual capacity he left an astonishing legacy: a multitude of people who confess Jesus Christ as their savior. In thirty years he changed the face of a nation and, in doing so, forever changed the destiny of that nation. And also the world.

And yet it is Americans who seem to think that it is for them alone that Saint Patrick hops over from Ireland every March 17 (with brief stopovers in Boston and Chicago) and triumphantly marches up Fifth Avenue, tying the City in green knots and inciting many of the half million frolickers to what Terence Cardinal Cooke calls "outrageous public behavior."

They are largely unaware that the saint's feast day is also being celebrated in such diverse places as the Pacific Islands, Canada, Europe, India, Africa, Australia, New Zealand, and China.

For all the distinction accorded this giant among men, few of his admirers can recount his life history or comment on his accomplishments. Most don't know that Patrick wasn't even Irish! If asked what Saint Patrick *did*, they'd probably reply, "He chased the snakes out of Ireland!"

The purpose of this book is to introduce the Saint Patrick's Day wayfarer to the fascinating life and influence of the man embraced by millions of one-day revelers and by the ever-faithful, a man whose 1,600th birthday will be celebrated in 1989. And yet, instead of contemplating how *long ago* he lived—having been born 389 years after Christ—let us visualize him stroking his beard, eyes blazing, pronouncing, "*Deo gratias,* there will be followers of Christ for a millennium and beyond—beyond!"

I am grateful to Father James B. Simpson, director of the Episcopal Book Club, for suggesting that my love for Ireland be translated into an anthology of Patricana. Family friendship with Father Simpson dates back to his visits with us in Dublin, where my late husband, Grant Stockdale, served as President Kennedy's first ambassador to Ireland. May he and all readers find the book to be revealing and even surprising.

—Alice-Boyd Proudfoot
Bronxville, N.Y.
1982

PATRICK

1 Ireland Before Patrick

BRONZE-AGE SETTLEMENTS

Very few Bronze-Age settlements are known in Ireland. But one unusual form of habitation which began to become popular towards the close of the period around 800 B.C. was the lake dwelling known as a crannóg, called after the Irish word for a tree. It was an artificial mound made up of branches, brushwood, earth and stone, located in the middle of or near the edge of a lake. Time and water have largely eroded Ireland's ancient crannógs, but at Craggaunowen in Co. Clare a recently completed reconstruction helps to give us a good idea of what these lake dwellings may have looked like in the Bronze Age. It ought to be said, however, that the majority of Irish crannógs probably date from the Christian period.

—Peter Harbison

EARLY IRELAND: 160–529

THE Irish believe—and we cannot gainsay them—that their island of "mists and mellow fruitfulness" was first peopled by Greeks and Scythians a thousand or more years before Christ, and that their early chieftains —Cuchalain, Conor, Conall—were sons of God. Himilco, the Phoeni-

An ancient crannóg at Craggaunowen, Co. Clare, as reconstructed by the Shannon Development Corporation

cian explorer, touched Ireland about 510 B.C., and described it as "populous and fertile." Perhaps in the fifth century before Christ some Celtic adventurers from Gaul or Britain or both crossed into Ireland, and conquered the natives, of whom we know nothing. The Celts apparently brought with them the iron culture of Hallstatt, and a strong kinship organization that made the individual too proud of his clan to let him form a stable state. Clan fought clan, kingdom fought kingdom, for a thousand years; between such wars the members of a clan fought one another; and when they died, good Irishmen, before St. Patrick came, were buried upright ready for battle, with faces turned toward their foes. Most of the kings died in battle, or by assassination. Perhaps out of eugenic obligation, perhaps as vicars of gods who required first fruits, these ancient kings, according to Irish tradition, had the right to deflower every bride before yielding her to her husband. King Conchobar was praised for his especial devotion to this duty. Each clan kept a record of its members and their genealogy, its kings and battles and antiquities, "from the beginning of the world."

The Celts established themselves as a ruling class, and distributed their clans in five kingdoms: Ulster, North Leinster, South Leinster,

Munster, Connaught. Each of the five kings was sovereign, but all the clans accepted Tara, in Meath, as the national capital. There each king was crowned; and there, at the outset of his reign, he convened the Feis or convention of the notables of all Ireland to pass legislation binding on all the kingdoms, to correct and record the clan genealogies, and to register these in the national archives. To house this assembly King Cormac mac Airt, in the third century, built a great hall, whose foundations can still be seen. A provincial council—the Aonach, or Fair—met annually or triennially in the capital of each kingdom, legislated for its area, imposed taxes, and served as a district court. Games and contests followed these conventions: music, song, jugglery, farces, story-telling, poetry recitals, and many marriages brightened the occasion, and a large part of the population shared in the festivity. From this distance, which lends enchantment to the view, such a reconciliation of central government and local freedom seems almost ideal. The Feis continued till 560; the Aonach till 1168.

The first character whom we may confidently count as historical is Tuathal, who ruled Leinster and Meath about A.D. 160. King Niall (c. 358) invaded Wales and carried off immense booty, raided Gaul, and was killed (by an Irishman) on the river Loire; from him descended most of the later Irish kings (O'Neills). In the fifth year of the reign of his son Laeghaire (Leary), St. Patrick came to Ireland. Before this time the Irish had developed an alphabet of straight lines in various combinations; they had an extensive literature of poetry and legend, transmitted orally; and they had done good work in pottery, bronze, and gold. Their religion was an animistic polytheism, which worshiped sun and moon and divers natural objects, and peopled a thousand spots in Ireland with fairies, demons, and elves. A priestly clan of white-robed druids practiced divination, ruled sun and winds with magic wands and wheels, caused magic showers and fires, memorized and handed down the chronicles and poetry of the tribe, studied the stars, educated the young, counseled the kings, acted as judges, formulated laws, and sacrificed to the gods from altars in the open air. Among the sacred idols was a gold-covered image called the Crom Cruach; this was the god of all the Irish clans; to him, apparently, sacrifice was offered of the firstborn child in every family—perhaps as a check on excessive population. The people believed in reincarnation, but they also dreamed of a heavenly isle across the sea, "where there is no wailing or treachery, nothing rough or harsh, but sweet music striking upon the ear; a beauty of a wondrous land, whose view is a fair country, incomparable in its haze." A story told how Prince Conall, moved by such descriptions, embarked in a boat of pearl and set out to find this happy land.

Christianity had come to Ireland a generation or more before Patrick. An old chronicle, confirmed by Bede, writes, under the year

Two-faced stone figure, presumably representing two Celtic deities, Boa Island, Co. Fermanagh, first century B.C.

431: "Palladius is ordained by Pope Celestine, and is sent as their first bishop to the Irish believers in Christ." Palladius, however, died within the year, and the honor of making Ireland unalterably Catholic fell to her patron saint.

—Will Durant

IRELAND **is a country in which prehistoric and historic monuments are not mere antiquities stored in the silence of the museum, but are embedded in the landscape and remain in intimate touch with the people of today. We shall never forget that white-headed peasant at Malinmore, in Donegal, who took us with eager pride to the huge dolmen in his meadow and almost invited us to say how beautiful it was.**

—Douglas J. Gillam

ANCIENT RECIPES

SALMON *Salmon has long been prized in Ireland: it features in myth and legend, notably Fionn MacCumaill (Finn MacCool) and the salmon which had eaten the hazelnuts from the Tree of Knowledge and thus gave that knowledge to the first person who tasted it when cooked.* It was the pièce de resistance at banquets given by the kings of Ireland, when it was cooked on a spit, after being rubbed with salt and basted with butter and honey.*

Baked Salmon with Cream and Cucumber

1 5-lb. salmon	½ pt. (1 cup) cream
3 heaped tablesp. butter	juice of 1 lemon
1 medium-sized cucumber	2 sprigs of parsley
salt and pepper	

Put the parsley in the cleaned gullet of the fish and rub the butter over the outside. Put the whole into a fireproof baking dish, season well and pour the cream around. Cover with foil and bake in a moderate oven (350° F. electric; gas regulo 4) for 10 minutes to the pound. Remove from the oven and add the peeled and cubed cucumber and the lemon juice. Baste well and put back in the oven, uncovered, for a further 15 minutes. Skin the fish before serving and pour over the sauce. The cucumber should still be a little crisp to act as a foil for the buttery salmon. It is excellent hot, but can also be served cold. Small cuts can be cooked in the same way, but should be left whole: a tail end is good for this method.

—Theodora FitzGibbon

COLCANNON *Traditionally eaten in Ireland at Hallowe'en or All Hallows' Day on 31st October, the vigil of Hallowmas or All Saints' Day.*

---

* Grilled salmon steaks served with cold butter pats mixed with pounded grilled hazelnuts is a discovery which links the past with the present.

It is thought originally to have been a Druidic festival, and the two chief characteristics of ancient Hallowe'en were the lighting of bonfires to honour the Sun God in thanksgiving for the harvest and the belief that it was the one night in the year during which ghosts and witches were most likely to walk abroad. It was also a Druidic belief that Saman, the Lord of Death, summoned together the evil souls that had been condemned to inhabit the bodies of animals. Indeed in parts of Ireland it is known in Irish as Oiche Shamhna, *"the vigil of Saman." From this name also comes "sowans"; the inner husks of oats after winnowing and threshing, which are allowed to ferment in salted water, drained, and the liquid is boiled up and eaten like porridge.*

Colcannon should correctly be made with kale, but is more often made with cabbage. A plain gold ring, a sixpence, a thimble or a button are often put into the mixture. The ring means you will be married within a year; the sixpence denotes wealth, the thimble a spinster and the button a bachelor, to whoever gets them.

1 lb. each of kale or cabbage, and potatoes, cooked separately	1 cup milk or cream
	4 oz. (½ cup) approx. butter
2 small leeks or green onion tops	salt, pepper and a pinch of mace

Have the kale or cabbage cooked, warm and well chopped up while the potatoes are cooking. Chop up the leeks or onion tops, green as well as white, and simmer them in milk or cream to just cover, until they are soft. Drain the potatoes, season and beat them well: then add the cooked leeks and milk.

Finally blend in the kale, beating until it is a pale green fluff. Do this over a low flame and pile it into a deep warmed dish. Make a well in the centre and pour in enough melted butter to fill up the cavity. The vegetables are served with spoonfuls of the melted butter. Any leftovers can be fried in hot bacon fat until crisp and brown on both sides.

—Theodora FitzGibbon

THE CELTS*

Long, long ago beyond the misty space
Of twice a thousand years,
In Erin old there dwelt a mighty race,
Taller than Roman spears;

* Selected verses.

Like oaks and towers they had a giant grace,
 Were fleet as deers,
With winds and waves they made their 'biding place,
 These western shepherd seers.

The Druid's altar and the Druid's creed
 We scarce can trace.
There is not left an undisputed deed
 Of all your race,
Save your majestic song,* which hath their speed,
 And strength, and grace;
In that sole song, they live and love, and bleed—
 It bears them on thro' space.

      —*Thomas D'Arcy McGee*

GOLD COLLAR

It was probably not until the last three centuries before Christ that iron began to replace bronze as the main material with which implements and weapons were made, and it is only then that we can truly speak of a prehistoric Iron Age in Ireland. In contrast to the Bronze Age with its thousands of axes and weapons, we know comparatively few bronze and gold objects which can be assigned to the Iron Age. However, among the few that we do know of, we find a number of beautifully decorated pieces carefully wrought by the hands of bronzesmiths and goldsmiths. One of the most handsome and artistic is the torque or neck ring which was found with a number of other interesting items at the end of the last century at Broighter in Co. Derry. It is made of tubular sheet gold, and has a very advanced construction to enable the two ends to be joined together. The tubular part of the ring is decorated with designs in raised relief, consisting of snail-like whorls from which a number of swelling lines emanate in a never-ending variety of tendrils. These are typical of the so-called La Tène style, the art style *par excellence* of the Celts, which developed on the Continent around the fifth century B.C. and later spread to Britain and Ireland.

      —Peter Harbison

The Destruction of Ancient Records
(Even Saint Patrick Was Guilty)

IT must be particularly lamented that much of the primitive state of Ireland and many of the transactions which occurred in it, previously to the introduction of Christianity, are wrapped up in a veil of almost impenetrable obscurity, and that the most laborious researches frequently terminate in little more than ingenious conjectures. The causes to which

---

* Refers to Ossian, the poet.

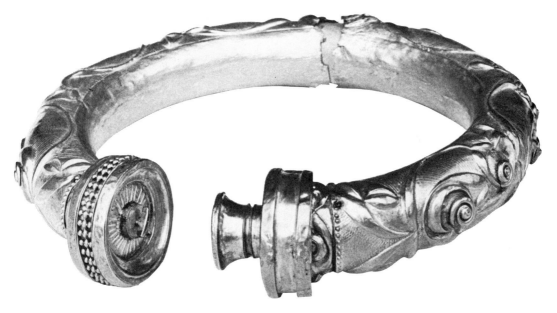

Gold collar, Broighter, Co. Derry, first to fifth century A.D.

these defects may be attributed are various, but the principal seems to be, the destruction of our ancient records; in the first place, by the pious zeal of Saint Patrick, and the other Christian missionaries, in their anxiety to destroy every vestige of heathen superstition; and, in the next, by the barbarous policy of the Danes and their immediate invading successors, the Anglo-Normans, by whom those venerable lights of antiquity were forever extinguished. Another, and no inconsiderable cause of the defects complained of, is that the most valuable of the remnants which escaped these devastations, and afterwards survived the wreck of time, are locked up from the inspection of the curious, in a language which few of the present day understand; a circumstance which has caused more misrepresentation and confusion on the subject of Irish antiquities, than any other whatsoever.

—James Hardiman, Esq.

2 In Pursuit of Patrick

WHAT IS A SAINT?

To speak in a dictionary manner, a Saint—with a capital "S"—is one of those persons recognized by the Church as having, by holiness of life and heroic virtue, attained a high place in heaven, and as being therefore entitled to the veneration of the faithful, fit to serve them as a spiritual model and able to intercede for them in the courts of God. The men and women thus recognized as Saints do not, of course, include all the holy, or exhaust all the possibilities of holiness. But of them we are certain.

The Saints would be the first to agree with Ambrose Bierce's definition in *The Devil's Dictionary*: "A saint is a dead sinner, revised and edited." Bierce, the skeptic, was referring, of course, to that cloyingly pietistic school of hagiography which depicts the Saint as a superhuman character, who is indeed constantly assaulted by temptation but is constitutionally unable to yield to it. It is a sheer invention of religiosity to depict a Saint as a human being of spiritual derring-do of which no mortal is capable.

The very meaning of the lives of the Saints for us lies in the fact that they were sinners like ourselves trying like ourselves to combat sin.

10

Patrick the Missionary. *See page 39 for comments on this painting by the artist, Sister Aloysius McVeigh.*

The only difference between them and us is that they kept on trying, precisely because they believed that the revision and editing of sinner-into-saint is done not by man's pen but by God's grace.

"I was like a stone lying in the deep mire," writes Saint Patrick, "and He that is mighty came, and in His mercy lifted me up, and verily raised me aloft and placed me on top of the wall."

—Clare Boothe Luce

BUT WHEN IS A SAINT A SAINT?

All men and women who devoted themselves to the religious life were, in ancient times, termed saints. There were three orders of saints: (1) the patrician, or secular, clergy (not referring to Saint Patrick but rather to persons of high social rank or noble family); (2) missionaries who traveled and preached Christ to all the land during the hundred years following the coming of Patrick; the monastic saints who, during the next hundred years, cultivated Christianity in, and radiated it from, their monastic schools; and (3) the anchorites, the hermit saints who, succeeding the great ones of the second order, cultivated Christ in solitude on lonely islands, on wild mountaintops, and in the impenetrable wilderness.

These last are described as "holy and shown as aurora; the second class, more holy, lighted the land as does the moon; and the first, most holy, were like the sun that warms the land by the fervour of its brightness."

Coming as he did from the land of the saints, it seems appropriate that the first canonized saint of Western Europe was an Irishman. He was Saint Lorcan O'Toole, patron of Dublin, who died in Normandy toward the end of the twelfth century. The accident of his place of death put him into line for the canonizing movement that was then beginning.

—Alice-Boyd Proudfoot

HOW DO YOU SPELL IT?

A visitor driving through Ireland may be puzzled at the inconsistencies in the spellings of place names. The names of towns on the map do not necessarily conform to the names on the signposts. Over and over people have written about the charm, the musical sound, the picturesqueness of towns such as Parknasilla, Lissadell, Clonmacnois, Lisdoonvarna.

The slight variations—for example, Glendaloch, Glendalough—arise from the same circumstances as their picturesqueness: They are, in general, Anglicizations of Irish descriptive names, (Glendalough: The Glen of Two Lakes). In the same way that personal names (Kavanagh, Cavanaugh) took different written forms in English according to taste and fashion and phonetics, the place names were written variously, with different versions earning local loyalties.

Even more curious may be the inconsistencies in the Gaelic and Latin spellings of people's names. Variations will be noted in: Brigid, Brighid; Colmcille, Columba, Colum Cille, Colum Kille; Kieran, Ciaran; Benen, Benignus; and others. Saint Patrick himself has been referred to as Sucat, Sochet, Magonis, Patraic, Padraig, Cothrighe, and Cothraige. Ancient writers, finding the name written as Cothraige, derived it as meaning "having served under four masters" in various places. But he shall continue to be known as he called himself in the first two words of his *Confession*—I, Patrick.

—Alice-Boyd Proudfoot

PATRICK, WERE YOU BORN HERE? . . .

This highly honoured and much revered saint—from whom the parish derives its name, and to whom the church was originally dedicated—is considered by the best authorities to have been born, if not at Kilpatrick at least in the vicinity, in the last quarter of the fourth century, whence he was carried off to Ireland, while yet a boy of 16 years, by Irish freebooters. There were at one time in the diocese of Glasgow six parishes deriving their name from St. Patrick, but we are told the most ancient and distinguished was Kilpatrick in the Lennox. Much controversy has arisen, and that for a long period, as to the birthplace of St. Patrick, Ireland and France having each their champions, Boulogne in the latter country claiming to be his natal place. The majority of critics now uphold the claim of Strathclyde. The Scotic freebooters from Antrim frequently ravaged the shores of the Firth of Clyde, and the Romans must have suffered much at their hands, as is evidenced by the numerous finds of Roman coins all along the Antrim coast. In the *Confession of St. Patrick*, which, from the rude and ungrammatical character of its Latin, is a strong evidence of its genuineness, the writer says:—"I, Patrick, a sinner, the rudest and the least of all the faithful, and most contemptible to very many, had for my father Calpornius, a deacon, a son of Potitus, a presbyter, who dwelt in the village of Bannavem, Taberniae, for he had a small farm hard by the place where I was taken captive. I was then nearly 16 years of age. I did not know the true God, and I was taken to Ireland in captivity with so many thousand men, in accordance with our deserts, because we departed from God, and we kept not His precepts, and were not obedient to our priests who admonished us for our salvation." In his *Epistle to Coroticus* St. Patrick further says:—"I was a freeman according to the flesh. I was born of a father who was a Decurio; for I bartered my noble birth—I do not blush or regret it—for the benefit of others." Decurians formed what might be called local Town Councils in every small town and village about the year 400.

While called Patrick, or Patricius, which was a common name among the Romans of Britain, he had, as Tirechan informs us, no less than three Celtic names—Succetus (Sucat), Magonus, and Cothraige (Cothrighe).

The dedications to St. Patrick in the locality are numerous. In the castle of Dumbarton there was a chapel dedicated to him from a very ancient date. Adam, the chaplain of the castle, appears as a witness to a deed in 1271, and in the Exchequer Rolls of this period payments to the "capella sancti Patricii infra Castrum" frequently appear. Robert III, in 1390, granted this chapel 10 merks sterling yearly, out of the burrow mails of Dumbarton. The Parish Church of Dumbarton is sacred to his memory, as well as a collegiate church for a provost, and six prebendaries, which was founded by Isabel Dunbar, of Albany, and Countess of Lennox, in 1450, in the burgh town.

In Strathblane Parish there is "St. Patrick's Well," which used to be held sacred, and on the 1st of May, up to the beginning of this century, many a pilgrim drank its healing waters.

From the evidence about the lands of Kilpatrick, there can be no doubt that, in the remote past, pilgrims came to worship at the shrine of St. Patrick in the village church, as the holder of the lands appears to have been under an obligation to receive and entertain those parties who came thither for that object. Duffgal, or Dougal, rector of the church about 1233, endowed the abbey with the land called Patrick's Seat, the locality of which it is now impossible to determine.

Besides the church dedicated to St. Patrick—which was said to be built on soil brought from Ireland in honour of its patron—we have St. Patrick's, or the Trees' Well, adjoining the church, which has been used until lately from time immemorial by the villagers, but now has been found unfit for use, and consequently ordered to be closed up. There is St. Patrick's Rock, near Erskine Ferry, on which, it is said, he was fishing as a boy when carried off to Ireland. Local tradition says erroneously, that St. Patrick was buried in his native place, but the Irish chroniclers tell us he lies buried in Downpatrick.

> In Down three saints one tomb fill,
> Patrick, Bridget and Columkille.

—John Bruce

. . . OR HERE?

A legend associated with Dumbarton Castle Rock relates to the patron saint of Ireland, Patrick, who was said to have been born there. The earliest reference to Dumbarton as St. Patrick's birthplace dates only from the eleventh century and is contained in a marginal gloss on a manuscript copy of a hymn to St. Patrick. The medieval chapel in Dumbarton Castle was actually dedicated to St. Patrick; and of the five medieval parish churches in Scotland with a similar dedication, the one nearest Dumbarton, at Kilpatrick, attracted a steady stream of pilgrims to the shrine of St. Patrick from the twelfth century. By the sixteenth century, the tradition that St. Patrick was born at Dumbarton Rock was commonly accepted. The question of the location of *Bannavem taburniae* (the name which St. Patrick himself gave to his birthplace in his *Confession*) has been debated by Dark Age specialists for almost a century but none has considered Dumbarton as even a remote possibility. St. Patrick, in his *Confession*, stated that his father, a decurion (a Romano-British official) owned a *villa*, or estate, on which several workers were employed and that his father was a deacon and his grandfather a priest in the Christian church. As St. Patrick's most recent biographer has pointed out, there is no evidence whatever that Roman villas ever existed in the area which later became the kingdom of Strathclyde, of which Dumbarton was the "capital." Most authorities have favoured regions much farther south for the saint's birthplace—Cumbria, South Wales, or southwest England.

—I. M. M. MacPhail

ST. PATRICK: HIS LIFE AND WORK

Early Life and Captivity

THE birthplace of a man who has achieved a signal place on a page of history for genius or for sanctity will always exercise a peculiar fascination for the human mind, as if, indeed, some spirit of the place had entered into his soul and dwelt there. To see the sights of field or mountain or sea which were the daily food of the child's mind, to catch the impressions which moulded its form and to grasp its early contacts with the common life of man, is a first and natural impulse as we set ourselves to study and to understand the story of a great life. St. Patrick himself has given us the name of his early home in Britain, but its exact location must be for ever a matter of conjecture. He tells us that as a lad he was brought up on a small farmstead by the village of Bannavem Taberniæ, which, Muirchu informs us, was "not far distant from our sea."

Somewhere near the western shores of Britain—perhaps at Dumbarton on the Clyde, perhaps farther South, on the shores of the Severn—the child who was to become the Evangelist of Ireland was born, and spent his early years. The exact chronology is a somewhat difficult problem, but the date may with some confidence be placed about the year 389 A.D.—not far from the memorable year when St. Augustine was baptised into the Christian Church by the venerable hands of St. Ambrose, and some twenty years before the Emperor Honorius withdrew from the province of Britain the last of the legionaries which protected its shores from the constant menace of Irish and Saxon raiders.

The home into which St. Patrick was born was a Christian home, and his family had a Christian tradition of at least two generations. But it was more than this. It was a clerical home. The principle of celibacy, which during the fourth century was slowly spreading over Christendom from the East as a reaction against the moral corruption of its decadent civilisation, was not at this date generally recognised in the Churches of the West. It need not, therefore, occasion any surprise to learn that both the father and the grandfather of St. Patrick were in Holy Orders. His father, Calpurnius, was a Deacon; his grandfather, Potitus, a priest. It is an interesting reflection that, had celibacy been imposed upon the clergy of the Church in Britain in the fourth century, Ireland would have lost her Patron Saint.

With the work of the ministry his father combined the duties of a small landowner, farming his own land, and the official rank of a *Decurio,* or urban councillor, whose duty it was to assist in the assessment and collection of the local taxation. His home would thus combine the three elements which above all others best make a home a successful training ground for character—frugal industry, a care for the things of the mind, and the fear of God. Much as we would like to know something of his mother, who first gave to her little child the foundation of his knowledge of the Scriptures, we know nothing save that her name was Concessa. A late tradition suggests that she was a sister or near relative of St. Martin of Tours, and much as we should like to believe that such a relationship existed with the great Gallic Saint, the story seems to be too good to be true.

Where the *Confession* is silent later legend has been busy with the family of Calpurnius and Concessa, and gives us the names of five sisters. It may be rash altogether to reject so possible a fact, and it may, indeed, have been that Sechnall, who wrote the famous hymn in his praise, was his nephew—the son of his sister, Liamain.

Like St. Paul, who had both a Jewish and a Roman name, St. Patrick had two names. In the home circle, where his parents familiarly talked in the British tongue, he was known as Sucat,* which, derived from a root meaning "warlike," may be taken as an unconscious prophecy of the future destiny of this warrior of the Faith. But, as in the case of St. Paul, the native name has been superseded by the Latin name of a Roman provincial, by which for all time he will continue to be known.

In the little farm near the Western coast of Britain the opportunities of early education in the troubled years of the end of the fourth century were circumscribed and probably limited to the simple instruction of a home where leisure for the training of the child was small. It was not until he had passed his twenty-second year—and six of them were spent in slavery—that the opportunity of learning came to the young man in the more spacious world of Gaul. Even for a robust mind like his, it is difficult in later life to build up the foundation of exact scholarship when this has not been previously laid in the discipline of early years at school. St. Patrick was acutely conscious of his defect, and with perhaps an excess of modesty refers to himself as "indoctus"

* Muirchu, Cap. i., gives *Sochet.*

and "rusticissimus"—an uneducated man brought up in country ways. However true this admission may be in general, no one can read his writings without realising that he had the formidable learning of the man of one book—and that book was the Bible. Doubtless his contemporary, Apollinaris Sidonius, would have regarded the literary style of the *Confession* and the *Epistle* with something in the nature of derision, but if they fail to reveal either an ample or a polished mind they do not fail to reveal something greater—energy of character, stability of courage, and, like John Ridd, a great power of abiding.

Over the home of St. Patrick all through his childhood hung the shadow of an ever-threatening menace, and life was haunted by fear. The cities of the Roman province of Britain tempted, by wealth beyond the dreams of their untamed avarice, the Picts of Caledonia and the Scottish freebooters from Ireland, whose undeveloped social system knew as yet no such thing as a city. The waving corn fields, which sent their surplus to supply the daily rations of the legions of the Rhine, were a perpetual invitation to the hungry raiders, whose boats lay along side the Irish coast, ever ready to descend in a lightning foray upon the shores of Britain. Sometimes these incursions were small affairs. Sometimes they were regular hostings.

A visitor who has stood amid the massive remains of the walls of the Roman city of Uriconium, near Shrewsbury, may still see the marks of the flames to which raiders from Ireland delivered that formidable fortress, and may calculate the numbers that must have taken part in its overthrow. The protection of the constantly threatened coastal frontiers of the province was the first and chief care of Roman policy. But as the strength of Imperial Rome declined, both the daring and the success of these uncivilised invaders grew.

Tradition has crowned the head of Niall, the High King of Ireland, as the most renowned of these Scottish freebooters—for the inhabitants of Ireland were then known as Scots—and it is probable that the fleet which swooped down upon the coasts near Bannavem Taberniæ, pillaged the country, and carried off several thousand captives, was planned by his mind and led by his sword. It would almost require the leadership of a king to collect a fleet large enough to execute so formidable a raid. But be that as it may, at the age of sixteen, Patrick was carried off into slavery in Ireland.

In his old age, moved by a conscience which his *Confession* reveals as acutely sensitive, he attributed this disaster to a judgment of God— "and I went into captivity to Ireland with many thousands of persons, according to our deserts, because we departed away from God, and kept not his Commandments." But history, with a truer perspective, will pronounce a milder verdict, and see in the event an example, not of the judgment, but of the providence of God.

When the raiders returned to Ireland, their ships laden with booty and with captives, the lad Patrick went into slavery in the house of "a certain chieftain, a heathen man, and a harsh" whose name was Miliucc. Until Dr. Bury—influenced by critical considerations which lie about the *Confession*—sought to identify the scene of his memorable captivity with Croagh Patrick and the Wood of Foclath, in Mayo, no one questioned the accepted scene of his captivity at Slemish, in Co. Antrim. Croagh Patrick has, doubtless, long been the most popular Patrician sanctuary in Ireland, but it has never invaded the rights of Slemish to be considered the spot where the captive Patrick tended his master's flocks. The northern tradition, as represented in the pages of Muirchu, places the captivity at Slemish. More important as evidence is the agreement of the Connaught tradition as given by Tirechan. Had this sacred spot been within the frontiers of Connaught, Tirechan, the Connaught man, would certainly have staked out its claim in no uncertain manner. He does nothing of the kind. He accepts the claim of Slemish. It would seem to be in the highest degree hazardous to reject so universal and so tenacious a tradition—a tradition which knows no rival.

And further, the northern tradition provides a clear and human motive for a curious episode at a later date in the life of the Saint. When he returned in the year 432 and landed in Co. Wicklow, he made an immediate dash to the distant north, instead of beginning his mission where he found himself. If Slemish had indeed been the scene of his six weary years of captivity so many years before, it would be an altogether natural—almost inevitable—impulse that he should first seek to revisit the unforgotten places, to see again the familiar faces, and to carry out literally the evangelistic command to do good to those who despitefully use us. Without the simple clue of this very human motive his rush to the North would remain inexplicable.

Both the father and grandfather of St. Patrick were in Holy Orders. His father, Calpurnius, was a deacon; his grandfather, Potitus, a priest. It is an interesting reflection that, had celibacy been imposed upon the clergy of the Church in Britain in the fourth century, Ireland would have lost her Patron Saint.

Travellers by rail from Belfast to Portrush may see from their carriage window, not far from the town of Ballymena, a curiously dome-shaped hill rising abruptly in the valley of the Braid on their right. Although the hill is little more than fourteen hundred feet in height, yet its loneliness gives it a dominance and its shape a dignity which does not fail to impress the imagination. This hill is the Mons Miss where the ancient authorities tell us that the captive Patrick tended the flocks of his master, Miliucc. The name, Slemish, by which it is known to-day is but a combination of the Irish word, Sliabh, or mountain, and the ancient name, Miss. Names are proverbially stubborn things, and not only has the name of this historic hill been preserved down the centuries, but a smaller hill on the other side of the Braid river, some three miles distant, now called Skerry, is clearly the Mount Scirte, where, Tirechan tells us, the angel of the Lord visited him in his dreams and the Scirit of Muirchu where the angel spoke to him.

Patrick Taken Prisoner as a Lad. *A detail from the great storied window dedicated to him at Saint Patrick's Cathedral, New York.*

PLACE OF CAPTIVITY

Patrick's place of captivity was close to the village of Broughshare, five miles from Ballymena, in the valley of the Braid, near the Hill of Slemish. There is a townland in the valley still called Bally-lig-Patrick, the townland of Patrick's Hollow. Here is a cave built with remarkable strength; it has had

VERNON REGIONAL
JUNIOR COLLEGE LIBRARY

at least three compartments, and one of them is supplied with air by a chimney. The river Braid, originally called Braghad, a gullet or windpipe, and used to signify a gorge or deeply cut glen, forms the boundary between the parishes of Racavan, or Rathcavan, on the south and Skerry on the north of the river. There are in the district the ruins of a cluster of ancient buildings, formerly surrounded by a deep ditch and parapet, and the adjoining locality is known in the county as Saint Patrick's Chapel.

—John Bruce

We may thus identify not only the scene of the captivity of Patrick, but also the little hill which the lad used as his oratory and where he had the earliest of those vivid spiritual experiences which were crystallised in his memory as dreams and visions. This is not the place to enter into a discussion upon these curious phenomena, nor to question the reality of an experience which St. Patrick claims to share with the Hebrew Prophets, with St. Paul, and with the goodly fellowship of the mystics. He believed that God revealed to him His will. He believed that the voice he heard was a voice from God and something more than an echo of his own commonsense. Amid all the wonders which our accustomed eyes forget to see as miracles we do well to preserve at least the grace of an open mind. "Oh, your voices, your voices," said the petulant Charles in Bernard Shaw's great play; "why don't the voices come to me? I am king, not you." "They do come to you," replies Joan, "but you do not hear them. You have not sat in the field in the evening listening for them. When the Angelus rings you cross yourself and have done with it; but if you prayed from your heart, and listened to the thrilling of the bells in the air after they stop ringing, you would hear the voices as well as I." In the time of St. Patrick there was no Angelus to thrill in the ears, but on the little hill of Skerry he prayed and sat in the field in the evening listening for the answering voice. Here is his own account by which we may know what manner of man the lad was.

"Now, after I came to Ireland, tending flocks was my daily occupation, and constantly I used to pray in the day time. Love of God and the fear of Him increased more and more, and faith grew, and the spirit was moved, so that in one day I would say as many as a hundred prayers, and at night nearly as many, so that I used to stay even in the woods and on the mountain to this end. And before daybreak I used to be roused to prayer, in snow, in frost, in rain; and I felt no hurt, nor was there any sluggishness in me—as I now see, because then the spirit was fervent within me."

On the hillside of Skerry, because Patrick was listening for it, he heard the voice of God. The homesick lad may have often brooded over plans of escape, but the immediate impulse came from a guidance which he believed to come from above. As he slept at night he heard a voice saying to him: "Thou fastest to good purpose, thou who art soon to go to thy fatherland." Again, after a short time: "I heard the answer of God saying to me, 'Lo, thy ship is ready.' "

When Patrick, escaping from Slemish, fled from his master, we are told that he was obliged to make a journey of some two hundred miles through the perils of an unknown land before reaching the port where he found the promised ship. In those rude days the difficulties and the dangers of that journey for the young runaway slave must have been formidable and have made no small demands upon both courage and determination. The name of the port is not given, but we may fairly conjecture, both from its distance and from the fact that the mouth of the river Vartry was a famous place of embarkation, that the port was Inverdea, or Wicklow. There the fugitive found a ship just at the point of slipping her moorings. The ship was a merchant vessel, with a cargo of the famous wolfhounds, so prized at this time for the sports of southern Europe. He at once got into touch with the Captain and offered his services as a super-cargo, but no bargain was struck. For some reason the shipmaster was annoyed, and replied roughly and angrily: "On no account seek to go with us."

It was a bitter disappointment; and as Patrick turned back disconsolately to the hut where he was lodging, on the way he began to pray. As he prayed he heard himself loudly hailed—"Come quickly, for these men are calling thee." Evidently the sailors had had a discussion on the matter and had come to the conclusion that a servant of a chieftain would understand well the management of the dogs, and would be a valuable addition to their company and well worth his passage. Whatever the reason, they now determined to take him on board, saying: "Come, for we will receive thee in good faith; make friends with us in any way thou desirest." And so in the company of this rough crew and with the characteristic hope "that some of them would come into the faith of Jesus Christ, for they were heathen," Patrick sailed from the shores of Ireland.

In Gaul and Britain

On setting sail from Ireland, Patrick and his companions were at sea for three days, encountering very heavy weather* on their voyage. If their intention had been to reach a British port, the storm drove them out of their course. It is more probable, however, that their objective was not Britain, but Gaul, whence they could transport their wolfhounds by land to the profitable markets of the south. Whatever their intention, it seems to be clear that when they touched land they found themselves on the western coast of France, and there are indications

---

* This is suggested by Muirchu, Cap. ii., though not mentioned in the *Confession*. To reach France would imply a strong following wind.

that their place of landing may have been Bordeaux.

On shore the troubles which beset the party were even greater than the risks they had run in the gale at sea, for the fury of the barbaric hosts of the Vandals and the Sueves, which a few years before swept over this region of Gaul, had devoured the land as a swarm of locusts. A journey overland, instead of passing through a peaceable and fertile province where ordered government secured protection and prosperous cities offered hospitality to the traveller, was now a matter of adventure and of peril. The land through which they journeyed was a desert, stripped to the bone. For twenty-eight days the party wandered on through this devastated country. Food, even for the dogs, failed them. Hunger threatened and overcame them.

Patrick had not been with the party so long without having impressed them as a man who was in touch with God and the things which lie about the unseen; for in their extremity the shipmaster, who had previously shown his hostility, turned for help to him and implored his prayers to deliver them out of their distress. "How is this, O Christian? Thou sayest that thy God is great and almighty; wherefore then canst thou not pray for us, for we are in danger of starvation? Hardly shall we ever see a human being again." In the true evangelistic spirit the youthful Patrick accepted the challenge and took his advantage of the occasion. "Then, said I plainly to them, 'Turn in good faith and with all your heart to the Lord my God, to Whom nothing is impossible, that this day He may send you food in your journey until ye be satisfied, for He has abundance everywhere.' " That day a herd of pigs was discovered which saved from starvation the hungry travellers and preserved the famished remnant of their dogs.

After this signal event the lot of Patrick was a better one, for he had now become a person of some account in the little band, as he himself tells us: "After this they rendered hearty thanks to God, and I became honourable in their eyes." It is evident that they were now passing out of the devastated track of the barbarians, as, for the remaining fourteen days of their journey, they had food and dry quarters until they reached human habitation once again. This episode Patrick refers to as his second captivity. He was now twenty-two years of age in the year of our Lord 411.

Hitherto both the sequence of events and the chronology have been straightforward and simple, but for the next twenty-one years which lie between the arrival of Patrick in southern Gaul and his mission to Ireland in the year 432 it is by no means easy to determine with anything in the nature of compelling certainty, the exact order of events or the dates which may reasonably be assigned to them. When one authority omits an episode given by another, he may make it almost impossible to reconcile dates. When one authority places an event in Gaul and another in Britain, although we may feel certain that the event did take place, yet we may be puzzled to reckon *when* it took place. The authorities claimed for this period are many and varied. Sometimes, as in the case of Muirchu, they are not quite consistent with themselves. Scholars have collected and collated every shred of evidence that can be obtained with that meticulous care which Mr. Sherlock Holmes devoted to the study of cigarette ashes, and yet with regard to the exact setting and sequence of some facts which are accepted as true, there remains a margin of conjecture.

And then, too, the ancient writers had an aggravating way of dealing in round numbers which serves to confuse the modern historian who demands accurate figures. During this period there is a number of well-established facts and episodes which no one would care to dispute. To place them in their exact and appropriate setting is a delicate problem, for the clues are at times perplexing and at times broken. But, none the less, scholarship has been fairly successful in collecting the fragments of the mosaic scattered throughout the early Patrician literature and piecing them together into a coherent and reasonably trustworthy picture. In its main outline the story is a true story; in the smaller details there may be room for a divergence of opinion.

Having parted from the shipmaster and his companions in Southern Gaul, there is a gap in the narrative of his *Confession*. Passing over the intervening years Patrick wrote, "And again, after a few years, I was in Britain with my kindred, who received me as a son." Where was he, and what was he doing during those intervening years before he returned to his native land and his own people? His silence is broken by an echo of his own voice preserved in the Book of Armagh. He spent these years visiting Gaul and Italy and the islands in the Tyrrhene Sea. Tirechan also had it on the authority of Bishop Ultan that "he was for thirty years in one of those Islands which is called Aralanensis." The "island" which is called "Aralanensis" is today known as Lérins; and although it would be impossible to press so long a period as thirty years into the structure of his biography, yet there can be no room for doubt that Patrick spent some years of his early manhood, when his mind took on its mature mould, at one of the most famous seats of Christian learning and piety in Western Europe in the fifth century.

It is almost impossible to exaggerate the change that had in so brief a time been effected in the fortunes of the young slave by a series of adventures which, did we not believe in Providence, would suggest the vivid fictions of the Arabian Nights. But a few months ago Patrick was a lonely slave lad herding flocks on the slopes of Slemish and offering up his simple prayers at the rock of Skerry in the rain and the wind of our bleak northern land, without the opportunity of learning, without conversation, save that of a brutal master and his rude and heathen fellows, without hope and without future. Now we find him transported to life in a community in which he found companionship with some of the most active intellects of Europe, in close touch with the deepest Christian piety of the time, no longer at the fringe, but near the heart,

THE TREE THAT BLOOMS AT CHRISTMAS

St. Martin of Tours was visited by St. Patrick on his journey to Rome. And a remarkable legend is still told of that visit.

About 20 miles from Tours the railway stops at Gare St. Patrice on its way to Angers. The Commune is also called after St. Patrick.

Above the Gare or station on the side of a hill which rises from the banks of the Loire is the famous tree which bears the famous "Flowers of St. Patrice."

The tradition is that St. Patrick travelling from Ireland to visit St. Martin of Tours lay down to rest under this tree. It was Christmas. The cold and fierce north wind which sweeps the Loire valley was blowing so the tree shed its blooms to protect him.

And each year since it blooms at Christmas. This it does even though there is frost and snow.

—The Rev. George Quinn

of Christendom, then pulsating with the vigour of Jerome, Ambrose and Augustine. From the little rocky island of St. Honorat, lying in the Bay of Cannes, the writer has seen the very sight which met the eyes of Patrick when he raised them from his book—the blue waters of the Mediterranean sparkling in the sunshine, and in the distance, upon the mainland, the encircling bastion of the Maritime Alps and the Esterelles.

It may be well to dwell for a moment upon the time spent by Patrick in the community of Lérins in order to emphasise the fact that, in spite of his own modest depreciation of his learning, he was a man with qualifications for his mission other than personal piety and zeal. He had lived in a close and personal touch with the more spacious intellectual life of his day, and the movements which were then sweeping through the Church. Under the influence of men like Jerome, Ambrose, and Martin of Tours, religious communities were being established over Italy and Southern Gaul for the encouragement of piety and learning in an age of decadence and decay. The monastic idea was, as we say, "in the air."

Moved by this impulse, a rich convert from Paganism, named Honoratus, retired to the little island of Lérins about the time of the birth of Patrick, and around him grew up a community which became the most renowned in Southern Gaul. In time it achieved something of the status of a great University, for the exigencies of the time compelled its inmates not merely to devote themselves to ascetic practice, but to direct the intellectual ferment of the day. And so Lérins became a centre of learning and of theological enquiry. But its learning was no cloistered and sterile scholarship. There was an atmosphere of freedom and independence of thought on the great questions which were then agitating the minds of men. It refused to follow with servility the authority of any great name, and two of its most famous sons Lupus and Faustus—who, like St. Patrick, came from Britain—are found on opposite sides of the great Pelagian controversy. So many bishops did Lérins give to the Church in Gaul that it came to be known as "the nursery of bishops."

No one would venture to claim for Patrick a place beside Hilary or Vincentius or Cassian in the province of intellect, but the mention of their distinguished names will serve to indicate the kind of *milieu* in which he found himself, and will enable us to appreciate the profound impression that Lérins must have made upon a young man who now found himself so unexpectedly in this famous school. If it did nothing else it must have brought home to him the advantages in that age of the monastic system for the confirmation and the propagation of the Faith—a system which was afterwards so highly developed in the peculiar fabric of the Celtic Church in Ireland. How long Patrick remained at Lérins it is impossible to say. But one thing we may say with confidence. The Patrick who left the little sunny island with its books and its prayers "after a few years" and returned to his kindred in Britain was a very different man from the raw and uncouth youth who had fled from the rude homestead at Slemish in the valley of the Braid.

Anyone who has been accustomed to live in the humid air and amid the fresh green of our more northern latitude finds the climate of the Riviera peculiarly trying as Spring passes into Summer. The heat and the dryness and the dust bring by contrast almost intolerable longings for the shade of the chestnut and the sight of a primrose. It was, no doubt, just a feeling of ordinary human homesickness and the wish to see his relatives once again that sent Patrick along the road back to Britain. Whether or no his parents were alive to greet their son on his return we are not told, but his kinsfolk welcomed his "as a son," and besought him, after such experiences, never to leave them again. It was during this visit to his home that one of those trivial events occurred which so often in human history serve to warp a career into new and unexpected channels.

Psychologists tell us that we may discover in our dreams an uprush from that mysterious region of our personality which lies beyond the threshold of our conscious desires and thoughts. It may, indeed, have been that the dream which determined the whole future career of

Patrick was but the climax of a purpose that had been slowly and perhaps unconsciously forming in his heart. It was a dream that changed the history of the man, and with him changed also the history of a whole people. "And there verily I saw in the night visions a man whose name was Victoricus coming as it were from Ireland with countless letters. And he gave me one of them, and I read the beginning of the letter, which was entitled, 'The Voice of the Irish'; and while I was reading aloud the beginning of the letter, I thought that at that very moment I heard the voice of them who lived beside the wood of Foclath which is nigh unto the Western sea. And thus they cried, as with one mouth, 'We beseech thee, holy youth, to come and walk with us once more.' And I was exceedingly broken in heart, and could read no further. And so I awoke."

The simple pathos of the dream touched the heart of the dreamer, for though a stout heart it was ever tender. He must have pondered long over a call which seemed to come from God, for again the invitation came in a more compelling form. "And another night, whether within me or beside me, I cannot tell, God knoweth, in most admirable words which I heard and could not understand, except that at the end of the prayer he thus affirmed, 'He Who laid down His life for thee, He it is Who speaketh in thee.' And so I awoke, rejoicing."

His mind was finally resolved. Like St. Paul, he had received and recognised a call direct from God. A divine command had come to him to become the evangelist of the Irish people. And so once again he left his native country to seek that preparation and training which he felt he needed to fulfil worthily the task which God had laid upon his shoulders.

Before the Mission: At Auxerre

Up till now the story of the life of St. Patrick produces upon the reader the impression of a thing of fragments—a series of uncoordinated episodes determined apparently by the chance of external events. It reads as if he had been drifting through life at the mercy of any fitful tide in the affairs of men. But from the time at which we have now arrived, when in his dreams he heard the pleading voice of the Irish and the more commanding voice of Christ Himself, we become conscious of a signal change. His life, formerly the sport of outward chance, now comes under the austere direction of an inward impelling purpose. No longer blown about as on a drifting raft, his hand is on a rudder, and he steers a clear course for a definite haven. His soul is absorbed with a single passion—

> He is crazed by the spell of far Arabia,
> It has stolen his mind away.

But while this is so, for some years there appears to have been something in the nature of shrinking from the mission to which he was thus beckoned. His years at Lérins had made him acutely conscious of a defective education which as yet made him incapable of the commanding authority imperative for the founder of a Church. And, furthermore, his sensitive conscience appears to have been at this time thrown into a shadow by the continual remembrance of some youthful fault which haunted his soul, as the trivial errors of Bunyan tortured that great and pure soul. And so, like St. Paul, when the divine call came, he went into retirement for study, for thought and for communion with God. Leaving his family in Britain—for they were against his purpose—he set forth once again for Gaul.

Although the confused chronology of our records for this period may leave room for hesitation, yet it appears to be most probable that his undoubted connexion with Auxerre is to be placed at this period of his life. There seems to have been some early tie between the See of Auxerre and the British Church, and had Patrick sought counsel as to where he could most conveniently seek preparation for the ministry and the mission on which he had set his heart, no doubt he would have been advised to betake himself to Auxerre. And if it be the case, as Dr. Bury suggests, that there is evidence that some Christians of Irish nationality resorted thither for theological study, this would be a decisive reason why Patrick should elect to pursue his own study there. The very distance of Lérins from Ireland, his objective, would be against his going thither at this period of his career, and it is doubtful if its peculiar *ethos* would have afforded a suitable training-ground for one whose work was to deal with people and problems very different from those which lay about the shores of the Mediterranean. We may, therefore, with some confidence say that from the time of his departure from Britain until setting forth his mission to Ireland in 432 Patrick was preparing himself for his work, intellectually and spiritually, at Auxerre, which was then springing into fame as a centre of Christian activity under the direction of its famous bishop, Germanus, who, according to early custom, had been elected to the See by the voice of the people on the death of the fifth bishop, Amator, in the year 418.

Whether he was there continuously during all these intervening years our evidence does not permit us to state. Muirchu tells us that on his departure from Britain "he found—the choicest gift of God—a certain very holy Bishop, Germanus, ruling in his city of Alsiodorum. With him he stayed no little time, just as Paul sat at the feet of Gamaliel." And that Germanus was his tutor is confirmed by the line of the hymn, *Genair Patraicc*: "He read the Canon with Germanus, this is what writings narrate." We may take it that besides the Canon of the Scriptures his study included also the Gallican Liturgy—a form differing in many respects from the Roman use. It was not the Roman but the Gallican Liturgy that was introduced into Ireland and used in the early Celtic Church. When subsequently the Anglo-Saxons of Northern England were evangelised by the Celtic apostles from Ireland, these imported with them this Gallican Liturgy which they had inherited from St. Patrick, and when the Irish missionaries from Lindisfarne met the Roman mission working in the South from Canterbury there at once arose between them a conflict on this very point. In the Eucharist, the very central point of Christian worship, the traditional use of Armagh differed from that of Rome.

Of the nature and range of Patrick's studies we have no direct information, but, as has already been indicated, from his wide knowledge of the Scriptures, he must have devoted much time to the acquisition of so remarkable a command of the books of the Bible. He quotes freely and aptly from the pages of the Old Testament, the New Testament, and the Apocryphal Books. There are indications, however, that his studies were not confined to the sacred text alone. Early in the *Confession* there is incorporated a credal profession of faith which has been identified as an extract from the Commentary on the Apocalypse by Victorinus of Pettau, and parallels have also been drawn between some passages from his pen and the teaching of Irenæus. But it would appear that the subtleties of theological controversy had little attraction for a mind of his mystical cast, for we find no reference to the current controversy on the nature of divine Grace in which his master, Germanus, took so prominent a part. And perhaps more remarkable still in one who in his teaching laid so strong an emphasis upon the doctrine of the Trinity, Patrick makes no remark upon the theological controversies on the Incarnation which disturbed and distracted Christendom from Nicæa to Ephesus, and which must have been the subject of keen debate amongst the theologians of Lérins. His own personal apprehension of God was so immediate, so vivid, and so sure that he took little interest in its verbal formula, but with a mind at unity with itself devoted the full energy of his spirit to the practical task of turning the souls of men from darkness to light.

The chapters in the *Life* of Muirchu which tell of St. Patrick's admission into Holy Orders present so confused an account that it is difficult to arrive at a convincing conclusion. Into that intricate problem it is not possible for us now to enter. It must suffice to say that the most satisfactory solution appears to be that Patrick received the Orders of Deacon and Priest early in his stay at Auxerre from the hands of the bishop, Amator, who died in the year 418; that subsequently as a Priest he studied under Germanus, his famous successor, in the See of Auxerre; and that in the year 432, on the eve of Patrick's departure on his mission to Ireland, Germanus conferred upon him episcopal consecration.

That so long an interval as fourteen years should have intervened between the acceptance of the call to Ireland and the actual landing upon its shores to fulfil the divine commission may well occasion something akin to surprise. Time was passing. Life is brief. Why did Patrick, who showed himself so active and resolute when the work was in hand, seem to hesitate and linger? As has been indicated, the *Confession* reveals Patrick in his youth as a man of singularly delicate conscience and, as such, acutely sensitive to criticism. Some youthful indiscretion at the age of fifteen, confessed to a friend, had been divulged and was bandied about by gossiping tongues. Doubts as to his moral fitness sprang up, and with the doubts came delay. Doubts also as to intellectual capacity to lead a mission which were entertained by his friends increased his own sense of unworthiness and reinforced his reason for delay. Trust in God had not yet overcome distrust in self. Looking back as an old man the perspective of the years showed him that the very virtue of modesty had been allowed to become a snare. "And the Lord showed mercy upon me thousands of times, because he saw in me that I was ready, but that I did not know through these revelations what I should do about my position, because many were forbidding this embassage. Moreover, they used to talk amongst themselves behind my back and say, 'Why does this fellow thrust himself into danger amongst hostile people who know not God?' They did not say this out of malice; but it did not seem meet in their eyes, on account of my illiteracy, as I myself witness that I have understood. And I did not quickly recognise the grace that was then in me. Now that seems meet in my eyes which I ought to have done before." But when his hour did strike, Patrick was not found wanting.

ACCORDING to legend King Conor in A.D. 74 died with rage on hearing of the Crucifixion, but in fact the Gospel was introduced to Ireland by Saint Palladius, in A.D. 431. He had some limited success in Kerry, and ever since Kerry men have boasted that they were Christians before the rest of Ireland; the rest of Ireland usually replies that Kerry men had to be converted twice, and even then it didn't take properly.
—Walter Bryan

In the pages of the eccentric Chronicle of Prosper, of Aquitaine, there is found, under the year 431, the following entry, which is the first reference in literature to the existence of Christianity in Ireland: "Palladius, ordained by the Pope Celestine, is sent as the first bishop to the Scots who believe in Christ"—the Scots being the name then employed for the inhabitants of Ireland.

To the history of Britain that of Ireland presents a complete and significant contrast. For better or worse, Ireland never became a

Christianity broke out at several dates depending on which St. Patrick arrived first.

In 1941 the late Professor T. F. O'Rahilly put forward the opinion that there were two Patricks, each working about thirty years as a missionary in Ireland; the elder, who died in 461, was known as Palladius; the younger, Patrick the Briton, who came at about the time of Palladius and who died in 493.

province of the Empire and never underwent the discipline of subjection to the imperial system. Agricola had reported to his master that the spectacle of an independent island so near their shores had a disturbing effect upon the provincials of Britain, and undertook to be responsible for winning and holding Ireland to the Empire with a single legion. But the matter went no further than the despatch, and Ireland remained uninvaded and unconquered—a country moving in a lonely orbit of its own almost below the horizon of the civilised world.

But although outside the political and social system of Europe, nevertheless, Ireland touched the Empire at two points. In commerce no country can be quite off the map. The hand of God had placed the island between the two provinces of Britain and Spain, and if Christian legionaries did not carry the story of Christ to the shores of Ireland, it is more than probable that the traders who touched at its ports did. There must have been many ships like that in which Patrick made his escape trading with Gaul and Spain, and amongst their crews there must have been not a few Christians—and Christians in those days were not in the habit of hiding their light under a bushel.

While Ireland touched the Empire slightly through trade, it also touched it, as we have seen, vigorously through war. The perpetual forays upon the coast of Britain meant captives. We can hardly think that the lad Patrick was the only Christian that was brought into slavery in Ireland. There must have been many hundreds of Christian provincials from Britain in slavery in various parts of the country, and even so small a leaven would serve to leaven the whole lump. The story of the early history of the Church in Rome itself is an indication of the influence that may be wielded by the humble witness of pious folk in a state of servitude. These considerations prepare us for the statement that while at this time there was no organised Church in Ireland, yet there were believers in Christ to be found scattered throughout the island.

The story of the Roman mission under Palladius is brief and soon told. It lasted but a year and ended with his death. Late and un-certain tradition strives to lift the veil which shadows the beauty of his feet upon the mountains as he brought his good tidings. Possibly they may be traced on the side of a Wicklow hill rising from the Vale of Avoca. It may be that he has left a memorial on the holy hill of Donard. But the missioner from Rome has left no authentic or en-during impress upon either Ireland or her Church. In his death Muirchu sees the preventing hand of God. The evangelist of his country was to be one sent by a higher authority than any upon earth—one who had heard a call from heaven, but was now lingering by the waters of the Yonne. In these few lines he tells the story of Palladius: "But God prohibited him, because no one can receive anything from earth unless it were given him from heaven. For neither did those wild or rough people readily receive his teaching, nor did he himself desire to spend a long time in a land not his own; but he returned to them that sent him. Returning then hence, he crossed the first sea; and, continuing his journey by land, he died in the country of the Britons."

—G. A. Chamberlain

3

The Mission Begins

ST. PATRICK: HIS LIFE AND WORK *(cont'd.)*

The Beginning of the Mission

ONE day in the memorable year of our Lord 432 two travellers disembarked from their ship on the northern coast of Gaul. These were Augustinus and Benedictus, companions of Palladius on his mission to Ireland, who brought the melancholy tidings of his retreat and death. Either through the misfortune or the fault of its leader the official mission from Rome had drawn to a rapid conclusion, and the people of Ireland were once again as sheep without a shepherd. To Patrick and his bishop, Germanus, the news must have come as a blow. They had looked upon Palladius and his little band as the vanguard of the army of the Lord; and now the leader was dead and his followers in retreat. Honour and policy alike demanded that the breach should be filled, and filled immediately. The memory of the voice of the Irish and the voice of Christ Himself which had never ceased to haunt the mind of Patrick must have immediately suggested that now the hour had struck, and that he was the man to carry forward once again the retreating standard

of the Cross. A perpetual shame would sear a conscience which would shrink at such a moment. The moment called for definite and immediate decision, and Germanus and Patrick rose to the occasion. They determined that Patrick should set forth at once to the work for which God had so manifestly called him and for which he had been for so long endeavouring to prepare himself. Without delay Germanus consecrated him bishop, and sent him forth with his blessing to the task of evangelising the Irish people.

The mother church of all Christendom was an upper room in a street in the city of Jerusalem. The mother church of Irish Christianity was a humble barn in Maginis by the southern shore of Strangford Lough.

Immediately after his consecration, Patrick embarked on a ship prepared for him and set sail for Britain. On his arrival his one concern was to reach Ireland with the utmost speed, so "dispensing with everything that could delay his journey on foot, except what the requirements of ordinary life demand (for no one seeks the Lord by sloth), with all speed and with a favouring wind, he crossed our sea." Whether or no he set upon his adventure alone, we cannot say. It may have been that he brought with him as companions or as servants a few Gauls, but the probability is that he undertook the pioneer work unaided and alone. There is no site in the Patrician history of which we can be more certain than his landing place in Co. Down, on the shores of Strangford Lough.

On landing at the mouth of the River Slain, Patrick and his little party concealed their boat and set off to explore the neighbourhood with a view to obtaining a resting place. The advent of a stranger is even to-day something of an event in an Irish countryside, and the tidings have a way of spreading and of gaining a wealth of detailed colour in the telling that has been turned to considerable dramatic effect on the stage of the Abbey Theatre. As the travellers were wandering along the banks of the Slain they were detected by a swineherd who, with that suspicion of a stranger which is the characteristic of the peasant in every land, instinctively put the worst construction upon their presence and rushed off to inform his master of the approach of a band of thieves and robbers.

Dichu, the master, was one of those petty chieftains who held an important and influential place in the social hierarchy of the times, and his high rank is indicated by the fact that he not only owned cattle, but also held possession of land. The first impulse of Dichu was to set upon the strangers and kill them in obedience to the instinct which makes preservation the first law of our being. But he, as Muirchu puts it, "although a heathen, was of a good natural disposition," and when face to face with the party he "beheld the countenance of St. Patrick" his malign purpose changed and "the Lord turned his thoughts to good." And so the kindly Dichu became the first Irish host and the first Irish convert of St. Patrick. In the terse words of our narrative, "Patrick preached the faith to him; and there he believed in Patrick before anyone else did; and there the Saint rested with him not many days." The mobile nature which had responded readily to the personality of the Saint, is represented as having yielded with a like rapidity to his preaching, and the process of his conversion was but a matter of days.

It would appear that as we have in Patrick *the man*, so in the times when he set foot upon the shores of Ireland we have also *the moment*. We have seen that there was already a leaven of Christianity in the land. Traders brought something of it to the coasts from Christianised Spain and Gaul. Hundreds of captives torn, like Patrick himself, from Christian Britain must have accustomed the inland households to the story of the new and beautiful faith. There may well have been a restlessness, a disintegration in the old superstitions; a vague feeling that sooner or later a reckoning would have to be made with the faith which was sweeping over and transforming the mighty Empire of Rome. Sailors, traders and captives would bring accounts of those strange figures with shaven head which they had encountered in all the provinces of the Empire. It may well have been that a kind of Messianic expectation had been evolved which would serve to prepare the way for the advent of Patrick. There is an obscure poem in archaic Irish which may be taken as an indication that some such expectation was abroad:

> Adze-head* will come
> With his crook-headed staff
> With his house† holed for his head.
> He will chant impiety from his table in the east of his house.
> His whole household will respond to him, So be it, So be it.

And we doubtless listen to the echo of an apprehension which they were unable to conceal when Muirchu tells us of a prophecy of the magicians of "the coming of a certain foreign religion, in the manner of a kingdom with a certain strange and harmful doctrine, brought from a long distance across the seas, proclaimed by a few, accepted by many, and honoured by all; one that would overturn kingdoms, slay kings that resist it, lead away multitudes, destroy all their gods, and, having cast down all the resources of their art, reign for ever and ever."

PATRICK THE MISSIONER

> Saint Patrick was a preacher
> With honey in his throat.
> They say that he could charm away
> A miser's dearest pence;
> Could coax a feathered creature
> To leave her nesting note
> And fly from many a farm away
> To drink his eloquence.
>
> No Irishman was Patrick
> According to the story.

---

* This curious phrase refers to the tonsure of the whole head which was customary in the early centuries.

† This refers to the *Paenula*, the ordinary cloak of the Roman citizen, which was sleeveless, with an aperture in the centre through which the head was passed.

The speech of Britain clung to him
(Or maybe it was Wales).
But ah, for curving rhet'ric,
Angelic oratory,
What man could match a tongue to him
Among the clashing Gaels!

Let Patrick meet a Pagan
In Antrim or Wicklow,
He'd talk to him so reachingly,
So vehement would pray,
That Cul or Neall or Reagan
Would fling aside his bow
And beg the saint beseechingly
To christen him that day.

He won the Necromancers,
The bards, the country herds.
Chief Aengus rose and went with him
To bear his staff and bowl.
For such were all his answers
To disputatious words,
Who'd parry argument with him
Would end a shriven soul.

The angry Druids muttered
A curse upon his prayers.
They sought a spell for shattering
The marvels he had done.
But Patrick merely uttered
A better spell than theirs
And sent the Druids scattering
Like mist before the sun.

They vanished like the haze on
The plume of the fountain.
But still their scaly votaries
Were venomous at hand.
So three nights and days on
Tara's stony mountain
He thundered till those coteries
Of serpents fled the land.

Grown old but little meeker
At length he took his rest.
And centuries have listened, dumb,
To tales of his renown.

For Ireland loves a speaker,
So loves Saint Patrick best:
The only man in Christendom
Has talked the Irish down.

—*Phyllis McGinley*

In Ulaid

There is a common saying that every Irishman claims to be descended from a king and, although we may smile at the pleasantry, yet behind it there is sufficient justification to rescue the dictum from the region of complete absurdity. The truth is that in the political and social organisation of Ireland at the time when it emerges into the light of history there was a multiplicity of petty tribal chieftains who were known as kings. The frontiers of these small states correspond roughly to our present baronies, and each, within its own boundaries, enjoyed an almost complete self-determination.

These small tribal states, though moving in little orbits of their own, yet formed a kind of primitive League of Nations around more august and spacious names.

What we may be permitted to term the super-kings of Connaught, of Munster, of Ulster and of Leinster (south of the Liffey)—to use the modern names—formed the nuclei of these larger political groups, while they themselves recognised an undefined supremacy of the King of Meath. Even in those far-off days Ulster had managed to secure for itself a wider degree of local independence, for within its boundaries we find no less than three superkings—the king of Aileach, or north Ulster to the Bann; the king of Oriel, or south Ulster; and the king of Ulaid (Ulidia), comprising roughly the modern counties of Antrim and Down. The royal hierarchy of Ireland thus consisted of the Ard-ri, or High King of Tara; the six super-kings; and a large number of tribal kings. The nature of this supremacy appears to have been expressed in personal precedence and such tribute as could be obtained. It does not appear to have involved any right of interference with the customs or the policy of the tribes.

There is, however, one fundamental principle which seems to have been universally recognised in the social structure of early and tribal Ireland, and had so important a bearing upon the policy of St. Patrick that it ought to be grasped when we seek to understand the story of his mission. Land appears to have been in theory the property of the tribe, and no land could be alienated without the consent of the chieftain. To build a church; to establish a simple monastic community; to endow a religious establishment of any kind, it was essential to gain, if not the conversion, at least the goodwill, of the chieftain. The person of the king of each district was the strategic point which must be won if the army of the Cross was to make any advance. In this respect the knowledge of the lie of the social land gained by St. Patrick during his six years at Slemish stood him in good stead. He knew that a failure to win the goodwill of the chieftains would mean failure all along the line. Nothing in his career in Ireland could compare for a moment in importance with his plan to win over the High King in his palace at Tara. To capture Tara for the Cross was to outflank the whole position of the enemy. And it is possible that it was a sense of the overwhelming significance of his victory in Royal Meath that led Tirechan to pass over in silence the episode of Patrick's brief rush into Ulidia and to make him land after touching at Inis-Patrick, upon the shores of Meath.

We must now return to St. Patrick, whom we left with Dichu by the River Slain, on the shores of Strangford Lough. Leaving his boat in charge of his new convert, Patrick pushed on by land through Down and southern Antrim, making his way towards Slemish. But rumour had preceded him, and with rumour had come fear. Miliucc, we have been told, was a harsh master, and it may well have been that the memory of old cruelties towards the slave lad with his strange religion came vividly into his memory when he heard the unwelcome tidings that his former slave was making his way north, bent, no doubt, upon some condign and terrible revenge. In an age when the minds of men lived in an atmosphere of magic, when the spells of the sorcerer were potent and terrible realities, the thought of that revenge would take on colours more sinister than we find it easy to conceive in our age.

It may have been that Miliucc, like the inhabitants of Moscow at the approach of Napoleon, burned his house and his possessions so that his unwelcome visitor who had come to bring his sin to remembrance might speedily be compelled to beat a retreat from his neighbourhood, while he fled to the temporary refuge of the woods. Or it may have been literally, as Muirchu records the tradition, that "when Miliucc heard that his slave was coming to see him, to the end that he should, at the close of his life, adopt, as it were by force, a religion which he disliked, fearing lest he should be in subjection to a slave, and that he should lord it over him, he committed himself to the flames, at the instigation of the devil and of his own accord. Having collected around him every article of his property, he was burnt up in the house in which he had lived as king."

The first sight that met the astonished eyes of Patrick when the old familiar shape of Mount Miss grew visible above the northern horizon was the smoke rising to heaven from the flaming homestead—a smoke which in a moment blotted out the picture his imagination must have often painted of a triumphant scene of reconciliation and of conversion. It was a bitter disappointment. So stupefied was he that for several hours he could not speak. Then with "sighs and tears and groans" he reproached his old master with having done this deed "lest he should become a believer at the close of his life, and serve the everlasting God." As we pause to look at this scene of long ago we are conscious of the simple elements of irony in the despair of the stout old heathen—in fear where no fear was; and of tragedy in the tears of the Saint who had been in a moment disappointed of his long deferred hope. And perhaps along with our sympathy for the Saint we need not be ashamed to extend a little also to the sinner.

There was nothing now to retain Patrick any longer in Antrim, for the ashes on the slope of Slemish marked the frustration of his immediate purpose. Accordingly, without further delay, he retraced his steps to Mag-inis—the "island plain" which lay around the great fortress of Dun Lethglasse—afterwards transformed into Dun Patrick —where so recently he had left his first convert, Dichu. "And there," Muirchu tells us, "he stayed many days; and he went round the whole countryside, and chose (clergymen), and did deeds of love; and there the faith began to grow."

It seems to have been that Patrick possessed that quality of character which every man would fain call master—authority. That he had in a high degree courage and tenacity and patience we have already seen. That he lacked any pretence to intellectual brilliancy he himself confesses and deplores. It is not, however, to nimble wits that the elusive force of authority adheres, but rather to slow, strong and purposeful character that has turned to good account the uses of adversity.

"When I painted Saint Patrick, I wanted to depict him as a man in his prime, a man of zeal and courage faced with the conflicting forces of the paganism of his time. These (represented by the converging arcs in the painting) are not annihilated by the saint; instead, as far as they can serve, even enhance, his design for Christianity, he weaves them into the fabric of the Celtic church. Patrick's faith in Christ lights the way for a never-ending line of missionaries who up to the present day have not ceased to preach Christ."

—Sister Aloysius McVeigh

The mother church of all Christendom was an upper room in a street in the City of Jerusalem. The mother church of Irish Christianity was a humble barn in Maginis by the southern shore of Strangford Lough. By virtue of his rank, Dichu was in a position to make over his barn to Patrick as his church. It was but a poor structure of wood, but if the rough timbers which heard the first chants of the Irish Church and saw the first Eucharist celebrated under an Irish roof have long ago perished, the site still remains holy ground; and in the parish church at Saul Christian people of the Church of Ireland at this very day hear Sunday by Sunday the same Gospel, profess the same Creed and receive the same Sacrament. The name Saul enshrines the far-off memory of these early days—for Saul is but *Sabhall,* which in Irish means a barn.

We have now brought Patrick to the critical moment when he is about to launch his first and greatest offensive against the forces of Irish heathenism, and this would seem to be the natural place to pause and take a brief notice of that peculiar form of religious belief and practice which he found in possession of the land and which he was destined to overthrow.

The form of heathenism by which St. Patrick found himself opposed was low and rudimentary in type. There was no clear and articulated form of belief in a supreme God, though there appears to have been a vague belief in gods whose functions were undifferentiated and uncertain. There was nothing to correspond with the celestial hierarchy of Greece and Rome. Where there is no defined god, there can be no prayer rising to heaven, no temple, no regiment of priests, no formulated creed. Nor does there appear to have been any kind of organised cult which was universally recognised and might serve either as a bond expressing a racial solidarity, or as a sanction for personal or tribal morality.

Contact with the Unseen, which is the definition of religion in its broadest sense, seems to have been local and tribal. And contact with the Unseen was established through the great elemental powers of Nature, which cannot fail to be recognised as potent influences upon the daily life and business of man—the more so in a primitive state of society when Science has not yet taught the secret of conquering Nature by understanding and obeying her hidden laws. The sun, striding like a giant across the heavens on his daily course; the life-giving water, rising mysterious and clean from the darkness of the well; the fire, whose devouring strength nothing can resist; the wind, with its moods of tenderness and of terror—it was through these that contact of some sort was established with the Unseen background of things. Some presence and spirit was felt to be moving and abroad in each of them and to claim the recognition of men. Altars in the open air were erected in their honour, idols were placed for adoration, and the powers of Nature were invoked to give sanction to the sworn word. "The elements passed a doom of death on Laoghaire, to wit, the earth to swallow him up, the sun to burn him, and the wind to depart from him. So that, in the words of the Four Masters, "the sun and wind killed him because he had violated them."

It seems unlikely, that the primitive Irish minds had as yet been able to abstract the idea of spirit from the natural phenomena with which they found it in close association. They would appear to have inferred that the two are one, an inference which by enslaving spirit to its material environment, is the heart and essence of idolatry. Such a mental climate has always been found favourable to the belief in and the practice of magic, for magicians merely carried the logic of this belief one step farther. They claimed to know the recondite secrets by which it was possible by words or by acts to compel the spirit inevitably to act as they required.

> And daily in their mystic ring
> They turned the maledictive stones.

Where a claim so terrible is conceded by the superstition of an unquestioning public opinion, a powerful weapon is placed in the hands that can wield it. This power in Ireland was firmly established in the hands of a spiritual aristocracy known as the Druids, who now emerge in our story as the protagonists of the ancient philosophy of life against the invasion of the Gospel of Christ.

The influence of this powerful caste, however, was not based alone upon their spiritual pretensions to foretell the future and to weave spells. Whatever secular knowledge was possessed was possessed by them. To them the kings deferred in matters of tradition and law as to a Cabinet, while over the common people their skill in rousing passion through the songs of their heroes gave them the sway of the demagogue. Clad in white, and with that curious tonsure across the forehead from ear to ear which was destined to become the Christian tonsure of the Celtic Church both in Ireland and in Britain, a college of Druids must have presented a venerable and impressive sight, and one calculated to reinforce the real source of their religious power—the power of fear. Until fear of the Druidic order had been exorcised from the minds of the native Irish and until the power which was founded on that fear had been openly challenged and overthrown, the issue between Christianity and Paganism would hang in the balance. This was the strategic point, and a victorious challenge here would disarm all opposition and remove the only vital obstacle to the Gospel.

Meath

The scene of our story now shifts from the island plain of southern Down, where we left St. Patrick directing the work of evangelisation, to the Kingdom of Meath and Royal Tara. During the early days of the spring there arose a high debate in the little Christian community as to where they should celebrate the first Easter Festival. As by an inspiration there flashed into the mind of the Saint the bold project of making

Aerial view of portion of the Hill of Tara, Co. Meath, the seat of the high kings of Ireland. The view shows in the foreground two ring-forts (dwelling sites), the Forradh and "Cormac's House." In the top left-hand corner the Rath of the Synods, occupied from the second to the fourth century A.D., may be seen, and just below it a mound known as "the Mound of the Hostages"—actually a Bronze Age burial site.

Easter the date of his great strategic movement against the very citadel of the enemy. "It seemed good to Saint Patrick, inspired by God as he was, that this great feast of the Lord, which is the chief of all feasts, should be celebrated in the great plain where was the chiefest kingdom of those tribes, which was the head of all heathenism and idolatry; that this unconquered wedge should be driven at the outset into the head of all idolatry by the mallet of a mighty work joined with faith." The appeal of the heroic needs no further argument, and, in the simple words of the chronicler, "so it came to pass."

Leaving his good friend Dichu, Patrick and his companions—there were eight of them—carried their boat once again to the sea and launched her in the waters of Strangford Lough. Passing along the coast they soon made the natural harbour of the mouth of the River Boyne, where the little party disembarked and, leaving their boat, proceeded on foot across the plain along the bank of the river, crossing the very spot which, centuries after, was to be a battlefield whereon another issue in the history of the country was to be decided. That day's walk brought Patrick and his companions some twelve miles to the hill of Slane which, rising from the plain of Breg, dominates the surrounding country. On this hill they pitched their tent, and doubtless before the setting of the sun were able to descry across the waters of the Boyne, flowing beneath them, the outlines of Royal Tara, ten miles to the south, where Laoghaire, the High King of Ireland, then held his court. That night, like the Passover of the Hebrews, was long to be remembered in the annals of the Irish race as one of those decisive moments which mark at once the end and the beginning of an epoch.

What, then, were King Laoghaire and his court doing at Tara on this Easter Eve; and why, in the grandiose language of Muirchu, were "gathered together kings, satraps, leaders, princes, and chief men of the people; and, moreover, magicians and enchanters and augurs and those who sought out and taught every art and every wile"? It was one of those occasions when the kings and leaders of the people were wont to assemble to celebrate with their Druids a high and solemn religious festival. On the first day of summer the festival of Beltane was observed by the lighting of a fire at Tara. It requires the gift of no vivid imagination to picture the strange and moving beauty of this solemn ritual, when in the deepening darkness of the night no hand might kindle a light until the gleam from the royal hill of Tara proclaimed once again the resurrection of the life-giving Sun from his winter's death.

It was while awaiting, in the darkness of a March night, this dramatic climax of their ceremonies that, to the horror and amazement of the expectant court, there flashed across from the hill of Slane the challenge and the insult of the Paschal fire lit by the hands of St. Patrick. "And when all the nobles and elders and magicians had been gathered together, the king said to them, 'What is this? Who is it has dared to do this impiety in my kingdom? Let him die the death!' And all the nobles and elders made answer, 'We know not who has done this thing.' "

But the inwardness of that rival light was not hidden from the eyes of the more astute magicians. The legend reveals to us that the Druidic order grasped the fact that the hand that lit that light from Slane was defying them all and all they stood for, and that the fight now to be fought would be a fight to the finish. They could not fail to have heard of the religion of Christ which was sweeping the whole civilised world, nor could they fail to have heard that a Christian Bishop had already landed on their shores. Sooner or later the clash was inevitably destined to come; and, in that defiant light flashing from Slane to Tara on that Easter Eve, they knew that the issue was already joined. For when consulted that night by the perplexed King Laoghaire they replied in the language of prophecy, "Unless it be put out on this night on which it has been lighted up, it will not be put out for ever. Moreover, it will overcome all the fires of our religion. And he who kindled it . . . will overcome both all of us and thee too."

At this point the page of Muirchu assumes an almost Homeric vividness and vigour as the ancient legend which he had from the lips of Aedh, Bishop of Sletty, carries down to us in its own way the story of this battle of the giants. We may, perhaps, in our superior manner, sometimes smile at the medium of miracle in which the picture is painted, but none the less, no sympathetic imagination can fail to realise the truth embodied in the tale which, as it would be spoiled by a paraphrase, is here given in full from the admirable translation of Dr. White.

> And St. Patrick was called to the king outside the place where the fire had been kindled. And the magicians said to their people, "let us not rise up at the approach of this fellow; for whosoever rises up at the approach of this fellow will afterwards believe in him and worship him."
>
> At last Patrick rose; and when he saw their many chariots and horses, he came to them, singing with voice and heart, very appropriately, the following verse of the Psalmist: "Some put their trust in chariots and some in horses; but we will walk in the name of the Lord our God." They, however, did not rise at his approach. But only one, helped by the Lord, who willed not to obey the words of the magicians, rose up. This was Ercc, the son of Daig, whose relics are now venerated in the city called Slane. And Patrick blessed him; and he believed in the everlasting God.
>
> And when they began to parley with one another, the second magician, named Lochru, was insolent in the Saint's presence, and had the audacity, with swelling words, to disparage the Catholic faith. As he uttered such things, St. Patrick regarded him with a stern glance,

as Peter once looked on Simon; and powerfully, with a loud voice, he confidently addressed the Lord and said, "O Lord, Who canst do all things, and in Whose power all things hold together, and who hast sent me hither—as for this impious man who blasphemes Thy name, let him now be taken out of this and die speedily." And when he had spoken thus, the magician was caught up into the air, and then let fall from above, and, his skull striking on a rock, he was dashed to pieces and killed before their faces; and the heathen folk were dismayed.

The discomfiture of their champion in this debate not unnaturally enraged both the King and his followers, and in their anger they were about to rush upon the Saint and kill him. But the moral power of courage had already sapped the strength of his opponents. As they were about to attack him Patrick rose up undaunted before them with the words: "Let God arise, and let his enemies be scattered; let them also that hate Him flee before him." Before this unruffled courage his enemies quailed. It seemed as if the earth beneath their feet had given way and the approaching dawn of that Easter morning had turned again to night. And so, in confusion, they fled from the unequal contest. "And straightway darkness came down, and a certain horrible commotion arose . . . and they rushed in headlong flight."

As Laoghaire next day was feasting in his palace with "the kings and princes and magicians of all Ireland" and when "some were talking and others were thinking of the things which had come to pass," St. Patrick with five companions made his appearance upon the scene. "When, therefore, he entered the banqueting-hall of Temoria, no one of them all rose up at his approach save one only, and that was Dubthach-maccu-Lugir, an excellent poet, with whom there was staying at that time a certain young poet named Fiacc, who afterwards became a famous bishop, and whose relics are now venerated at Sleibti . . . and the Saint blessed him, and he was the first to believe in God that day."

The name of this young pupil of St. Patrick's first convert at Tara is of more than passing interest to the historian. In after years the hands of the Saint were laid in consecration upon the head of Fiacc, who became the first Bishop of Sletty. It was from Aedh, a successor in the See of Fiacc, that Muirchu derived his account of what happened at Tara in these early days; and there can be little room to doubt the facts which lie behind the tradition thus handed down from an eye-witness and preserved in the ancient See of Sletty.

The Lighting of the Fire

PATRICK made straight for the citadel of Tara and arrived at the Hill of Slane, ten miles away, on the evening of Easter Saturday. This was the day of the year on which it was his duty to light the paschal fire. But it was also a pagan festival to celebrate the beginning of summer, this being symbolized by the extinguishing of all fires throughout the country; a ceremonial fire was then lit by the Druids, from which all the other fires were re-ignited. It was a crime punishable by death to allow any fire until this was done, as Patrick well knew.

Preparations for the Druid ceremony were in full swing when a light was seen on the distant Hill of Slane, rapidly becoming a great glow in the darkening sky. The Druids ran to the king in anger, crying with a strange foreboding, "If that fire be not put out, it will burn forever."

The king and his Druids, in eight chariots, sped to Slane, where a great crowd of people had already gathered. Patrick came through them to meet the king, singing: "Some in chariots and some on horse, but we in the name of the Lord." The words were from the Bible, but the tune was his. The king was impressed by Patrick's courage, the people were charmed by the song, the Druids conceded defeat and the Church had entered into its estate in Ireland.

Or so the story goes. In fact the conversion of Ireland was by no means as sudden and complete as that account implies. The kings of Ireland remained pagan for another two hundred years, and even as late as 1844 votive offerings of flowers were placed by country people on the altar at Mount Collan in County Clare to the pagan sungod, Lug.

—Walter Bryan

THE RUNE OF SAINT PATRICK

Tara today in this fateful hour
I place all Heaven with its power,
and the sun with its brightness,
and the snow with its whiteness,
and fire with all the strength it hath,
and lightning with its rapid wrath,
and the winds with their swiftness along their path,
and the sea with its deepness,
and the rocks with their steepness,
and the earth with its starkness:
    all these I place,
by God's almighty help and grace,
between myself and the powers of darkness.

—*Anonymous (from the Gaelic)*

The Blessing of Saint Patrick

IN the noted work, *The Book of Rights*, ascribed to his disciple Benignus, is found the "Blessing of Saint Patrick," which some think is one of Patrick's poems:

The Blessing of God upon you all,
Men of Erin, sons, women,
And daughters; prince-blessing,
Meal-blessing, blessing of long life,
Health-blessing, blessing of excellence,
Eternal blessing, heaven-blessing,
Cloud-blessing, sea-blessing,
Fruit-blessing, land-blessing,
Crop-blessing, dew-blessing,
Blessing of elements, blessing of valour,
Blessing of dexterity, blessing of glory,
Blessing of deeds, blessing of honour,
Blessing of happiness be upon you all,
Laics, clerics, while I command
The blessing of the men of Heaven;
It is my bequest, as it is a Perpetual Blessing.

In a series of events in which he repeatedly defeated the magicians, St. Patrick broke forever the opposition of the Druids. Laoghaire would appear to have adopted an attitude of benevolent neutrality towards the new Faith, and the pages of history indicate a progressive and steady increase in the number of the converts and the founding of churches. The very place names of Meath tell us of the activity of the Christian Church. At Donagh*-Patrick—the Church of Patrick—arose a church known as the Great Church of St. Patrick. It was small indeed as we today reckon the dimension of churches, being but sixty feet long. In Dunshaughlin we have a corruption of Domnach Sechnaill— the church of Sechnall, where the first hymn composed in Ireland was written, in honour of St. Patrick and during his lifetime. Tradition claims for Trim the honour of having been founded by St. Patrick twenty-two years before Armagh. Tirechan gives us very precise details of his activity in the northwestern region of the kingdom of Meath. Crossing the river now known as the Inny, Patrick reached the region known then as Tethbia. Here he consecrated Mel, who, in the list of the Bishops of the Church of Ireland, is the first Bishop of Ardagh. With his own fingers he pointed out the site of Rahan church—still one of our parishes in the Diocese of Meath—and our authority tells us that here he ordained to the ministry Gosact, the son of his old master, Miliucc. Doubtless, as Patrick laid his hands upon the head of his friend, his thoughts wandered back to the old days at Slemish, when, as boys, they had played together on the northern hillside, and wondered at the strange vicissitudes of life which had led to that ordination service. And we, looking back through the centuries, may

* Donagh = Dominica, is always used of a Church, the foundation of which St. Patrick laid, or pointed out, on the Lord's Day.

"Blessing of God upon you all—sons, daughters, of Erin."

also see another illustration of that personal ascendancy and deep affection which our Saint seemed so naturally to establish in the hearts of those with whom the changes and chances of this mortal life brought him into contact.

—G. A. Chamberlain

HIS SONG

The "Lorica of Saint Patrick" is well known in the version of Mrs. Cecil Frances Alexander, which finds a place in the Hymnal of the Church of Ireland and is a favorite ordination hymn in the hymnal (on page 268) of the Episcopal Church in the United States. It is written in that uncouth Irish which the saint learned as a lad in Slemish.

Lorica, is Latin for "breastplate," and the repetition of the word was supposed to guard a traveler like a breastplate from spiritual foes, thus ensuring divine protection.

The hymn, also called "Deer's Cry," was set to music as a sacred cantata by Sir Robert Stewart, professor of music at the University of Dublin, and was performed for the first time in Saint Patrick's Cathedral, Dublin, on Saint Patrick's Day, 1888. Mrs. Alexander's translation appeared the following year.

In its vigorous lines we see Patrick's vivid and intense grasp of the central Christian doctrine of the Trinity—then the storm center of the religious world. We sense the equally vivid belief in the reality and potency of evil against which God and His servants did battle. We feel the unshakable courage of the man. We feel his sense of Nature. And, above all, we feel the steadying influence of the pervading presence of Christ Whom, as a breastplate, he had bound unto himself. Here is Christianity that is strong, direct, vigorous and simple.

In the hymnal the congregation is instructed to sing the song *with energy,* which is doubtless the way Patrick himself sang it.

—Alice-Boyd Proudfoot

THE LORICA OF SAINT PATRICK

I bind unto myself today the strong Name of the Trinity,
By invocation of the same, the Three in One, and One in Three.

I bind this day to me forever, by power of faith, Christ's Incarnation;
His baptism in the Jordan river; His death on the cross for my salvation;
His bursting from the spiced tomb; His riding up the heav'nly way;
His coming at the day of doom: I bind unto myself today.

I bind unto myself the power of the great love of the cherubim;
The sweet "Well done" in judgment; the service of the seraphim;
Confessors' faith, apostles' word, the patriarchs' prayers, the prophets'
    scrolls;
All good deeds done unto the Lord, And purity of virgin souls.

I bind unto myself today the virtues of the starlit heav'n,
The glorious sun's life-giving ray; The whiteness of the moon at even,
The flashing of the lightning free; The whirling wind's tempestuous
    shocks;
The stable earth; The deep salt sea, around the old eternal rocks.

I bind unto myself today the power of God to hold and lead.
His eye to watch, his might to stay, his ear to hearken to my need;
The wisdom of my God to teach, his hand to guide, his shield to ward;
The word of God to give me speech, his heav'nly host to be my guard.

Christ be within me, Christ behind me, Christ before me,
Christ beside me, Christ to win me, Christ to comfort and restore me,
Christ beneath me, Christ above me, Christ in quiet, Christ in danger,
Christ in hearts of all that love me, Christ in mouth of friend and
    stranger.

I bind unto myself the Name, the strong Name of the Trinity;
By invocation of the same, the Three in One and One in Three.
Of whom all nature hath creation; Eternal Father, Spirit, Word:
Praise to the Lord of my salvation, salvation is of Christ the Lord.

Amen.
—Translated by Mrs. Cecil Frances Alexander

Patrick sang it when the ambuscades were laid for him by Laoghaire, in order that he should not go to Tara to sow the Faith, so that
on that occasion they were seen before those who were lying in ambush
as if they were wild deer having behind them a fawn (Patrick's young
psalmist, Benin) and "Deer's Cry" is its name.

—From an ancient Irish Preface

The "strange" Saint Patrick statue in Saint Patrick's Cathedral, Dublin. This statue of the saint is probably an effigy of a fourteenth-century cleric, with the head added at a later date.

"DEER'S CRY," OR "THE BREASTPLATE OF SAINT PATRICK"

Patrick made this hymn; in the time of Loegaire mac Neill it was made, and the cause of its composition was for the protection of himself and his monks against the deadly enemies that lay in ambush for the clerics. And it is a lorica of faith for the protection of body and soul against demons and men and vices; when any person shall recite it daily with pious meditation on God, demons shall not dare to face him; it shall be a protection to him against all poison and envy; it shall be a guard to him against sudden death; it shall be a lorica for his soul after his decease.

4

The Mission Continues

ST. PATRICK: HIS LIFE AND WORK *(cont'd.)*

Connaught

HAVING established himself in the Kingdom of Meath, and having secured not merely the neutrality but also the respect and the goodwill of the High King of Ireland, Patrick now devoted his attention and his energy to the evangelisation of the western lands beyond the Shannon, to which so many years before the voice from the wood of Fochlath had called him.

It would appear that the route of the first missionary journey across the Shannon struck northwards through Roscommon, where the Saint founded the church of Aghanagh—still the name of the parish—near Boyle, and also Shancoe, to the west of Lough Arrow. His footsteps may be traced thence to the neighbourhood of Ballymote, where the parish of Taunagh still perpetuates the name of a parish founded by St. Patrick, on to the sea near the site of the town of Sligo. Here, perhaps because it marked the extreme limit of his progress, he consecrated

52

Patrick's Cross on the Rock of Cashel. *The earliest stone carving of the saint is this one in Cashel, Co. Tipperary, in which the full-length figure is incorporated into the side of a cross. Even though it is worn and disfigured, the elongated body, with its hand raised, imparts a feeling of great dignity. The cross is fitted into a base that was used for the coronation of the kings of Cashel.*

Bron as Bishop for the service of a church founded under the shadow of Knocknaree. Thence he would seem to have turned and proceeded almost due south through the counties of Sligo and Mayo, when swinging to the west—evangelising and founding churches as he went—he at length found himself on that desolate peninsula on the north shore of which the rugged peak of Crochan Aigli overlooks Clew Bay, which will be forever associated with the name of Patrick.

Late Legend, as illustrated by the *Tripartite Life,* has thrown around the simple dignity of St. Patrick's withdrawal to the mountainside for prayer and for communion with God, after the exhaustion of his period of toil in his service, fancies which have sunk deep into popular imagination. It was here that, with the aid of his miraculous staff (the *baculum Iesu*) given by our Lord Himself in one of the islands of the Mediterranean, Patrick assembled all the snakes and venomous creatures and drove them into the sea. It was here that demons, in the shape of flocks of black birds, tormented the Saint until he flung his bell at them and shattered it. Of such things Tirechan knows nothing; and how much more impressive are the simple words of his narrative, "And Patrick journeyed to Mount Egli, to fast on it forty days and forty nights, observing the discipline of Moses and of Elijah and of Christ."

The track of another expedition into what is now known as Roscommon emerges as we study the placenames in the pages of Tirechan. Crossing the River Shannon in the neighbourhood of Lake Bofin, some dozen miles south of Carrick-on-Shannon, the Saint made his way into the plain of Glass, which lies about Moyglass. In this district the village of Kilmore to this day perpetuates the memory of the Cell Mor —the great church—which he founded. Pushing northwards he found himself in the great plain—Mag Ai—which stretches over the central area of the modern county. A few miles brought his footsteps to Ailfinn —the White Rock—where one of the most important of his foundations was made. The little community of three which was here established had as its first head a Bishop named Assicus, who, like Tubal Cain, was "an instructor of every artificer in brass and iron." Assicus may be regarded as the father of that Irish ecclesiastical art which moved along so unique a line of development and produced such works of beauty as may still be seen in the Ardagh Chalice. Square patens of curious design made by his hands were long preserved in Elphin, which, as we know, ultimately became the seat of a diocesan Bishop and gave its name to his diocese.

At Elphin St. Patrick found himself within a short distance of one of the most famous strongholds in Ireland—a place which was to the Kings of Connaught what Tara was to the Kings of Meath. The earthen mounds at Crochan, still raised above the surrounding plain, are to-day all that is·left to remind us that here kings lived and died and were buried. The secular story of the place where a palace looked down upon a tomb and where the King dwelt beside his ancestors is not our immediate concern. But Rathcrochan comes within the ambit of our story as the scene of one of the most interesting and curious of the earliest legends of St. Patrick.

That there are inconsistencies in the story and a certain artificiality in its structure will not escape the notice of the attentive reader. But, none the less, the story bears upon its surface the stamp of very early date and it gives us in a vivid way—what it was designed to give those who first heard it—a genuine impression of the kind of teaching given by St. Patrick and the articles of the Christian faith upon which he laid his emphasis. And it also gives us a flavour of the Natural Religion of the Pagan Irish, who looked to see God in the sea and the river and the mountain and the valley. How far the legend may be regarded as "foreshortened history" and as confining to the limits of a day what may have been spread over years, we shall not pause to conjecture, nor shall we spoil the story by paraphrase.

THE CONVERSION OF KING LAOGHAIRE'S DAUGHTERS

Then St. Patrick came before the rising of the sun to a fountain which is called Clebach, on the side of Crochan looking towards the sunrising. And they sat beside the fountain.

And lo, two daughters of King Laoghaire, Ethne the fair and Fedelm the golden-haired, came to the fountain to wash in the morning, as is the wont of women. And they found beside the fountain the holy synod of bishops with Patrick. And they were at a loss to know where they were, or in what shape they were, or of what people they were, or to what country they belonged. But they judged them to be fairy men, or to be of the earth gods, or to be an apparition.

And the girls said to them: "Where are ye? and whence come ye?" And Patrick said to them: "It were better for you to confess the true God, our God, than to ask questions about our race."

The elder girl said: "Who is God? And where is God? And whose is God? And where is His dwelling? Has your God sons and daughters, gold and silver? Does He live for ever? is He beautiful? Had His Son many foster fathers? Are His daughters dear and beautiful to the men of this world? Is He in heaven or in earth? in the sea? in the rivers? in the mountains? in the valleys? Tell us the knowledge of Him. How shall He be seen? How is He loved? How is He found? Is it in youth, is it in old age, that He is found?"

Then St. Patrick full of the Holy Spirit, answered and said: "As for our God, He is the God of all men. He is the God of heaven and earth, of sea and rivers; He is the God of sun and moon; of all the stars. He is the God of the lofty mountains and of the lowly valleys. God above the heaven and in the heaven and under the heaven, has

His dwelling around heaven and earth and sea and all that in them is. He inspires all things; He quickens all things; He transcends all things; He sustains all things. He gives its light to the sun; He veils the light and knowledge of the night. He made fountains in the parched land, and dry islands in the midst of the sea; and He appointed the stars to serve the greater lights.

"He hath a Son, co-eternal with Himself. The Son is not younger than the Father, nor the Father older than the Son; and the Holy Spirit breathes in them; nor are the Father, Son and Holy Spirit divided.

"Now I wish to unite you to the heavenly King, inasmuch as ye are daughters of an earthly King. Believe."

And the girls said, as with one mouth and heart: "That we may be able to believe on the heavenly King, do thou teach us with the utmost care. That we may see Him face to face, do thou direct us; and we shall do whatsoever thou sayest."

And Patrick said: "Do you believe that by baptism ye cast away the sin of your father and mother?" They answer: "We believe."

"Do ye believe in repentance after sin?" "We believe."

"Do ye believe in life after death? Do ye believe in a resurrection at the Day of Judgement?" "We believe."

"Do ye believe in the unity of the Church?" "We believe."

So they were baptized; and a white veil was put over their heads. And they demanded to see the face of Christ. And the Saint said to them: "Unless ye taste of death, ye cannot see the face of Christ, nor unless ye receive the Sacrifice." And they answered: "Give us the Sacrifice, that we may see the Son our Spouse." And they received the Eucharist of God, and they slept in death. And they placed them in one bed, covered with garments. And their friends made a wailing and great lamentation.

It will be remembered that in his *Confession* St. Patrick tells how in his dream as he read a letter entitled "The Voice of the Irish," he seemed to hear "the voice of them who lived beside the Wood of Fochlath, which is nigh unto the western sea," calling, and we have seen how from that decisive hour his whole life was devoted to the preparation for and fulfilment of his response to that haunting cry. It has been reckoned that St. Patrick was already some thirteen years in Ireland when, on his second return to Tara from his journeyings in Connaught, a chance conversation overheard opened up the possibility of a complete and literal fulfilment of the task which was given him. Near the Palace of Laoghaire he happened to hear a conversation between "two noblemen . . . and one said to the other . . . 'Tell me thy name, I pray thee, and that of thy farm, and of thy plain, and where thy house is?' And he replied: 'I am Endeus, the son of Amolngaid . . . from the western shores, from the plain of Domnon, and from the Wood of Fochlath.' "

We can well imagine the thrill with which Patrick must have heard again that name which must have been vividly in his memory as the goal of his endeavour—the only Irish place name in the pages of the *Confession*. "Now when Patrick heard the name of the Wood of Fochlath, he rejoiced greatly, and said to Endeus, the son of Almongaid: 'I, too, will go with thee, if I am alive, because the Lord bade me go.' " Endeus demurred and refused to permit the Saint to accompany him, saying that they would both be killed. "Then the Saint said: 'Of a truth thou shalt never reach thy country alive, if I come not with thee,

---

"You have departed from this world to go to paradise. Thanks be to God."

—Saint Patrick

---

nor shalt thou have eternal life; because for my sake thou didst come hither.' "

Patrick set out with Endeus and his party, and with them arrived in safety in the land of Amolngaid, the name of which is perpetuated to this day as Tirawley. History records almost nothing of what happened during what the Saint must have regarded as the climax of his mission. But where history is silent, topography speaks. The "Great Church" which he founded—Domnach-Mor—is our Donaghmore, and near it lay the Wood of Fochlath. Not far from Killala the map still shows the townland of Crosspatrick; and the "meeting place of the sons of Amolngaid," where St. Patrick built a square church of earth, may be identified in the name and the situation of Mullaghfarry. With the evangelisation of the country around the Wood of Fochlath, the mission of St. Patrick in the West was brought to a conclusion.

THE ENCHANTMENT OF CASHEL

So deep a hush lay over the plain of Tipperary that I could hear the dogs barking as far away as Rosegreen and Cahir. The setting sun was almost warm over the plain, and not one whisper of wind moved the grass.

Before me, in the centre of the Golden Vale, rose Cashel of the Kings, that mighty rock, lonely as a great ship at sea, lifted above the flat lands as Ely lifts herself above the fenlands of Cambridgeshire. It is strange that one of Ireland's most sacred relics should have been planted by the devil. Every school-child in Tipperary knows that when the devil was flying home (apparently to England) across the plain of Tipperary, he took a savage bite out of the northern hills in passing, but dropped the rocky mouthful in the centre of the Golden Vale.

It is a fact that, if you look in the right direction towards the

The Rock of Cashel. *This citadel of Irish Christianity, today a national monument, rises sheer out of the level farmlands of Tipperary. Saint Declan, a sixth-century disciple of Saint Patrick, built the first church on the site. In the thirteenth century the cathedral was built, including a round tower and Cormac's Chapel, the finest surviving example of Irish Romanesque. The cathedral was burned by the Earl of Kildare in 1495 because he thought the archbishop was inside. It was later restored, but finally abandoned in the eighteenth century.*

Slieve Bloom Mountains, you can see the gap in the remote hills which Cashel, it seems, would exactly fit. They call it the Devil's Bit.

The Angelus bell was ringing in the still evening as I took the steep path to the ancient stronghold of the Kings of Munster.

On top of this high rock, surrounded by a stone wall, is all that is left of a royal city of ancient Ireland. The man who unlocks the gate and admits you to a wide space of hummocky grass and the ruins of palace and churches points to a rough stone on which is an ancient cross.

"That," he tells you, "is where St. Patrick baptized King Aengus in the olden days."

In Cashel they still remember the story of the baptism of King Aengus. I like the familiar way people in Ireland talk about the heroes and kings of antiquity. They might just have left them round the bend of a lane. They say that when King Aengus was baptized on the ancient coronation stone of the high kings at Cashel, St. Patrick was old and feeble, and in order to support himself he drove the spiked point of his crozier firmly into the earth. When the ceremony was over St. Patrick and those who stood round saw blood in the grass. The crozier had transfixed the foot of the king. The saint asked Aengus why he had not cried out in pain, and the king replied that he had heard so much about the sufferings of our Lord that he would have been proud to bear the agony, even had he not considered it part of the ceremony.

More wonderful than the round tower of Cashel, more interesting than the vague lines of the ancient palace, more beautiful than the roofless shell of the cathedral is King Cormac's Chapel, the most whimsical, the most strange and the most remarkable little chapel in the British Isles.

If you visit Ireland only to see this astonishing building you will not have crossed the sea in vain. It is the strangest sight to one accustomed to Norman churches in England, built by the Normans—apparently with a chisel in one hand and a drawn sword in the other! Durham Cathedral, which is the greatest Norman Church in England, holds something of Flambard's sternness in its stones. Even small chapels, like St. John's in the Tower of London and that practically unknown underground chapel in the Black Keep at Newcastle, are essentially grim. They appear to have been designed by architects who had just composed a fortress. But Cormac's Chapel on Cashel is the only piece of gay Norman architecture I have seen. One might almost call it Norman architecture with a sense of humour! There is nothing else quite like it in the world.

What is the explanation? It is the only great piece of Norman work in the British Isles not built by Normans. It was built half a century before the Normans invaded Ireland by those much-travelled Irish monks who, in the early days, went out from their monasteries to every part of Europe. These monks tried to copy something which they had admired very much in France, but it worked out with a Celtic difference: they put into this chapel—into its rounded dome—toothed arches, something quite original, which you will find only in the *Book of Kells* and the Shrine of St. Patrick's Bell.

"And do you not see something strange about the chapel?" asked the guide.

I followed his glance, and noticed that it is at a slightly different angle from the nave, symbolizing the drooping of Christ's head on the Cross. This is the earliest declination I remember to have seen.

The guide took me up into a stone room above the chapel which was a library in the days when Cashel was the Tara and the Armagh of the south.

Professor Macalister comments on the diminutive Irish churches in *The Archaeology of Ireland*:

> The small size of the early Irish churches has frequently been commented upon; we all remember how Thackeray in his *Irish Sketch Book* waxes merry over the miniature cathedral at Glendalough. But it must be remembered that the stone buildings, which survive, were in all likelihood the smaller and the poorer structures; and further, that the provision of a building for the reception of the laity as well as the clergy was not necessarily contemplated by the builders. In a large number of cases the people attending Mass remained outside the building, as may still frequently be seen in the country parts of Ireland.

Most people who see these churches must be fascinated by the skilful construction of the stone roofs.

> The double roof of the main portion of St. Kevin's Kitchen is an example of an ingenious mode of construction which seems to have been a native Irish invention [says Professor Macalister]. It is also found in the ancient chapel in the cathedral church at Killaloe, in St. Colum Cille's house at Kells, in Cormac's Chapel at Cashel, and in one or two other buildings. It was a device for obtaining a high-pitched sloping roof, such as a rainy climate required, without running the risk of the thrust of the roof pressing the walls outwards and so bringing the whole structure to ruin. After the side walls were erected, a centering of timber was constructed, forming a vault, the extrados of which was covered with timber planking or of brushwood. Upon this centering a stone vault was constructed, and well grouted with liquid mortar, which ran through the joints and accumulated above the brushwood, of which it retained an impression. (There is a fine example of this in the sacristy vault of Clonfert Cathedral.) When the mortar was thoroughly set, the centering was removed; the result was that the church was covered in, as it were, with a solid lid, with flat top and with a vaulted under side. On the upper surface of this "lid" the sloping roof was erected. There was, in consequence, no outward thrust at all; all the weight of the roof pressed vertically downward; a building of no considerable size could thus be set up without any buttresses. A chamber was formed in the roof, which could be reached with a ladder through an opening left in the vault.

Professor Baldwin Brown has studied the mechanics of this form of roof and concludes with these words: "Though they have in most cases been considerably restored in recent times, their vaults seem to have remained firm, and have not been reconstructed, while in no case has any buttressing of the external walls become a necessity. The fact reflects no little credit on the Irish mason, who not only evolved a novel scheme of construction, but carried it out with perfect success into practice."

I could return again and again to Cormac's Chapel and never exhaust its singular charm. What, I wonder, would Irish architecture be like if this translation of Romanesque into Gaelic had been allowed to go on? It is, in my opinion, one of the architectural tragedies of the world that the Irish did not, or were not permitted to, develop this style but were forced to adopt the Gothic, which never suited them.

The Gothic in Ireland differs from that of the neighbouring countries in a remarkable and important circumstance [says Professor Macalister]. Elsewhere the Gothic styles were an organic growth, passing from stage to stage in a natural evolution. In Ireland Gothic was a transplanted sapling, which never became acclimatized.

To the last the native architects could never master the principle of Gothic; just as they could never master the English language. They forced both to conform to the Celtic idiom. The language spoken throughout Ireland is still Irish, with English words substituted for the corresponding Irish words; and it is on the syntactic anomalies thus produced that the inventor of "Irish" jokes depends for his livelihood, although his attempts at producing the real idioms of this extremely difficult language are, as a rule, fatuous beyond conception. The architecture practised in Ireland throughout the Middle Ages was, in like manner, Celtic, with a Gothic veneer. In consequence, we find in Irish medieval churches an endless succession of anomalies; churches with the transept longer than the nave, as at the Black Abbey, Kilkenny; capitals with the abacus cut into delicate flowers, as at Corcomroe, Clare; arch-mountings twisted into ropes, as at Clonmacnois; pointed arches with keystones, as in a small church on the Aran Islands; want of symmetry in groups of window-lights, as at Glenagra (Limerick) or in a church on Inis Clothrann in Loch Ree; a chancel roofed with a barrel vault at right angles to the main axis of the building, as at Kilmaine (Mayo) : there seems to be no limit to the indifference to the "rules of the game" which the Irish architects display when designing Gothic churches. . . . But just as a foreigner speaking English often hits upon a phrase which is not English in the least—which would never enter the head of a native of England to concoct—and yet which is strikingly expressive, so the Irish architects not infrequently produce a bold stroke of originality out of their very inexperience and independence of tradition.

If I were an Irishman I would haunt Cashel of the Kings, for there, and there alone, is visible a link with the Gaelic Ireland which, subjected to invasion and oppression, has stubbornly survived: the Ireland of the *Book of Kells*, the Ardagh Chalice, the Cross of Cong, and the Tara brooch. All these things prove a rich and imaginative national life which never had the opportunity to develop. And if the

Walter Scott whom Ireland needs so badly should ever arrive I think it is to Cashel that he should go for his first book.

Where, I wonder, is the Walter Scott of Ireland? He has a richer store of romance ready for him than ever Scotland gave to the writer who made the whole world love Scotland. It would seem a duty to give to the world the best and the finest qualities of the Irish character: the reckless gallantry, the courage, the humour, the pathos, and the spirituality. It is a task that awaits genius. Let him go to Cashel.

The view from the perilous wall which is on a level with the cone of the round tower is one of the grandest in Ireland. I can compare it only with the view down over the Links of Forth from the height of Stirling Castle. All round is the fat, green country of the Golden Vale: the thin roads crossing running through the fields; the farms; the little belts of woodland and, to the southward, hills.

When it grew dark a great yellow moon swung up over Tipperary plain and hung in the sky above Cashel. The dogs were howling far off in distant farms. Little knots of young men idled and talked at the street corners, laughing and joking and speaking English woven on a Gaelic loom. And on the hill I looked up at the ancient ruins of Cashel of the Kings, rising darkly against the stars. It was silent, empty, and locked for the night, and the moon's light was over it, falling down on it like a green rain.

It rode in moonlight over Tipperary like a haunted ship.

—H. V. Morton

CASHEL

Behind charred doors and splintered glass the smoke,
Acrid and tainted has the stench of vileness.
Dark walls (begrimed by fire where Inchiquin
Piled corpse on corpse before the tortured altars,
The naked dead painting their shame with blood)
Enclose a charnel house of hate gone mad.

Aseptic time has mellowed Guernica
To lichened peace and mouldering effigy,
Where lark-song fills a gap of roofless sky
And cloudland, seen through eyeless arch.

In Kansas City kodachromes are shown
Picturing where Corc, the son of Aengus, stood
Impaled by Patrick (tactless accident).
"They crowned the King of Munster on that stone."
"Who?" "Why, Brian Boru." "Say, just who was he?"
"Oh Sadie, listen! That guy says some Earl

Set fire to it before. He claims he did it
Only because the Bishop was inside."
The cameras click, and way back home in Yonkers
Poppa will show it with the Changing of the Guard.

—*R.L.*

One little human episode does more to illustrate the character of the saint than all the later legends composed to do him honor. It speaks to us of his affection for an humble servant who had been a faithful companion in labor and in danger. His driver, whose name was Totmael, died in Murrisk—the plain between Croagh Patrick and the sea. "And he buried Totus Caluus the driver; and he heaped stones about his tomb, and he said, 'May it so remain forever; and it shall be visited by me in my last days.' "

CLIMBING CROAGH PATRICK

When Lent came in the year A.D. 441 St. Patrick retired to a great mountain in Connaught to commune with God. He fasted there for forty days and forty nights, weeping, so it is said, until his chasuble was wet with tears.

The medieval monks possessed detailed accounts of St. Patrick's fast. They said that to the angel, who returned to him every night with promises from God, the saint said:

"Is there aught else that will be granted to me?"

"Is there aught else thou wouldst demand?" asked the angel.

"There is," replied St. Patrick, "that the Saxons shall not abide in Ireland by consent or perforce so long as I abide in heaven."

"Now get thee gone," commanded the angel.

"I will not get me gone," said St. Patrick, "since I have been tormented until I am blessed."

"Is there aught else thou wouldst demand?" asked the angel once more.

St. Patrick requested that on the Day of Judgment he should be judge over the men of Ireland.

"Assuredly," said the angel, "that is not got from the Lord."

"Unless it is got from Him," replied the determined saint, "departure from this Rick shall not be got from me from today until Doom; and, what is more, I shall leave a guardian there."

The angel returned with a message from heaven:

"The Lord said, 'There hath not come, and there will not come from the Apostles, a man more admirable, were it not for thy hardness. What thou hast prayed for, thou shalt have . . . and there will be a consecration of the men of the folk of Ireland, both living and dead.' "

St. Patrick said:

"A blessing on the bountiful King who hath given; and the Rick shall now be departed therefrom."

As he arose and prepared to descend from the mountain, mighty birds flew about him so that the air was dark and full of the beating of wings. So St. Patrick stood, like Moses on Sinai, and round him all the Saints of Ireland, past, present, and to come.

In this we can see the Irish belief in the inflexible determination of their saint: "a steady and imperturbable man." And it was said that while upon this mountain in Connaught St. Patrick banished all snakes from Ireland.

This mountain, Croagh Patrick—or Patrick's Hill—lifts its magnificent cone 2,510 feet above the blue waters of Clew Bay. It is Ireland's Holy Mountain. Once a year in July a pilgrimage is made to the little chapel on the crest. Atlantic liners drop anchor in Galway Bay, bringing Irish-Americans who wish to ascend the mountain for the good of their souls. As many as 40,000 pilgrims have climbed the mountain in one day; and many of the more devout remove their shoes and socks and take the hard path barefoot.

The morning broke dangerously clear and fine. I took a stout stick and prepared to climb the mighty flank of Ireland's Sinai. As I approached it, admiring the high pattern of wheeling clouds over its head, I could see far off the little Mass chapel like a cairn of stones on the crest.

I plodded on over a rough mountain path worn by the feet of the faithful century after century. A wind blew in from the Atlantic bringing rain with it, and in a few moments the earth was hidden in a thin grey mist. I was disappointed, but went on in the hope that the sky would clear in time and give me what must surely be the grandest view in Ireland.

There are few experiences more uncanny than climbing a mountain in mist and rain. As I went on and up, the mist grew thicker, and the drizzle fell in that peculiar persistent Irish way that wets you to the skin before you are aware of it. Above me was this grey wet pall, below me the same mystery; only the rocks under my feet were real, and there was no sound but the falling of water and the click of a dislodged stone rolling behind me down the path.

There is something terrifying, at least to me, in the mists that cover mountains—mists that hide you know not what; mists that cut a man off from the world and deny him the sight of the sky. To be lost on a mountain in mist is to experience all the horror of panic, for it seems to you that you might lose the path and go wandering vainly in circles answered only by a mocking laugh which seems to hide in all mountain

Saint Patrick on Croagh Patrick

mists. But I consoled myself by the thought that Croagh Patrick is a holy mountain from whose ravines and gullies all demons have been banished. Suddenly, right before me rose a white figure, and I looked up to a statue of St. Patrick.

The saint, I discovered, stands there to hearten pilgrims, for the real climb begins behind him. The path ends. The climber ascends, picking his way over a steep gully, the loose stones sliding beneath his feet; and as I went on the joy of climbing in rain came to me, so that I loved the wetness of my cheeks and hair and the movement of the mist which told me that I was in a great cloud that hid Croagh Patrick from the eyes of men.

I came to a cairn of stones: one of the Stations of the Cross. And as I stood there asking my Catholic ancestors what to do about it I heard a voice, and out of the mist came an unlikely and preposterous sight. A middle-aged woman was painfully descending the path. She looked exactly as though some one had taken her up in the very moment of buying six yards of *crêpe de Chine* at a Grafton Street draper's and had blown her on top of Croagh Patrick. No sooner had she become startlingly clear in the narrow circle of my vision than another figure materialized from the mist: her husband. He also was incredible. He wore a bowler hat. It seemed so odd to encounter a bowler hat on a holy mountain. We said what a bad day it was. They asked if there were any more people coming up behind me. They told me it was their first pilgrimage. The woman was worried. She had lost a rosary among the stones. If I found it would I post it to her in Limerick? I thought how strange it was to English eyes: two solid, middle-aged people of the comfortable kind going off together to pray on the summit of a holy mountain.

"God be with you and bless you," they said gravely; and I went on into the damp cloud.

Onward in the mist I went, hot and weary and happy; once I thought I had found the lost rosary, but it was only a piece of torn shoelace that had fallen into a hollow of the rocks. I passed another Station of the Cross and soon found myself on the peak of Croagh Patrick, 2,510 feet above Connaught, with the mountains of Mayo north of me, the blue Atlantic west of me, and south the mountains of the Joyce Country and the Twelve splendid Pins of Connemara. But, alas, not one glimmer of it shone through the wet cloud that hung over the holy mountain. . . .

On the summit of this height is a little Mass chapel. I was told in Connemara how this building was made. Cement in seven-pound bags was carted to the foot of the mountain and every pilgrim regarded it as an act of devotion to carry one of these to the top. Many a man, I was told, made the ascent more than once for the honour of carrying up material for the construction of this tiny oratory.

I went inside and knelt down. The place was very small and ice-cold. A young priest knelt in prayer. The wind howled round the little building in soft gusts, and I wondered what it felt like to be there in the great storms that swept in from the Atlantic. Even though the walls of the little chapel cut off the sight of moving mists there was something in the air of the chapel that told of a chilly solitude far from the comfortable earth. I was conscious that, outside, the mountain mists were sweeping past; the cold air told of a remote solitude; the rudeness of the little sanctuary was that of a shrine built on an outpost of the world. The kneeling priest never moved. He might have been carved in stone. He reminded me of some knight keeping vigil before the altar.

I tiptoed out, and sitting on a wet stone, ate the sandwiches and the cheese that I had brought with me. I sat there wet through, longing and hoping against hope that the clouds would rise and show me the distant earth. The wind that sweeps over the head of Croagh Patrick is the cruel whistle that comes to all great mountains; and in the sound of it, even though you cannot see two yards before you, is a message of height, of dizzy drops, of jagged gullies and awful chasms.

It was on this height, as told by the medieval monks, that St. Patrick flung his bell from him only to have it returned to his hand; and at each sound of the bell the toads and the adders fled from Ireland. . . .

I went down over the wet stones. I came gratefully to the white statue of the saint. I had left the clouds above me, but the rain was falling, blotting out the sea and the hills.

—H. V. Morton

THE early Irish Church, on its own, arrived at some doctrines which seem so sensible that one regrets that the Roman Branch did not see fit to accept them. It should, for instance, be more generally appreciated throughout Christendom nowadays that while the rest of the world is undergoing the horrors preceding Doomsday, Ireland will not only be spared that anguish but will have a friend at court. Exactly one week before it will have been covered by a soft green flood, while the inhabitants are being judged by Saint Patrick.

The Venerable Bede pointed out, "Almost all things in the island are good against poison. Indeed it has come to our knowledge that when certain persons had been bitten by serpents, the scrapings of the leaves of books brought out of Ireland were put into water and given them to drink, which immediately expelled the spreading poison and cured the swelling."

—Walter Bryan

EXPULSION

A legend, wafted over seas and lakes,
Says St. Patrick drove out Ireland's poisonous snakes.
What would St. Pat, were he around today,
Do about the I.R.A.?

—The Rev. Francis C. Lightbourn

Giraldus Cambrensis, secretary to Prince John, visited Ireland in 1187 and reported:

THERE are neither snakes nor adders, toads nor frogs, tortoises nor scorpions, nor dragons. It produces, however, spiders, leeches and lizards; but they are quite harmless. . . . It does appear very wonderful that, when anything venomous is brought here from other lands, it never could exist in Ireland. For we read in the ancient books of the saints of that country, that sometimes, for the sake of experiment, serpents have been shipped over in brazen vessels, but were found lifeless and dead as soon as the middle of the Irish Sea was crossed. Poison also similarly conveyed was found to lose its venom, disinfected by a purer air.

Nevertheless a frog was found, within my time, in the grassy meadows near Waterford, and brought to court alive before the Warden there and many others. And when the Irish had beheld it with great astonishment, at last Duvenold, King of Ossory, beating his head and having deep grief in his heart, spoke thus: "This reptile is the bearer of doleful news to Ireland." And he further said that it portended without doubt the coming of the English, and the subjugation of his own nation.

THE WEARING OF THE GREEN

The wearing of Shamrock is certainly the best known of the various Saint Patrick's Day customs and large quantities of it are specially shipped from Ireland to all parts of the world in the weeks preceding March 17th. It is wrongly said of the symbolic plant that it never flowers, that it is not a clover and that it will not grow on alien soil. It has slender creeping stems and small neat leaves and is now generally accepted by botanists as being *Trifolium minus.*

But although the legends associated with it trace its use back to Saint Patrick himself, the earliest recorded reference to its use as a badge does not occur until the seventeenth century when Thomas Dinely, an English traveller through Ireland, noted in his *Journal:*

"The 17th day of March yearly is Saint Patrick's, an immovable feast when ye Irish of all stations and condicons wear crosses in their hats, some of pins, some of green ribbon, and the vulgar superstitiously wear shamroges, 3-leaved grass which they likewise eat (they say) to cause a sweet breath. The common people and servants also demand their Patrick's groat of their masters, which they goe expressly to town, though half a dozen miles off, to spend where sometimes it amounts to a piece of 8 or cobb a piece, and very few of the zealous are found sober at night."

—Anonymous

THE SHAMROCK FOR GOOD LUCK

In olden times the shamrock was highly regarded as a defense against the malevolent power of witches. Irish peasants plucked the leaf before venturing across lonely moors where banshees wailed and fairies were wont to spirit away the souls of travelers, and many of its apotropaic powers are still believed in parts of Ireland. If a farmer plucks a sprig and takes it home, all will go well with his cattle on May Day. The colleen who surreptitiously conceals a leaf in the shoe of her departing lover can be certain of his return. When plucked with a gloved hand and carried secretly into a house where an insane person resides, the magical shamrock will cure the patient. Emigrants leaving Ireland commonly carry a sprig to ensure good luck.

—Anonymous

Wedgwood collector's plate, introduced in 1981. Sage green on Jasper white, it is hand-ornamented with shamrocks and a figure of Saint Patrick with church and crozier.

SCRAMBLED SHAMROCKS

It is well known that Saint Patrick introduced the shamrock as a symbol of Ireland by using it as a visual aid to explain the mystery of the Trinity (which accounts for the fact that many Irish children think of God as small, green and vaguely triangular), but unfortunately the fact seems to have been so well known that nobody bothered to write it down until about 150 years ago. Indeed the first mention in literature of the shamrock in connection with Ireland was in the 16th Century, when English writers reported it to be part of the Irish diet. I realize this is disturbing news, like the French finding a frog's leg foisted on them as a national symbol, or like the Americans discovering that their eagle is really a turkey, but I'm afraid there is worse to come. Not only is the shamrock not peculiar to Ireland, but the Irish themselves are not sure which plant it is. They think they know, but not so long ago an interfering naturalist carried out a sort of shamrock census. One March he wrote to people all over Ireland asking for specimens of the True Shamrock that Grows in Our Isle, and then planted them and waited for them to flower. The obnoxious busybody then claimed to identify no less than four different varieties of trefoil, none of them unique to Ireland. In fact the word shamrock in Irish simply means "little clover." And, to pile horror on horror like Pelleas on Melisande, I read some years ago that the home crop had failed and supplies were being imported from Czechoslovakia. Oh well, I suppose it doesn't do to worry too much about trefoils.

In any event retribution was not long delayed, because shortly afterwards the Irish lost a case they had taken against a German firm for using the shamrock as a trademark. I am still waiting for fate to overtake the Japanese, who produce great quantities of fake Irish souvenirs. Admittedly they mark them with a statement of origin, but since there are two official languages in the Republic of Ireland all they have to do is stamp them "Made in Japan" in Gaelic, and very pretty it looks too.

—Walter Bryan

Armagh

Upon the hill around which the little city of Armagh has grown stands its Cathedral—small, indeed, as cathedrals are reckoned, but dignified and homely. Within the walls of the Cathedral is the seat of the Primate of the Church of Ireland, the successor of St. Patrick in the See of Armagh, which he founded in the year of our Lord 444. During the many centuries which composed what is known as the Celtic period, when the Church of Ireland moved in a strange orbit of its own within the ambit of the still unbroken Church of Christ before its Primates were induced to receive the pall from Rome; during the four centuries after the English invasion, when the old Celtic ways gradually gave way before the strength and vigour of the invader briefed from Rome; on, past the great cleavage of the Reformation period, a Cathedral on that venerable site has contained the seat of the Primate of the Church of Ireland. It is an inheritance which has come down through the strange vicissitudes of national history, and is an outward and visible link uniting us to-day with our spiritual ancestry of fifteen centuries.

Why St. Patrick came to choose Armagh as the site of his Church and religious house must remain a matter of conjecture. It would be but natural to surmise that, as he regarded himself as the Bishop of all Ireland, he would have selected a more central site and one more accessible. The fact that Laoghaire, though well disposed, did not embrace the Christian faith may have deterred the Saint from selecting so obvious a site as Tara. Armagh lay within the kingdom of Oriel, and there is evidence of St. Patrick's missionary activity there as well as in Ulaid.

We have seen that his own work lay almost entirely in Ulster, Connaught and Meath, and it is possible that such a site as Armagh may have seemed to him a suitable and convenient centre to keep in touch with the districts with which he had been already in personal contact. The time had come to consolidate and to organise the conquests he had already made. He may well have felt that a policy of an "intensive shepherding" of the northern area would be more fruitful than a dissipation of energy by attempting to embrace the South, with which his personal connection had been, at best, but slight. If, as may well have been the case, Daire was not merely a king, but a person of character and weight in public life, it would be of considerable advantage to have his support and goodwill.

That St. Patrick intended his foundation at Armagh to be regarded in a peculiar sense as his own See, and to occupy a commanding position in the ecclesiastical organisation of Ireland, can hardly be questioned, as it would be impossible otherwise to account for the claims it consistently made and the position it actually attained. Into the long story of the struggle of Armagh to hold its pre-eminence and assert its authority we cannot now enter; but the fact that its Bishops did make such a claim would indicate that they had good grounds for believing that such a commanding position was theirs by right and bequeathed to them by the founder of the See and Church.

In the quaint and naive stories which lie about the foundation of Armagh in the pages of Muirchu there is no hint of any such original intention thus to elevate Armagh into anything in the nature of a diocese, to say nothing of a primacy. We are simply told that "in the country of Airthir" there was "a certain rich and honourable man named Daire. To him Patrick made request that he would grant him some place for the exercise of religion." But it seems reasonable to surmise that, once St. Patrick was established here, the advantages of the situation would before long make themselves felt if, as has been suggested, he desired to consolidate the Church in those districts where he himself had laid the foundation. And so what began as "a place for the exercise of religion" came to be regarded as the See of the Saint and the centre of the Church. St. Patrick, says our story, had set his heart upon a piece of high ground which was known as Ardd-Machæ, or the height of Macha. On this high ground stood two ridges, the loftier of which bore the name of the Ridge of the Willow— Druim Sailech. It was for this ridge on Ardd-Machæ that St. Patrick made request from Daire, its owner. Daire was unwilling to give this site, but gave another upon lower ground. With this the Saint had, for a time, to be content. "And there," we read, "St. Patrick dwelt with his people."

Rights of property are a fruitful source of friction in Ireland to this day, and it would appear that at first the relations between Daire and St. Patrick's little community were disturbed by a disagreement about grazing rights. The memory of this discord and hasty tempers has been vividly enshrined in the primitive legend of the horse of Daire:

> Now some time after there came a groom of Daire's leading his admirable horse, to graze on the grass lands of the Christians. And Patrick was offended at the horse trespassing in this way on his ground; and he said, "Daire has done a foolish thing in sending brute beasts to disturb the little holy place which he gave to God." But the groom was "like a deaf man and heard not, and as one that is dumb who doth not open his mouth"; he said nothing, but went away, leaving the horse there for the night. But on the next day, when the groom came in the morning to see the horse, he found it dead already. So he went back home in grief, and said to his lord, "See, that Christian killed my horse; he was annoyed at the disturbance of his place." And Daire said, "Let him be slain, too; go ye now and kill him."
>
> And as they were going forth, a death stroke, quicker than a word, fell on Daire. And his wife said, "This death stroke is on account of the Christian. Let someone go quickly, and let his blessing be brought to us, and thou wilt be cured; and let those who went forth to kill him be forbidden to do so, and be called back." So two men went forth to the Christian; and concealing what happened, they said to him, "Lo, Daire is sick; may something from thee be brought him, if haply he may be healed." St. Patrick, however, knowing what had happened, said, "Certainly." And he blessed some water, and gave it to them, saying, "Go, sprinkle your horse with water, and take him

VERNON REGIONAL

JUNIOR COLLEGE LIBRARY

with you." And they did so; and the horse came to life again, and they took him away with them, and Daire was healed by the sprinkling of the holy water.

IRELAND'S FIRST HYMN

One of the earliest, if not the earliest, of the documents illustrative of the life of Saint Patrick is the hymn *"In laudem S. Patricii,"* ascribed to Saint Sechnall, "the first hymn that was made in Ireland," according to the ancient Irish Preface.

The Annals of Ulster state that Sechnall died at the age of seventy-five in 447. The hymn was probably written earlier than Saint Patrick's own Latin writings. In it Patrick is spoken of as still alive, and although the eulogy is extravagant, no miracles, save those of the grace of God, are ascribed to him. It is revealing, though, that in the minds of his contemporaries there had grown an intense reverence for the man and a realization of the work he had already accomplished.

Sechnall is mentioned by Tirechan in a list of bishops consecrated by Saint Patrick and his name is preserved in Sechnall's Church in Co. Meath. It is there that the hymn is said to have been composed. According to the Irish Preface, Sechnall wrote it to make his peace with Patrick, who was displeased at a remark of Sechnall's that was reported to him: "A good man were Patrick, were it not for one thing, that he preaches charity so little."

When Sechnall recited the hymn to Patrick, the latter was so well pleased with it that he said, "Thou shalt have this boon: everyone who shall recite it at lying down and rising up shall go to heaven." "I accept that," said Sechnall, "but the hymn is long and not everyone will be able to commit it to memory." "Its grace," said Patrick, "shall be on the last three capitula [verses]."

One of the Four Honors due to Patrick in all the monasteries and churches of Ireland, according to the *Book of Armagh,* is that "his hymn should be sung during the whole time [three days and three nights] of his festival."

The hymn itself consists of twenty-three quatrains, each beginning with a different Latin letter (Audite, Beata, Constans, etc.). At the risk of not going to heaven, the compiler has chosen only two stanzas:

Steadfast in the fear of God, and in faith unshaken
Upon him, as upon Peter, the Church is built.
His apostleship he has received from God.
Against him the gates of hell prevail not.

Christ chose him for Himself to be his Vicar on earth,
Who from twofold slavery doth set captives free;
Of whom very many he redeems from slavery to men,
Countless numbers he releases from the dominion of the devil.

—Alice-Boyd Proudfoot

INVOCATION
by Caelius Sedulius (fifth century)

Sedulius was an Irish bard who travelled to Rome and there composed the first Christian epic, *"Carmen Paschale,"* or "Easter Song." A selection:

Ope me the way that to the City bright
Leads forth; let Thy Word's lamp be light
To guide my footsteps through the narrow gate,
Where the Good Shepherd feeds His sheep, elate:
There first the Virgin's white lamb entered
And all His fair flock followed where He led!
With Thee how smooth the way: for Nature all
Thine empire owns! Thou speak'st, her fetters fall
And all her wonted shows new forms assume:
The frozen fields will into verdure bloom
And winter gild with grain: if Thou but will
'Mid budding Spring the swelling grape shall fill,
And sudden labor tread the bursting vine.
All seasons answer to the call Divine!

However our enlightened age may be disposed to brush aside these facile miracles of healing, there can be no doubt that there was a serious disagreement, which, like many another, sprang out of some trifle. Those who have suffered that most irritating of torts—a trespassing animal—will have a large sympathy for the angry Saint; and we may well feel that even the temper of Job himself would give way had he to deal with that stolid groom. No Irishman will be disposed to think less of St. Patrick, because, in such circumstances, he grew hot.

Daire, after his recovery, bore no malice in his heart against his neighbour, and the story of the making up of the quarrel is not only the most delightful of all the Patrician legends, but gives us an explanation of how the Cathedral of Armagh came to be built on the site of the Ridge of Willows.

And after these things Daire came to pay his respects to St. Patrick, bringing with him a wonderful bronze pot, holding three gallons, that had come from beyond the seas. And Daire said to the Saint, "Lo, this bronze pot is for thee." And St. Patrick said *"Graza-*

*cham."** And when Daire returned to his own house, he said, "That is a stupid man, who said nothing more civil than *Grazacham* in return for a wonderful bronze, three-gallon pot." And Daire then proceeded to say to his servants, "Go, and bring us back our pot." So they went and said to Patrick, "We are going to take away the pot." Nevertheless, St. Patrick that time too said, *"Grazacham,* take it away." And they took it away. And Daire questioned his companions and said, "What did the Christian say when you took back the pot?" And they answered, "He just said *Grazacham.*" Daire answered and said, *"Grazacham* when it is given! *Grazacham* when it is taken away! His expression is so good that his pot must be brought back to him with his *Grazacham.*" And Daire came himself this time and brought the pot to Patrick, saying, "Thy pot must remain with thee; for thou art a steadfast and unchangeable man; moreover, as for that parcel of ground which thou didst once desire, I give it thee now in so far as I possess it; and do thou dwell there."

The truth lurks in this charming story that Daire came in the end to respect the Saint as a man of strong purpose and firm character; and he appears, like so many with whom St. Patrick came in touch, to have been impressed by something of forcefulness and power in his personality. The result was that Daire relented in the matter of the site and gave the desired Ridge of the Willows of Ardd-Machæ to Patrick and his community, which this day remains a "place for the exercise of religion."

Running through the literature of Celtic Christianity there is to be noticed a singularly delicate vein of tenderness towards animals. We have, for example, the well-known story of the old horse of St. Columba, and of the robin of St. Malo. The third of the trilogy of legends which lie about the founding of Armagh in the pages of Muirchu is a beautiful little episode which so resembles what the human memory always treasures that one can have little doubt that it represents faithfully one of those small and unconsidered trifles in life which serve to reveal perhaps more faithfully than larger matters the quality of a soul.

And they went both of them out, St. Patrick and Daire, to inspect the admirable and acceptable gift that was being offered; and they ascended that high ground, and found a hind with her little fawn lying where now stands the altar of the Northern Church in Ardd-Machae.

And St. Patrick's companions wanted to take the fawn and kill it; but the Saint did not wish this to be done, and would not allow it; nay, on the contrary, the Saint himself took the fawn and carried it on his shoulders. And the hind followed him, like a gentle and

---

* This curious word represents a hurried pronunciation of the Latin *gratias agam* = Thank God.

tame sheep, until he let the fawn loose in another wood situated on the north side of Ardd-Machae.

In the story of the cession of Armagh to St. Patrick already given it will be observed that Daire is represented as introducing a qualification. The words run: "I give to thee now, in so far as I possess it." In the peculiar social system of ancient Ireland ownership of the land does not appear to have vested absolutely in the noble owner. Both the tribe and the descendants of the proprietor had also rights and a vested interest in the property. These rights public opinion would not permit to be alienated, nor would there be provision in the law for absolute ownership. The consequence was that the monastic establishments founded in Ireland as centres of piety and missionary enterprise were obliged to adopt a constitution which would fit them into the social fabric of the tribes, and which differentiates the Celtic monasteries from those that sprang up in lands dominated by Roman law and a society based upon its foundation.

In the Irish monasteries the rights both of the descendants of the proprietor and of the tribe were conserved. Side by side with the abbot, the descendant of the original owner in some cases exercised an authority. In other cases the abbot could be appointed only from the family of the founder. To enter into the complicated and varied constitution of the Irish monastic system lies outside our immediate province, save to point out that it was moulded by the curious form of secular society in which it sprang up, and developed along lines quite independent of similar institutions within the frontiers of the Roman Empire. That St. Patrick and his successors should have fashioned the Church of Ireland along these lines was, in the circumstances, a necessity. There were in Ireland then no cities to form centres from which, as in the Empire, might radiate evangelisation and education, and the monastery was an attempt to create something which, in a tribal state of society, would fill this void.

But while this is so, and while it is true that in after years the monastic element developed so largely as to eclipse the diocesan and to subordinate the Bishop to the Abbot, there is no reason to conclude that this was so in the time of St. Patrick or that he had such an intention in his mind. That he consecrated many bishops is a fact. Tirechan, who gives the number as 450, mentions no less than forty-five by name. To eight of them he assigns certain churches in Connaught. This would indicate that he intended them to have episcopal jurisdiction over defined areas, and the numbers would suggest that the areas corresponded to the small tribal divisions of the country. Dr. Bury, who has studied this question with minute care, is probably right when he says that "Patrick's organisation was from one point of view monastic, from another episcopal. It was monastic in so far as many of the churches in the various regions were connected with religious communities of a monastic character . . . but this did not prevent it being episcopal, in the sense that there were episcopal districts or dioceses. There was not a body of bishops without Sees, who went round visiting churches promiscuously, but each bishop had his own diocese."*

Many centuries were to roll away until the diocesan system, as we know it, was to be established by the masterful hands of later ecclesiastics when, under foreign influence, they brought Ireland into the spiritual empire of Rome, and the pall—never before seen in Armagh—was added to the ancient vestments of the successors of St. Patrick. And more centuries were to pass before the Primacy of the See of St. Patrick was acknowledged without challenge by the occupants of the See of Dublin.

"The church of the Irish, or rather of the Romans; in order to be Christians like the Romans, you should chant among yourselves at every hour of prayer that praiseworthy cry, Kyrie eleison, Christe eleison. *Let every church which follows me chant* Kyrie eleison, Christe eleison. *Thanks be to God."*

—Saint Patrick

Death and Burial

A note in the *Book of Armagh* draws four analogies between the life of St. Patrick and the life of Moses. Both heard the voice of an angel speaking; both fasted forty days and forty nights; both lived for one hundred and twenty years; of both no man knows the sepulchre. The tradition that the Saint lived for one hundred and twenty years also appears in the pages of Muirchu. On the other hand, Tirechan and the Annals of Ulster† approximate to show a shorter life and an earlier death. Into the complex calculations as to the exact chronology of his death, this is not the place to enter; but it would appear that if we accept the date 461 as the date of his death our calculation will not be far wide of the true mark.

Common sense suggests that it would indeed be improbable that one who had spent his life under the continual strain of danger and toil would long survive the allotted span of human life. If, as seems most probable, the date of his birth was the year 389, the year 461 would mean that he died at the age of seventy-two. The greater age is not only in itself improbable, but arouses our suspicion as an artificial attempt to add to the obvious analogies to the career of Moses. If, then, we

---

* J. B. Bury, *Life of St. Patrick,* Appendix, p. 379.
† The Annals of Ulster also give another date: A.D. 493.

accept this most probable date an interesting conclusion follows. It will be remembered how the Saint had designated the lad Benignus, "who was most dear to him and trusty," as his successor. In the ancient lists of the succession in Armagh the name of Benignus appears as his successor and is assigned a period of ten years in the See. As Benignus died in 467, this would mean that St. Patrick resigned his pastoral staff into the hands of his beloved disciple in the year 457, or some four years before his death.

It may indeed well have been that, unlike Moses, he felt his eye grow dim and his natural force abated as he approached his three score years and ten; and that he desired a time of rest and quiet before he went hence and was no more seen. What more probable than that he should seek retirement amongst his old friends on the pleasant shores of Strangford Lough where he had made his first converts and built his first church? It is to such scenes of earlier life that the hearts of men turn with longing when they begin to hear the call of their Long Home.

So natural a surmise is confirmed by the pages of Muirchu. The tradition he preserves tells us that as the Saint felt the near approach of death he was living at Saul, amidst the friends of earlier days and beside the Barn which is the Mother Church of Ireland. But Patrick wished to die at Armagh, "which he loved beyond all other places," and sent a message "that many men should come to him, and bring whither he wished to go." But again the divine voice intervened, and it seemed as if the angel said: "Return unto the place whence thou camest, that is to Sabul." On March 17th, as Easter was drawing nigh, Patrick received his last Communion from the hands of Bishop Tassach and died at Saul. And it was said that on the day of his death and for twenty days afterwards there was no night in the province where he was buried. It may well have been that, in their grief, his people forgot to sleep, and it is recorded that on the nights of his funeral "men guarded the body, praying and singing psalms."

The legends preserved by Muirchu, which lie about the burial of the Saint, leave us in some perplexity as to his last resting place. It is quite clear from these stories that Armagh was anxious to obtain the body of St. Patrick. "At the time of his death, a sore contention, amounting even to war, arose concerning the relics of St. Patrick, between the Ui-Neill and the men of Airthir on one side, and the men of Ulaid on the other." But no fight took place, as the waters of Strangford Lough are said to have overflowed and separated the contending hosts. In another foray it is said that the men of Armagh thought that they had captured the wagon on which the body had been placed, but when they "got as far as the River Cabcenne, at that point the body was not present with them." It is, therefore, clear that the natural desire of Armagh was frustrated, and that wherever the mortal remains of the Saint lie, they do not rest in Armagh. The claim of Downpatrick would appear to receive support from a very definite statement embodied in a legend, were it not for the suspicion that the legend arose from a desire to substantiate that claim. It is related by Muirchu that an angel gave St. Patrick the following advice with regard to his burial:

> Let two unbroken oxen be chosen, and let them go whithersoever they will, and in whatever place they lie down, let a church be built in honour of thy poor body.
>
> And as the angel said, restive bullocks were chosen, and they drew a wagon, with a litter firmly fixed on it in which the holy body was yoked to their shoulders. And oxen from the herds of Conail, from the place that is called Clocher, on the east of Findubair, were made glorious by being chosen for this purpose. And they went forth, the will of God guiding them, to Dun-Lethglaise, where Patrick was buried.

In the absence of any conflicting tradition, this might well be taken as decisive in favour of Downpatrick, which is Dun-Lethglaise. But in point of fact there is a conflicting tradition. In the note attached to Tirechan's memoir in the *Book of Armagh* another tradition is given:

> Colomb-cille, under the inspiration of the Holy Spirit, showed the place of Patrick's burial; he confirms (the tradition as to) where it is; that is, in Sabhul Patrick, that is, in the church nearest the sea.

The question naturally arises, how we are to account for the survival of the legend of his burial in so insignificant a place as Saul in competition with an important royal seat such as Downpatrick near by, unless the story was true? Miracle is invoked to explain why the Saint should be buried at Downpatrick, but no miracle is needed to explain why St. Patrick should be buried where he died, and in the one spot in Irish ground where, next to his beloved Armagh, we may well believe he would wish his mortal remains to rest. But it matters, indeed, but little where that dust now lies, for the memory of that tireless and heroic spirit is for all time enshrined in the hearts of the Irish people.

—G. A. Chamberlain

5

Patrick the Man

PATRICK THE MAN: A PORTRAIT FROM HIS OWN LIPS

SAINT PATRICK was no man of letters such as Saint Paul. How much he wrote is unknown and all that we possess from his pen are two short texts: his *Confession* and his *Letter to the Soldiers of Coroticus*.

But he has stamped his image forcefully in these writings for they convey the sort of man he was: a preacher of potency rather than a cultured writer, gifted with the suggestive power of the spoken word while at the same time humbly apologising for his lack of learning; but above all dedicated and humbly triumphant over his detractors in his conviction of being a chosen instrument of God.

The two writings which have been handed down to us were both written in the sense of duty in face of challenge. The Saint himself speaks in the *Letter to the Soldiers of Coroticus* of an earlier letter to the same soldiers which apparently failed to have the effect on them that Patrick desired. And one of his letters written as part of his pastoral duties is known to have existed at one time. This was directed to the

Saint Patrick in the Act of Confirmation

Bishops of Mag Ai and reproved them for conferring Holy Orders without his permission.

These writings lend a picture of a man "rusty in Latin," as he
himself confesses, rich in usage of the Scriptural idiom but averse to
writing and preferring the spoken word.

There are other fragments that survive in later annals but some of
them are uncertain and others have been wrongly attributed to the
Saint.

The remarkable *Lorica,* or *Breastplate of Saint Patrick* as it has
been called, is first attributed to Saint Patrick in the Book of Armagh,
which was compiled about the beginning of the ninth century by a
scribe named Ferdomnach whose partiality, to say the least, has caused
him to be discounted in many aspects of Patrician scholarship.

The *Lorica* was a prayer in early Irish in the form of an invocation
of the Holy Trinity against the powers of evil and witchcraft. And,
according to legend, it is the prayer Saint Patrick is supposed to have

recited as he made his way, invisible from all dangers, to Tara for his first encounter with the druids.

Whether or not it is the Saint's, it is a powerful invocation that has a wonderful ring of faith:

> Christ for my guardianship to-day:
> Against poison, against burning,
> Against drowning, against wounding,
> That there may come to me a multitude of rewards;
> Christ be with me, Christ be before me,
> Christ be behind me, Christ be in me,
> Christ be beneath me, Christ be above me,
> Christ be to right of me, Christ be to left of me,
> Christ in lying down, Christ in sitting, Christ in rising up,
> Christ be in the heart of every person who may think of me,
> Christ be in the mouth of every one who may speak to me.
> Christ in every eye which may look on me,
> Christ in every ear which may hear me.

Then there are the *Canons,* pastoral instructions dealing with the organisation of the Irish Church. These bear the signature of Patrick along with those of other bishops—Auxilius, Secundinus and Benignus —of the Church. But though they may be endorsed by Saint Patrick they are not necessarily his writings.

Finally there are the "Dicta Patricii," or "Sayings of Patrick," found in the *Book of Armagh.* They are probably authentic in that they were pious sayings of which Patrick was fond, as he shows in his *Confession.*

So, we come back to the *Confession* and the *Letter to the Soldiers of Coroticus* for an assessment of St. Patrick through his writings.

Both of them are alive with the author's righteous indignation. Indeed, one gets the picture of Patrick as a man with strong temper, quick of tongue, rich of phrase, as tough as Saint Peter but as humble as St. Francis. And here and there one receives insight into his positive faith, unshaken in face of ecclesiastical critics, that he had been entrusted by Divine Will with the conversion of the Irish.

Looking first at the *Letter to the Soldiers of Coroticus* it is evident that it was preceded by a first letter sent by a priest to Britain to remonstrate after a raiding party of soldiers had carried off a number of newly baptised converts from Ireland to sell them into slavery.

The soldiers were those of the British prince Coroticus or Ceretic, founder of the Welsh principality of Cardigan.

Patrick in the second *Letter* roundly castigates the soldiers, but then he develops his argument as an answer to criticism made against him by certain groups of the clergy in Britain whom he accuses of currying favour with the supposedly Christian ruler. He calls on the British priests to boycott Coroticus and his soldiery:

> Whence therefore, ye holy men, humble of heart I beseech you earnestly, it is not right to pay court to such men, nor to take food or drink with them, nor ought one to accept their alms-givings, until by doing sore penance with shedding of tears they make amends before God and liberate the servants of God and the baptised handmaidens of Christ, for whom He died and was crucified.

In this boycott appeal to his brethren in Britain Patrick speaks of his common nationality with them: "his own" have done this thing to the "flock of the Lord, which verily was growing up excellently in Ireland with the greatest care."

Then he turns directly on the prince: "You have delivered the members of Christ as it were into a house of ill-fame. What manner of hope in God have you, or whoever consorts with you or holds converse with you in words of flattery?"

And, as grief convulses his writings in compassion for the butchered ones and the women given into slavery and subjection, Patrick lets himself go in one of the rich Biblical passages of which he appears to have been fond as a preacher. For he speaks of the dead: "You have begun to remove to where there shall be no right nor sorrow nor death any more, but ye shall leap like calves loosened from their bonds, and ye shall tread down the wicked and they shall be as ashes under your feet."

And he ends his *Letter* with the prayer: "Peace to the Father, and to the Son and to the Holy Ghost. Amen."

The *Letter* was directed by Patrick to be read in all the churches, and even in the presence of the prince. But whether it had the effect of bringing Coroticus to repentance we shall never know.

There is a legend that the prince turned into a fox and "like water that floweth away," was never seen again.

And thus we come to the *Confession,* which is the closest we can truly get to a picture of the man Patrick.

Undoubtedly it was dictated to his scribe by the Saint when he was aged. But it is the work of a live mind, an alert intellect.

The writer introduces himself at the start: "I, Patrick, a sinner, the most unlearned and least of all the faithful and despised by many. . . ."

Then he continues to inform us about his parents and his family background: "My father was Calpornius, a deacon . . . ." And he traces his genealogy back to his great-grandfather.

He tells how he was carried off by the Irish raiders when he was sixteen. But he sees it as a just punishment for a youth who in the secularised society of the then Roman world had been ungodly and without any real spiritual experience. He looks back on his slavery as the merciful road to a better and holier life:

> And there the Lord opened the sense of my unbelief that I might at last remember my sins and be converted with all my heart to the Lord my God, who had regard for my abjection, and mercy on my youth and ignorance, and watched over me before I knew Him . . . and guarded and comforted me as a father would his son.

Then the plea of the Saint becomes more personal:

> For this reason I intended to write long ago but hesitated until now; I was afraid of being talked about, because I have not studied like the others who thoroughly imbibed law as well as Sacred Scripture and never in life changed their language but made a steady progress toward perfection. For my speech and word have been translated into a foreign tongue and it may be seen from the flavour of my words how little I am instructed in the art of words.

But then comes the flash of Patrick's powerful belief that he had been chosen for the Irish:

> I have thought it my duty to speak aloud in acknowledgment of the graces of God which a human mind can never estimate. . . . Therefore, be ye astonished ye great and little that fear God, and ye men of letters on your estates, listen and search. Who stirred me up, the fool, from the midst of those who are wise and expert in law, and powerful in word and in everything, and who inspired me, the most abject of the world, before others, to be the man who with fear and reverence and without blame might faithfully serve the people to whom the love of Christ conveyed and gave me for the duration of my life, if I were worthy, to serve them humbly and sincerely?

Next comes the most intriguing portion of the *Confession* in which the Saint, after telling briefly of his slavery in Ireland and his escape and subsequent return to his own people, comes to deal with his mission to the Irish.

He was attacked by some of his seniors. They called attention to a sin which Patrick had committed in his youth and which he had confided to "his dearest friend" who later betrayed his secret to his detractors.

> Many tried to frustrate this mission; even behind my back they would say: "Why does this fellow throw himself into danger among the enemies who know not God?"

But God called him. For he goes on to tell of the vision which consoled him. And in the end he was chosen as bishop to the Irish, for which he pours forth a song of praise.

The remainder of the *Confession* deals with his work among the Irish. He went into exile as he says for the love of God. He threw up the privileges of Roman citizenship.

He must have been a man of noble stature, else he would not have impressed the Irish by his appearance. He must have been fearless, yet humble. A great preacher who knew the Scripture by heart, yet without pedantry or pomp. A man of strict rule, who organised his mission like the Roman legions, yet who could cry out in anguish for the least of his brethren who suffered ill. And more than all, a man of extraordinary gifted faith, the same gifted faith that has marked the Irish out down all the centuries since the days of Patrick the Apostle.

—Seamus Brady

ST. PATRICK'S HOUSEHOLD

THE *Tripartite Life* gives us a brief account of the household of St. Patrick. The *Book of Leinster* and *Leabhar Breac* give somewhat the same list. These are particularly interesting as they give us some knowledge of the social life of the period and the many difficulties of St. Patrick's mission in Ireland.

St. Patrick so overshadowed his era that many people have not a true perspective of his helpers and companions.

Tirechan tells us: "A multitude of holy bishops, priests, deacons, exorcists, doorkeepers, lectors and youths whom he ordained" accompanied him to Ireland. With these came many relations. These having the faith and a knowledge of doctrine and laws were a great asset.

Moreover, he could count on their loyalty and place them in strategic positions to consolidate the work he had begun. The *Tripartite Life* tells us when St. Patrick was at Oran in Magh Aoi he was solicited by his Gallic disciples and followers to assign them situations.

We must remember that there were no towns, hotels, few roads, bridges. He had to encounter much hostility and danger. He had to provide food and clothing. There were no churches or equipment for them.

All these had to be made and he had to rely on his own resources. In fact, he copied the Irish kings of the time and formed his household on somewhat the same lines as theirs. This was necessary for prestige. If the king had such, the Bishop of the new religion should have the same. They were all necessary. The following is the list given in the *Tripartite:*

Sechnall, his bishop or Secundinus;
Mochta, his priest;
Bishop Erc, his judge;
Bishop MacCairthinn, his champion;
Benignus or Benen, his psalmist;
Coeman of Cell Riada, his chamberlain;
Sinell of Cell Dareis, his bell-ringer;
Athcen of Both Domnaig, his cook;
Presbyter Mescan of Domnach Mescain at Fochain, brewer;
Presbyter Bescna of Domnach Dala, chaplain or sacristan;
Presbyter Catan and Presbyter Acan, his two attendants at table;
Odran of Disert Odrain in Hui Failgi, his charioteer;
Presbyter Manach, his fire-woodman;
Rottan, his cowherd;
His three smiths, Macc Cecht; Laeban and Fortchern;
His three wrights, Essa, Bite and Tassach;
His three embroideresses, Lupait, Erc and Cruimtheris;
He also had three masons, Caeman, Cruineach and Luireach
    (neither these nor the following are in the *Tripartite Life*);
Presbyter Lugna—a priest, was his pilot (Flann);
Presbyter Brogan—his scribe.

Sechnall was placed over the church of Dunshaughlin in Co. Meath. He acted as Patrick's coadjutor and assisted him in his many functions in the government of the early Irish church. He was the son of Restitutus and Liemania.

He wrote the famous "Hymn of St. Patrick." It describes in a general way the holiness of Patrick's life, his divine mission to preach the gospel, his humility, his zeal in preaching, the feeding of the flock entrusted to his care, his chastity, his saintly life, his utter contempt of worldly fame, his love of the sacred Scripture, his constant prayer and of the daily sacrifice of the Mass. This hymn became a popular devotion and was especially sung on March 16, 17, and 18. The life of St. Declan tells us that he was the first Bishop buried in the soil of Ireland.

Mochta was one of the oldest and dearest disciples of St. Patrick. He was his intimate friend and was noted for his great learning and holiness. He was Abbot of Louth and this is still a parish in the diocese of Armagh.

Bishop Erc, Patrick's judge, was a Brehon before his baptism. He is described as one of King Laoghaire's pages. He was appointed by Patrick to the Commission of Nine for the purification of the Brehon code. The *Leabhar Breac* tells us: "Whatever he adjudged was just;

everyone who passes a just judgment, Bishop Erc's blessing succours him." He died at Slane, A.D. 512.

Bishop MacCairthinn was Patrick's champion, which means his strong man. There was need of a young active giant to help Patrick in his many dangers—the crossing of rivers and fords and many such physical dangers. The rude chieftains of the time often treated the companions of Patrick with violence and cruelty as when Cairbre drove his servants into the River Blackwater, or when they were stoned as happened at Enniscrone. Patrick placed Bishop MacCairthinn in charge of the church of Clogher.

Benignus, Patrick's psalm-singer came of a bardic family and had a hereditary gift of music and song. So he gave Benen charge of his church choirs with the duty of training his young ecclesiastics in the psalmody of the church. He, too, belonged to the Commission of Nine. The *Book of Rights* is attributed to him. He always belonged to Patrick's household and never had a church of his own. He was destined to be Patrick's successor in Armagh.

The lesser official, such as his bell-ringer, held an important office because in those days the bell was a symbol of jurisdiction, and the man who carried it had the authority of Patrick himself. The bell used was probably the famous Bell of the Will, now in the National Museum, Dublin.

His cook had not only to superintend the cooking of food for fear of poison, but generally had the difficult and onerous task of providing maintenance for the saint and his household.

Patrick's brewer: Every chief had a brewer to brew what was necessary for himself and his followers. The corn was ground with the quern or hand mill, and the whole process would have to be superintended by the brewer. The wine would have to be reserved solely for sacrifice and it would have to be imported. Mead and beer were the drinks of the early Irish.

His sacristan had to provide all the necessaries for the Mass, the proper celebration of divine worship on Sundays and Festivals and all other duties connected with ceremonial.

His attendants: The Irish saints were hospitable to strangers and every church and monastery had its guest ministers to look after the needs of the church and also of the poor who would come to them.

Odran, his charioteer, was the great saint who gave his own life to save his master when he was waylaid on his journey through Offaly. Another charioteer also died at the foot of Croagh Patrick.

It would appear that Patrick used the two-wheeled chariot; the body of wickerwork with a frame of wood was fixed to a tough holly axle-tree, the wheels shod with iron which had to be strong for the rough work.

His cowherd: On a journey, Patrick had to bring his cattle and sheep with him. They would feed on the grass as they went along. He would also have to look after his horses, for we know that they were stolen on one or two occasions. This meant constant vigilance.

His artisans: There were two kinds—the smiths who helped in the building of churches, the making of bells, cauldrons, the shoeing of his chariot wheels and his horses, and the more delicate metalworkers in gold, silver and bronze—Essa, Bite and Tassach.

Essa was his most skilful artificer. He it was who helped to make chalices and patens, altar stones and reliquaries. Bite was his nephew. Tassach was the holy Bishop who gave Viaticum to Patrick on his deathbed; his church is at Raholp, two miles from Saul.

His embroideresses; These made all the linen, the weaving and perhaps the clothing, not only for St. Patrick and his followers but all things necessary for the service of God and the many churches.

Lugna, his pilot, was also his nephew. He it was who went before Patrick and prepared the routes, was his guide, and undertook the provision of boats for the crossing of the many rivers and lakes.

Thus the household of Patrick as he moved around the country was self-sufficing. Churches, vestments, books, bells, food, clothing, fire, drink and transport were provided, showing in this way the wisdom and management of the patron saint.

—The Rev. George Quinn

ST. MACARTAN (MacCÁRTHAIN)

Among the followers of St. Patrick forming the company called St. Patrick's "household" was one Aedh Mac Cárthain known as the saint's *tréan-fhear,* meaning literally his "strong man," or what we would now call a bodyguard. His function was to protect the saint in time of danger, especially on his missionary journeys, and to carry him on his back across river fords or over rough ground. It is related that on one occasion when travelling in the territory of the Uí Tuirte, a sept of the Airghialla, the petty king of the region, known as Cárthan Mór (who, it has been suggested, may well have been a kinsman of Patrick's tréan-fhear) , drove the saint and his household out of the region. Mac Cárthain later became a bishop and the Martyrology of Donegal states that "Bishop Mac Cárthain used to carry him (Patrick) over every rugged place." It is said that when Mac Cárthain had grown old and was no longer able to carry out his function of "strong man" effectively St. Patrick commented on this fact. This gave Mac Cárthain the opportunity to remind the saint that while most of his companions who had served the saint faithfully had been rewarded by being promoted to the care of churches, he had been left unprovided for! Patrick soon afterwards appointed him bishop and set him over the church of Clogher (County Tyrone) , giving him, as a token of his esteem, the staff he himself had used in his journeys as well as some precious relics later encased in a shrine known as the Domhnach Airgid.

—Aer Lingus

Fragment of Saint Patrick's copy of the Gospels

His Gospels

WHAT is considered by the best authors to be Saint Patrick's copy of the Gospels is one of the most treasured possessions of the Royal Irish Academy. It is enclosed in a shrine called the "Domnach Airgid." The shrine is an oblong box, nine inches by seven, and five inches in height. It is composed of three distinct covers, in the ages of which there is obviously a great difference. The inner or first cover is of wood, apparently of yew, and may be coeval with the manuscript it is intended to preserve. The second, which is of copper plated with silver, is assigned to a period between the sixth and twelfth centuries, from the style of its scroll or interlaced ornaments. The figures in relief and letters on the third cover, which is of silver plated with gold, leave no doubt of its being the work of the fourteenth century.

—John Bruce

A LINK WITH SAINT PATRICK'S SISTER

The Island of Inchagoill (Island of the Stone) is situated in Lough Corrib, Co. Galway, and for scenic beauty and historic lore is the most interesting of the many islands on that lake. A translation of the name is the "Island of the Devout Stranger." A link with Saint Patrick's sister provides a lagniappe discovered in 1810.

Saint Patrick's Church is situated on the island and is a simple nave-and-chancel structure, except for the doorway which has an inclination of the jambs, typical of very early Irish church architecture and which comes down to us directly from the portals of the prehistoric stone forts.

"Island of the Stone" in Lough Corrib, Co. Galway, derives its name from this four-sided obelisk-like pillar. A few paces from Saint Patrick's Church, it is thought to be a memorial to the saint's nephew Lugna, the son of Patrick's sister Liemania. There are seven fishtail crosses on this stone, examples of the most ancient carvings of that sacred emblem now to be found outside the catacombs in Rome.

As the church is a ruin, there are no traces of any windows. There is another and later church called the Church of the Saints, probably eleventh century.

But the real archeological treasure of Inchagoill lies outside Saint

Patrick's Church, a few yards from the doorway. It is a stone pillar, a little over two feet high with one or two fishtailed crosses on each of the four sides. On one face is an inscription in old Irish, a translation of which is "the Stone of Lugnaedon, son of Limenueh." It is said to be a memorial to Saint Patrick's nephew.

Saint Patrick had a sister named Liemania, and her son was Lugnad. The genitive cases of those names are Limenueh and Lugnadeod, hence the discrepancies in spelling. Lugna, as he is most commonly referred to, was Patrick's pilot. It was he who reconnoitered, preparing the routes for the saint's journeys and he who undertook the provision of boats for the crossing of the many rivers and lakes, and acted as guide.

It was an officer from the barracks in Galway who, in 1810, stumbled upon the little monolith in the overgrown and neglected churchyard. According to Oscar Wilde, the fishtailed crosses "may be regarded

Saint Patrick's Church, or Tempull Padraig, on the "Island of the Stone," is built of large stones laid irregularly without mortar. It is 29 feet 7 inches long internally; 17 feet 11 inches in the nave; 11 feet 7 inches in the chancel; and 9 feet high. The door, squareheaded, is 6 feet high, its jambs formed of square, uncut limestone inclining inwardly. The style has been termed Cyclopean, and would be from about the fifth or sixth century.

as examples of the most ancient carvings of that sacred emblem now to be found in the British Isles or perhaps, if we except those in the Catacombs of Rome, anywhere in Europe." It is probable that Lugna is buried beneath the stone.

Mass is said each year on the Island by priests from Cong, Co. Mayo.

—The Very Rev. Patrick Eaton

THE SAINT'S CURSE

IN spite of the critical remarks against cursing usually delivered by Christian moralists, it was nothing unusual among those considered to be models of Christian living—the saints. Indeed Christ is seen in the Gospel as cursing a fig tree which he found unfruitful and it withered as a result. Further back one finds the "Cursing Psalms" which, as a rural wit once expressed it, "would raise the paint off a door, so violent are they!"

The hagiographers who passed on to us the accounts which we possess of the early Irish saints (circa A.D. 450 to 800) endowed their heroes with fearful powers of cursing. It may be suggested that all this was pure fiction, written down to give the saintly people added status in the eyes of their fellow Irishmen. If this were so, one must agree that the readers of the hagiographies were familiar with cursing and it is also possible that the early Irish saints also practised malediction in some cases. One just cannot dismiss the frequent mention of the saint's curse as being completely without historical foundation of any kind.

It is instructive at this time to recall the siting of the cursing stones in so many early Christian monastic sites. The accomplished cursers of the hagiographies may have found a thriving home-grown custom to practise and not some notion which came from abroad.

Saint Patrick

It is sometimes a source of wonder to readers of the life of the alleged Apostle of Ireland—Patrick—how radically different his personality is in the short autobiographical *Confessio* from that found in the *Tripartite Life of Saint Patrick,* written nearly four centuries later. In the intervening time, the humble harassed missionary has become a wonder-worker and a hurler of maledictions on anyone who impeded his triumphal journey through Ireland. It is worthwhile taking a look at the cursing clerical bully of the later work.

The total number of maledictions mentioned in the later work are about thirty. They vary from a curse placed upon an area where inferior yew wood grew—wood unfit to repair the saint's chariot—to a malediction placed on a tyrant who had ill-treated his slaves and refused to heed Patrick's entreaties on their behalf.

The story about the cruel slaveowner is as follows: Patrick approaches a group of slaves who are felling a yew tree. Their hands are bleeding profusely because, they explain to him, they had been forbidden to sharpen their tools sufficiently. This, by the way, may reflect something which came to the notice of the hagiographer in the late ninth century. Patrick went at once to the dwelling of the slaveowner who refused him a hearing. To bring him to heel, the saint fasted against him at the entrance to his residential site. When this proved unavailing, Patrick next spat on a stone and the spittle penetrated it. Then the saint cursed the stubborn slaveowner and said that his family would never produce a king or the heir to a king. To round off this story, the writer informs us that the stubborn man who had resisted the saint was drowned in a lake soon afterwards. Notice the part that fasting and a stone play in this story.

Some of the curses are monstrously frivolous. The saint comes to Inbhir Domnand, for example and finds no fish there. We are told simply that he utters a curse on it and that it lacks fish ever since then. The Hill of Usnagh, hallowed in pre-Christian Ireland, also suffers malediction when Patrick and his fellow missionary, Sechnall, collaborate in cursing the stones there:

> *"Maldacht,"* ol Patraic ("A curse!" said Patrick) *"for clocha Uisnigh,"* ol Sechnall ("On the stones of Usnagh," said Sechnall)
> *"Bith dano,"* ol Patraic, *"ni dénaither cid clocha fotraichi dib!"* ("So be it, indeed," said Patrick. "Of them not even heating stones will be made!")

It should be explained that heating stones were used to bring up the temperature of water for bathing in these times.

Personal violence to Patrick or his friends was also the reason for malediction. A certain family group were unlucky to stone Patrick and his people and they earned the following curse:

> *Mo débrod . . . no comlund i mbethi memais foraib ocus bethi for seilib agus for sopaib hi cach airiucht i mbed!* (My sorrow . . . you will be defeated in every engagement you take part in and in every assembly you attend you will be spat on and reviled!)

Some misguided wretch used a psalm book as missile with which he struck Patrick. On this fellow, the pious hagiographer tells us, Patrick put a curse which led to the loss of a hand later. And then one reads of the members of a family who whipped the servants of the saint. The curse inflicted on these people was that they would be barren henceforth. One gathers the opinion while reading the *Tripartite Life* that one did not touch or injure with impunity the good saint or his servants and friends.

There is one anecdote which concerns "pagans" specifically. It happened, we are told, that these people were digging a *ráth*—an earthwork around a domestic settlement—on a Sunday. For this breach of Christian sabbatarian laws Patrick uttered a curse against them. The result of this malediction was that a great storm arose which swept away the results of their labours!

One interesting story is related which concerns a curse which was eased. It is related that Patrick's horses were taken by the people in an area and, of course, the good saint rained down curses on them. However, luckily for them, they had a bishop who interceded on their behalf and the curse was eased. Then the story goes on: . . . *ro nig Máine cossa Pátraic cona folt ocus cona déraib ocus ro immaig na echu i fergorrt ocus glan a cossa ar honóir Pátraic.* (". . . Máine, the bishop, washed Patrick's feet with his hair and his tears and he set the horses on grazing ground and washed their feet in honour of Patrick.")

These anecdotes from the *Tripartite Life of Saint Patrick* may be seen as reflections of Irish life in the ninth century as seen from a monastery. Evidently it was understood that a great saint should be not only a great worker of miracles, but also a fulminator of curses on all who hurt or thwarted him or his followers. The biographer attempts to show the saint as equal to or even greater than the pagan heroes whose fame was in the mouths of the storytellers. The thought also occurs to one that the writer may have known of ecclesiastics in his own time who laid maledictions on their enemies and he surely heard plenty of stories of what happened or was alleged to have taken place in the past.

—Patrick C. Power

Patrick Introduced the Roman Alphabet

PRIOR to Patrick's teaching, the Gaels employed a twenty-letter alphabet called "Ogham." The sounds were represented by a combination of vertical or slanting lines, and read from top to bottom, as in Chinese. The Ogham script was used mostly on funerary boulders and slabs, which bore a Greek cross in a circle or a Latin cross with expanded ends, and the name of the person commemorated. It was Patrick who introduced the Roman alphabet to Ireland, yet he himself calls attention to the "rusticity" of his Latin.

—Alice-Boyd Proudfoot

AN EVEN-SONG

Patrick Sang This

May Thy holy angels, O Christ, son of living God,
Guard our sleep, our rest, our shining bed.

Let them reveal true visions to us in our sleep,
O high-prince of the universe, O great king of the mysteries!

May no demons, no ill, no calamity or terrifying dreams
Disturb our rest, our willing, prompt repose.

May our watch be holy, our work, our task,
Our sleep, our rest without let, without break.

—Translated by Kuno Meyer

PATRICK'S BLESSING ON MUNSTER

God's blessing upon Munster,
Men, women, children!
A blessing on the land
Which gives them fruit!

A blessing on every wealth
Which is brought forth on their marches!
No one to be in want of help:
God's blessings upon Munster!

A blessing on their peaks,
On their bare flagstones,
A blessing on their glens,
A blessing on their ridges!

Like sand of sea under ships
Be the number of their hearths:
On slopes, on plains,
On mountain-sides, on peaks.

—Translated by Whitley Stokes

Ogham Stone in Coolmagort, Co. Kerry

THE TEACHING OF ST. PATRICK

THE nature and content of St. Patrick's religious belief and practice may be gathered partly from his own writings, and partly from what we know of the doctrine accepted by the Church of the West in the early part of the fifth century A.D. We can form a good idea as to St. Patrick's belief and practice from what he incidentally says, and does not say.

There is one passage in the *Confession* (§4), which at first sight looks like a formal creed; it runs thus:—"There is no other God, nor was there ever any in times past, nor shall there be hereafter, except God the Father unbegotten, without beginning, from whom all things take their beginning, holding all things [*i.e.* Almighty], as we say, and his Son Jesus Christ, whom we affirm verily to have always existed with the Father before the creation of the world, with the Father after the manner of a spiritual existence, begotten ineffably before the beginning of anything. And by him were made things visible and invisible. He was made man; and, having overcome death, he was received up into heaven to the Father! And he gave to him all power above every name of things in heaven and things in earth and things under the earth; and let every tongue confess to him that Jesus Christ is Lord and God, in whom we believe. And we look for his coming soon to be; he the Judge of the quick and the dead, who will render to every man according to his deeds. And he shed on us abundantly the Holy Ghost, the gift and earnest of immortality, who makes them who believe and obey to become children of God the Father, and joint heirs with Christ, whom we confess and adore as one God in the Trinity of the Holy Name."

In view of the fact that the Celtic Churches were sound in the faith as to the Godhead and the Incarnation, we must hold that the omission in this passage of several clauses in the Creeds of Nicaea (A.D. 325) and of Constantinople (A.D. 381) is not due to heresy on St. Patrick's part. We know now that the basis of this section of the *Confession* is a passage from a Commentary on the Revelation by Victorinus, Bishop of Pettau* (martyred under the emperor Diocletian, A.D. 303-313). We learn from St. Sechnall's *Hymn in Patrick's Praise* that Patrick was a diligent student and expounder of the book of the Revelation.

We have here, then, not a formal creed, but St. Patrick's declaration of his doctrine of God. The doctrine of the Holy Trinity was, he tells us, (*Confession* §14), his *Rule of Faith.* When an ambassador for Christ has to deal, as Patrick had, with a people who "only worship idols and abominations" (*Confession* §41), he can speak only about the big things of the true religion. And hence St. Patrick was wont to present to the heathen Irish the sublimest conception of the essential nature of God.

The first thing that strikes the reader of St. Patrick's writings is the copious use he makes of Holy Scripture. His citations from it are astonishingly numerous, and he assumes a like familiarity with it in his

---

* A town in Jugo-Slavia.

readers. Christians were evidently encouraged, then, to read the Bible for themselves. It never occurred to any one of the faithful to call in question articles of the Creed—drawn from the Holy Scriptures by the Church, which has "authority in controversies of faith"—but, otherwise, all members of the Church, lay and cleric alike, in St. Patrick's time, read their Bibles for instruction and consolation, without any scared apprehensiveness of the danger of private judgment.

One of the most noticeable elements in the personal life of St. Patrick, as reflected in his writings, was the intensity of his devotion to our Lord Jesus Christ. He speaks of him as "Christ my Lord" (3), "Christ my God" (1), "Christ the Lord" (1). A specially striking passage is in *Confession* §24, an account of a vision:—"Whether within me, or beside me, I cannot tell, God knoweth . . . at the end of the prayer he thus affirmed, 'He who laid down his life for thee, he it is who speaketh in thee.' " This sense of the mutual indwelling of Christ and the human soul finds its supreme expression in the *Breastplate*,

> Christ with me, Christ beside me,
> Christ behind me, Christ in me,
> Christ under me, Christ over me,
> Christ to right of me, Christ to left of me,

> Christ in lying down, Christ in sitting, Christ in rising up,
> Christ in the heart of every person, who may think of me!
> Christ in the mouth of every one, who may speak to me!
> Christ in every eye, which may look on me!
> Christ in every ear, which may hear me!

St. Patrick knew of only "one mediator between God and man, Christ Jesus"; for him the only intercessors with God for man are Jesus Christ and the Holy Spirit.

The process of deterioration of Christian practice in the direction of creature worship—always attractive to the natural man—was in its earlier stage in the fifth century; and it had not gone further, in any instance of it, than a more or less rhetorical request to deceased holy persons that they, in their presumably higher sphere of existence, should continue to pray for those for whom they had prayed while on earth. But even of this practice there is no trace in St. Patrick's writings, though there are places in which a reference to it would have been natural, had he observed such a custom.

The Blessed Virgin Mary is not once named by him. She was at that time thought of as a peculiarly privileged human being, of exceptional sanctity; but nothing more. Excessive veneration for her began in connection with reaction from the Nestorian heresy, which affirmed that in Christ there were two Persons—human and Divine—as well as two Natures. The orthodox doctrine was briefly summed up in a title applied to the Blessed Virgin, Theotokos, *i.e.*, "She who gave birth to the Child who is God."

This technical term of theology, when used, and thought of, by the unlearned, lent itself to that perverted estimate of our Lord's human mother, which culminated in a baseless myth of her corporal Assumption into heaven—a figment of the sixth or seventh century—and in the subtle doctrine of the Immaculate Conception [of her soul]. This notion was rejected in the thirteenth century by Thomas Aquinas, the greatest of the Schoolmen, but defined as an article of faith by Pope Pius IX, in 1854.

As regards the state of the soul between death and the Judgment Day, St. Patrick speaks only of Hell and Paradise. Individual thinkers had suggested that there might possibly be an intermediate state in which such Christians as do not seem good enough to go straight to Heaven, while not bad enough to go to Hell, might gradually be cleansed from the stain of sin. But no authoritative declaration that there is a Purgatory was made until Pope Gregory the Great (died A.D. 604) affirmed it.

Indulgences, in the sense of remission, after death, of the punishment for sin, depend upon the doctrine of Purgatory; and were, of course, unknown in St. Patrick's time.

St. Patrick is a witness to the Apostolic three "Orders of Ministers in Christ's Church: Bishops, Priests, and Deacons." He speaks of himself as "a bishop, appointed by God, in Ireland" (*Letter* §1) and refers more than once to the episcopal functions of Ordination and Confirmation; the duties of the clergy (*clerici*) generally being to baptise and exhort the people.

The second order of Ministers he terms either *presbyteri or sacerdotes*. In the two places in which the latter word occurs, the "sacerdotal" functions specified are (a) public admonition of the people, and (b) the power of "declaring to God's people, being penitent, the absolution and remission of their sins." In connection with this latter function, it is to be noted that in the early Celtic Church, confession of sins was public rather than private; optional rather than compulsory; and absolution was not pronounced until after the penance assigned had been fulfilled. In the *Letter* (§7), St. Patrick warns people against having any dealings with Coroticus and his followers "until [doing] sore penance with shedding of tears, they make amends to God."

The "secular," or parish, clergy in Britain and Ireland were not compelled to be unmarried until some centuries later than St. Patrick's time. He himself states, without any comment, that his own father was a deacon and his grandfather a presbyter. On the other hand, the ideal for a Christian life which he set before his converts was that they should become "monks and virgins of Christ." The unreasonable notion that a pure unmarried life is, essentially, more pleasing to God than is a pure married life was strongly advocated by the Church leaders of the fourth century, and we cannot be surprised if St. Patrick shared in the opinions of those whom he venerated. The foulness of the pagan world in which the Church had at first lived naturally led to a reaction in Christian thought.

It cannot be denied that the service of God (Matt. xix., 12), no less than the service of the State (2 Tim. ii, 4), sometimes calls upon a man or a woman for special self-denial in this matter; and undoubtedly, in the dark ages, the monasteries preserved both Christianity and civilisation. "God hath made everything beautiful in its time."

Prominence is given in St. Patrick's writings to the sacrament of Holy Baptism and to Confirmation. It is not clear whether the unction alluded to in *Letter* §3, was administered in connection with Baptism or whether the unction is that of Confirmation, which in this instance followed the baptism almost immediately.

But the only reference in these writings to the sacrament of Holy Communion is in *Confession* §49, where, describing the enthusiasm of the "devout women" among his converts, he says, "They used to cast off their ornaments upon the altar." We know that in the early Celtic Church, as in the Gallican Church, the presentation of money and other precious things at the time of the Offertory was a prominent feature in the service of Holy Communion.

But we cannot argue from St. Patrick's silence about this sacrament that he attached to it no special importance. What is called "the argument from silence" is of force only when the matter about which an author is silent is of such a sort as that he must have mentioned it had he been aware of it. Thus St. Patrick's silence in the *Confession* about the Bishop of Rome is good proof that he had not been sent to Ireland by the Pope. Because the primary object of the *Confession* was to defend himself from the charge of presumption in having undertaken the task of converting the Irish. Now, although the claim of Rome to be "the mother and mistress of all churches" was not generally admitted in the fifth century, the Pope was sufficiently well thought of to make it impossible for any responsible person in the Western Church to challenge the action of a missionary commissioned by him. If St. Patrick had been sent by the Pope to Ireland, he need not have written the *Confession* at all; it would have been enough to point to his Papal credentials.

But there is no place in either the *Confession* or the *Letter* in which the context *demands* a reference to the Holy Communion. In letters to our friends, we do not mention matters which, however necessary, are part of the daily round. On the other hand, if the Mass had dominated St. Patrick's religious life to the same extent that it dominates the religious life of a modern Roman Catholic, he would hardly have avoided some mention of it.

In the absence of any statement by St. Patrick himself, it is reasonable to hold that his belief and practice as to the Holy Communion were those of the Church in which he had been educated, that is, the Church of Gaul, or France. It would be impossible, in the limited space of this tract, fully to discuss this great theme; it will be sufficient to comment on the implications of the term *altar*, by which St. Patrick designates the Holy Table.

The term *altar*, of course, involves the idea of a sacrifice; but it by no means follows that the sacrifice offered upon it is propitiatory. Under the Mosaic Law, the meal offering, the peace offering, the whole burnt offering, and the sin offering were all offered upon an altar; but the sin offering alone was propitiatory. The bread and wine, when placed by the officiating minister upon the Holy Table, correspond to the meal offering of the ancient Hebrews; when partaken of, after the consecration, they correspond (in one aspect of them) to the peace offering—(see I Cor. x, 17, 18); therefore it cannot be argued that because St. Patrick uses the term *altar* of the Holy Table, he held the Roman Catholic belief that "in the Mass there is offered to God a true, proper, and propitiatory sacrifice for the living and the dead." He could not, in fact, have held this belief; since it depends on the scholastic theory of transubstantiation, which arose in the dark ages, and did not harden into a dogma of the Western Church until A.D. 1215, at the Fourth Lateran Council.

The Eucharistic doctrine of the great divines of the fourth century —St. Patrick's elder contemporaries—St. Ambrose (died A.D. 397) and St. Augustine (died A.D. 430) was the same as that of our *Book of Common Prayer*. They taught that, by his "death upon the Cross," our Lord made "a full, perfect and sufficient sacrifice . . . for the sins of the whole world," and that the service of Holy Communion is "a perpetual memory," or memorial, of that one sacrifice, which itself can never be repeated. This is St. Paul's teaching, in I Cor. xi, 26, "Ye proclaim the Lord's death till he come." By partaking of the bread and wine, after they have been consecrated by Christ, acting through the minister of his Church, his body (I Cor. x, 16), the faithful communicant—beside other benefits—shares in the merits of the sacrifice of Christ. Consequently, a consecration by the priest and a communion of the people must always go together. This was what was taught by the most venerated teachers of the Church in St. Patrick's time.

Some centuries later, a confusion arose in men's minds between the idea of "the body (or flesh) and blood of Christ" and the idea of "the Person of Christ"; they came to be identified; so that it was declared by the Council of Trent (Session xiii) that, "after the consecration of the bread and wine, our Lord Jesus Christ, true God and man, is truly, really, and substantially contained under the species of those sensible things."

If this be accepted, it naturally follows that in the "sacrifice which is performed in the Mass, that same Christ is contained and immolated in a bloodless manner, who once offered himself in a bloody manner upon the altar of the cross" (Council of Trent, Session xxii).

This theory, and the practices which are its logical consequences, were unknown in St. Patrick's time. In the Celtic Church, reservation of the consecrated elements for the sick was practised, as in the primitive Church; there was no reservation for the purposes of worship. Communion was in both kinds: the chalice was not withheld from the laity. Celebrations were not daily: even in the monasteries, they were only on Sundays and Saints' Days, and on days especially appointed.

It is sometimes asked, if St. Patrick were to be restored to this life, with only the knowledge and outlook in which he lived here, in which of the two Churches would he find himself more at home, in the reformed Church of Ireland, or in the Church of Rome in Ireland? At first, we may be sure, he would feel a stranger in either communion. He would miss, in the Church of Ireland, the use of the Latin tongue. But it would not be hard to make him understand that, while Latin was the common language of all civilised people in his (Western) world, there were now other languages of civilisation, suitable for the expression of reverent worship. He would miss also, in the reformed Church, the use of the special Eucharistic vestments, universal in his day; and, perhaps, he might miss some details of ritual in public worship; and he would certainly resent the Protestant antipathy to monks and nuns.

On the other hand, when he came to realise the full content of present-day Roman teaching and practice, he would be deeply pained and shocked. He would soon discover that Romanism means a moral, spiritual, and even social, tyranny; that if the Church of Ireland had taken from him some things that were dear and precious to him, Rome had added to the Creed many doctrines which quite obscure the Apostolic faith, and constitute a burden intolerable to reason, "the lamp of the Lord within us"; and that she has been too tolerant of degrading superstitions, such as give great occasion to the enemies of Christ to blaspheme.

—The Rev. Canon N. J. D. White, D.D.

HE SPOKE THE IRISH TONGUE

That Patrick spoke the native tongue was an enormous advantage to him in converting the Irish to Christianity. He had learned and spoken the language from the ages of sixteen to twenty-two, when he was a young slave tending sheep in Slemish. One wonders, in fact, about the outcome of his mission had he not been able to speak Gaelic.

When we speak of the Gaelic language, we are referring to the Celtic tongue, often called "Old Irish" or just "Irish," and the terms are used interchangeably in modern Irish literature. Ireland, of course, is an English-speaking country, and has been for many centuries. Nevertheless, an abundance of Gaelic expressions have survived as Anglo-Irish terms. A few such words are *shillelagh, leprechaun, blatherskite, smithereen, whiskey, blarney, brogan,* and *colleen.*

Gaelic is still spoken in pockets of Ireland, most notably in the west of the country and on the Aran Islands. Gaeltacht (that is, Irish-speaking) areas in Galway, Kerry, Cork, Donegal, Meath, and Waterford all boast a drama tradition. Not only do they produce old Irish plays, they are constantly writing new ones, often of local interest. To encourage familiarity with the tongue, the Department of the Gaeltacht funds activities of a number of drama groups, including twelve local festivals, many single productions, and a National Drama Festival.

Although most of the schoolchildren learn the language, it is increasingly rare that a family speaks it at home. It speaks to them, however, on television, where a number of programs and commercials are in Irish.

Few of the Irish immigrants, except the early ones, spoke their native language. Its use was confined to sporadic tag words and old sayings. But it was their use of English, laced with Irish idiom, that gave the Irish an immediate advantage over the other newcomers to the United States, just as fluency in the Irish tongue sped Patrick on his mission.

—Alice-Boyd Proudfoot

THREE APPRAISALS
Patrick's Character

Probably it was Patrick's character, rather than his wonders, that converted the Irish—the undoubting confidence of his belief and the passionate persistence of his work. He was not a patient man; he could dispense maledictions and benedictions with equal readiness, but even this proud dogma convinced. He ordained priests, built churches, established monasteries and nunneries, and left strong spiritual garrisons to guard his conquests at every turn. He made it seem a supreme adventure to enter the ecclesiastical state; he gathered about him men and women of courage and devotion, who endured every privation to spread the good news that man was redeemed. He did not convert all Ireland; some pockets of paganism and its poetry survived, and leave traces to this day. But when he died (461) it could be said of him, as of no other, that one man had converted a nation.

—Will Durant

He Did Three Things

In appraising the "eminent significance" of Patrick in history, Professor Bury, one of the definitive Patrician scholars, observes:

> He did three things: He organized the Christianity which already existed; he converted kingdoms which were still pagan, especially in the west; and he brought Ireland into connection with the church of the Empire, and made it formally part of universal Christendom." As one of the means to this end he "diffused a knowledge of Latin in Ireland."
>
> —J. B. Bury, LL.D.

Stealing the Thunder

He spent thirty years in the country, by the end of which Christianity was the dominant religion, though paganism persevered for centuries more. He speaks of monastic communities both for men and women, but his own main work was in diocesan organisation, since that was the framework of the British Church he knew. Meanwhile others were spreading the monastic idea, and throughout the country monasteries were springing up. It was the combined work of possibly hundreds of Gallic and Welsh missionaries that sowed the seeds of the later bloom. Only Patrick has survived as a composite figure, and he appears to have stolen the thunder of his contemporaries and those who went before him.

—Brendan Lehane

6

Patrick's Writings and Muirchu's Life

AGIOGRAPHY is the writing and critical study of the lives of the saints. The word "haggle" has no roots in common with "hagiography" and yet the connection is undeniable. Hagiographers *do* haggle and, fortunately, scholarship is the better for it.

Although Patrick's life and work are extremely well recorded, hundreds of biographers, stepping in chronological quicksand, have struggled to accurately reconstruct or agree upon his movements during tantalizing gaps in the puzzle of his life.

And the quest goes on. It is entirely possible that at this very moment two or three Patrician scholars (probably in an Irish or American university or seminary) are huddled in animated disaccord over the meaning of one of Patrick's own rudely constructed Latin phrases.

For it is Patrick himself who tells us the story of his life—partial and fragmentary though it is—in his *Confession*. The title *Confession*,

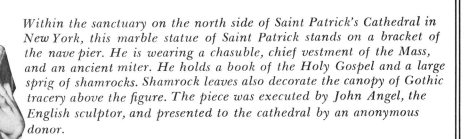

Within the sanctuary on the north side of Saint Patrick's Cathedral in New York, this marble statue of Saint Patrick stands on a bracket of the nave pier. He is wearing a chasuble, chief vestment of the Mass, and an ancient miter. He holds a book of the Holy Gospel and a large sprig of shamrocks. Shamrock leaves also decorate the canopy of Gothic tracery above the figure. The piece was executed by John Angel, the English sculptor, and presented to the cathedral by an anonymous donor.

as applied to the first of Saint Patrick's writings, must have been suggested by his own words, "I shall briefly set forth the words of my confession. . . . This is my confession before I die." But *confession* has not any penitential association here; it is an open and thankful acknowledgment of the goodness of God, a summing up of the net spiritual result of his mission work.

He wrote with two classes of readers in mind: his "kinsfolk" in Britain, who for the most part opposed his leaving Britain; and his "sons" in Ireland. For these latter the *Confession* was intended as "a legacy . . . , to strengthen and confirm their faith."

From references to homesickness for his family in Britain, one may wonder if Patrick ever felt completely at home in Ireland. He was "bound in the spirit" to remain there until his death, and was indeed faithful unto death to the charge laid upon him by God. But his mind was often in Britain as he was writing: "Those of *our* race who were born *there*." And: "A stranger, and an exile for the love of God."

His second important writing, *Letter to Coroticus*, was dispatched some twenty to twenty-five years after he had been working in Ireland. It protested the imprisonment and butchery of Irish Christians who had been captured on a raid and taken to Britain by Coroticus, a British king. This document, intent with outrage, is Patrick's second appeal to the king to release the captives. "Is it a crime," he cries out, "to be born in Ireland? Have not we the same God as ye have?"

Miraculously, his *Confession* and the *Letter to Coroticus* are the only documents that have survived from the British Isles in the century after the fall of Rome. Their authenticity is unquestionable, one fact on which his biographers *do* agree. Saint Patrick, humble man that he was, would no doubt have been stunned and wryly amused that his simple biography would survive for sixteen centuries. Had he known it, he might have been more precise and detailed, thus saving Patrician scholars endless centuries of hair-pulling (their own and each others').

The *Life of Saint Patrick*, written by a Leinster priest, Muirchu, is the most ancient reliable Latin biography that we have of the saint. It was probably written before 699, since Bishop Aed, who commissioned it and to whom it is dedicated, died that year.

That Muirchu set about his task with a clear-cut duty as a historian is evident in his preface. His *Life of Saint Patrick* drew upon the *Confession* and other contemporary texts, since lost. The narrative is primarily concerned with the saint's activities in Ulidia, the ancient kingdom that included the modern counties of Down and Antrim.

Muirchu's writings have come down to us in two manuscripts, neither of which is perfect; but since one possesses what the other lacks, the whole *Life* is accessible to the modern reader.

There is another document dealing with Patrick's life that might be earlier. It is the *Memoranda* of Bishop Tirechan, which scholars place between 664 and 668, a little over two hundred years after Patrick's death. Striving to preserve the saint's movements in Connaught, he obviously could not resist the temptation to embellish the saga with extravagant claims. In writing that Saint Patrick lived to be 120 years old, for instance, he was apparently attempting a comparison with Moses. His numerous corruptions of reality concerning Patrick have caused most scholars to discount a large body of his work and have long been grist for the lively Patrician mill. Though Tirechan's *Memoirs* add nothing but untruth to the study of Patrick, their importance lies in his history of the seventh and eighth centuries in Ireland.

And where are these important documents to be found? In that venerable volume, the *Book of Armagh*, which resides in the library of Trinity College, Dublin. Like the Bible, a miniature library in itself, it is a collection of writings copied by Ferdomnach, official scribe of Armagh, sometime between 807 and 846. Written in Latin in Irish miniscule script, with decorated capitals but without color, it contains: (1) *Life* by Muirchu; (2) *Dicta Patricii*, [*Sayings by Patrick*, presumably his]; (3) *Memoir* by Tirechan, (4) three petitions of Patrick; (5) five notes by the scribe; (6) records derived from the archives of Armagh respecting certain Patrician foundations in Meath, Connaught, and Leinster; (7) more notes by the scribe about Patrick; (8) *Liber Angeli*, an imaginative work in support of the claims of Armagh; (9) an incomplete copy of Saint Patrick's *Confession;* (10) a complete copy of the Celtic text of the Vulgate New Testament; and (11) *The Life of St. Martin* by Sulpicius Severus.

These writings, together with the saint's *Letter to Coroticus,* which is in the Bibliothèque Nationale in Paris, form the authoritative sources of knowledge about the life and work of Saint Patrick.

—Alice-Boyd Proudfoot

Saint Patrick's Confession *and his* Letter to Coroticus *are the only documents that have survived from the British Isles in the century after the fall of Rome.*

CLEARING AWAY THE RUBBISH

The mass of rubbish that has been piled about the memory of Patrick in ancient and modern times has done little positive harm, for Patrick is his own truthful witness, and Muirchu was a sober biographer. But negative damage has been considerable. Because the extravagance of Tirechan and his successors has been taken as serious evidence for the life of Patrick, who remains the patron saint of Ireland, their true importance has been undervalued; for though they contribute nothing but untruth and distortion to the study of Patrick and the fifth century, they are contemporary texts of the first importance for the history of seventh- and eighth-century Ireland and its beliefs. They take their place beside a great quantity of secular texts, of equal importance, but equally little studied. These texts deserve full examination, for in these centuries the detailed history of Ireland is considerably better documented than the history of England, or of most European countries; these are the years when Ireland was in the course of transformation from an alien barbarian island into a European nation, and in which all Europe was deeply indebted to the ferment of ideas that poured from Ireland. The neglected texts, misused for the wrong purpose, require proper consideration. They form a proper and significant part of the study of the formation of medieval Europe.

All this literature, important in its own right and its proper context, must be cleared away from the study of Patrick. His own writings and Muirchu's Life, combined with what else is known of the age in which he lived, together give a clear outline of his life and work. To understand them, it is necessary to explain their context and to remove the irrelevance and confusion that hides them. When they can be seen in their own right, Patrick's own awkward language speaks for itself. His courage and his fears, his resolution and his hesitations, his persistent devotion to a people whom he knew, understood and loved, and his determination to do all he could for their well-being on earth and hereafter, in disregard of all obstacles and all other considerations, are utterly remote from the ecclesiastical portrait of a plaster saint and a national idol. He is one of the few personalities of fifth-century Europe who has revealed himself with living warmth, in terms that men of any age who care for their fellows can comprehend. He is no more typical of his time than any other man in any other time; but through the eyes of Patrick men may penetrate beyond the headlines and the generalities of historians ancient and modern, may perceive something of the human problems that are common to their age and his and also something of the essential differences that distinguish one age from the other. Patrick's moving and intensely personal account of his life and troubles is much more than a story of the conversion of the Irish to Christianity; it touches the mainsprings of human endeavour and teaches not only the history of one period, but the substance of what history is about.

—John Morris

INTRODUCTION TO PATRICK'S *CONFESSIO**

THE *Confessio* is the more substantial of Patrick's two works. It is not essentially a confession of sins but rather a declaration of his personal mission to the Irish and a confession of praise and gratitude to the God who called him to that mission. Written to counter criticisms, it is a humble but powerful statement in justification of his work in Ireland; hence the fine concluding phrase: "and this is my declaration before I die."

Repeatedly Patrick draws attention to his own lack of learning and culture, to the "rusticity" of his Latin. For once this is not the Christian Latin author's deliberate choice of the "lowly style" (*sermo humilis*); nor is it the conventional self-abasing apology for poor style and grammatical inaccuracy even when neither is present. Patrick is struggling to express himself in a language which he has never wholly mastered. Latin had been a second language to him in childhood and his literary education was abruptly terminated when he was captured by Irish raiders at the age of sixteen. There is no certain reminiscence of any Latin author, Christian or secular, in his writing; the only book which he can be seen to know is the Latin Bible, which he quotes freely and which provides him with much of his vocabulary and phraseology.

—Allan Hood

* Also known as his "Declaration."

The opening page of Saint Patrick's Confessio, *F. 22 in the* Book of Armagh, *Trinity College Library, Dublin*

DECLARATION *(CONFESSIO)*
(Selected Paragraphs)

1   I, Patrick, a sinner, quite uncultivated and the least of all the faithful and utterly despicable to many, had as my father the deacon Calpornius, son of the late Potitus, a priest, who belonged to the town of Bannavem Taburniae; he had a small estate nearby, and it was there that I was taken captive. I was then about sixteen years old. I did not know the true God and I was taken into captivity in Ireland with so many thousands; and we deserved it, because we drew away from God and did not keep His commandments and did not obey our priests who kept reminding us of our salvation; and the Lord brought on us the fury of His anger and scattered us among many peoples even to the ends of the earth, where now I in my insignificance find myself among foreigners.

16   But after I reached Ireland, well, I pastured the flocks every day and I used to pray many times a day; more and more did my love of God and my fear of Him increase, and my faith grew and my spirit was stirred, and as a result I would say up to a hundred prayers in one day, and almost as many at night; I would even stay in the forests and on the mountain and would wake to pray before dawn in all weathers, snow, frost, rain; and I felt no harm and there was no listlessness in me—as I now realise, it was because the Spirit was fervent within me.

17   And it was in fact there that one night while asleep I heard a voice

saying to me: "You do well to fast, since you will soon be going to your home country"; and again, very shortly after, I heard this prophecy: "See, your ship is ready." And it was not near at hand but was perhaps two hundred miles away, and I had never been there and did not know a living soul there. And then I soon ran away and abandoned the man with whom I had been for six years, and I came in God's strength, for He granted me a successful journey and I had nothing to fear, till I reached that ship.

18 Now on the very day that I arrived the ship was launched, and I said that I had the wherewithal for my passage with them; and as for the captain, he was not pleased and replied sharply and with annoyance: "You will be wasting your time asking to go with us." On hearing this I left them to go to the hut where I was staying, and on the way I began to pray and before I had finished my prayer I heard one of them; he was shouting loudly after me: "Come quickly, they are calling you." And immediately I returned to them and they proceeded to say to me: "Come, we are taking you on trust; make friends with us in whatever way you wish" (and so that day I refused to suck their nipples because of the fear of God; however, I had hopes of their coming to faith in Jesus Christ, because they were pagans), and as a result I got a place with them, and we set sail at once.

19 Three days later we made land and we travelled through a wilderness for twenty-eight days, and they ran out of food and hunger overtook them, and the next day the captain approached me and said: "What about it, Christian? You say your god is great and all-powerful; well then, why can you not pray for us? We are in danger of starving; there is little chance of our ever seeing a living soul." I told them confidently: "Turn trustingly and with all your heart to the Lord my God—because nothing is impossible for Him; and this day He will send you food for your journey until you are fully satisfied; for He has an abundance everywhere." And with God's help it turned out so; lo and behold, a herd of pigs appeared in the way before our eyes, and they killed many of them and stayed there for two nights and fully recovered and had their fill of the pigs' meat, for many of them had collapsed and been left half-dead by the wayside; and after this they gave grateful thanks to God, and I gained great respect in their eyes, and from that day they had plenty of food. They even found some wild honey and offered me a piece; and one of them said: "It is a sacrifice." Thanks be to God, I tasted none of it.

22 Now as we travelled He provided us with food and fire and dry weather every day until on the tenth day we reached human habi-

tation; as I indicated above, we had travelled for twenty-eight days through the wilderness and on the night that we reached human habitation we had in fact no food left.

23 And again a few years later I was in Britain with my kinsfolk, and they welcomed me as a son and asked me earnestly not to go off anywhere and leave them this time, after the great tribulations which I had been through. And it was there that I saw one night in a vision a man coming as it were from Ireland (his name was Victoricus), with countless letters, and he gave me one of them, and I read the heading of the letter, "The Voice of the Irish," and as I read these opening words aloud, I imagined at that very instant that I heard the voice of those who were beside the forest of Foclut which is near the western sea; and thus they cried, as though with one voice: "We beg you, holy boy, to come and walk again among us"; and I was stung with remorse in my heart and could not read on, and so I awoke. Thanks be to God, that after so many years the Lord bestowed on them according to their cry.

God and Satan, the Great Realities

THERE is, in his writings, a display of genuine missionary spirit, which as it has roused many a Christian worker to action in the past, may well stir up many in our day also. Patrick everywhere displays an earnest trust and faith in the constant protection of a gracious Providence. His love for the souls of the men among whom he laboured, notwithstanding the ill-treatment he received at their hands, is remarkable. His honest simplicity and the contempt everywhere displayed for the riches of the world deserve far more general recognition than they have yet received. His acquaintance with the Holy Scripture, with the phraseology of which his Writings are thoroughly imbued, and his desire to conform his doctrine to their teaching, is significant. To him God and Satan, heaven and hell, were great realities; "he endured as seeing Him who is invisible" (Heb. xi, 27).

—The Rev. C. H. H. Wright, D.D.

26 And when I was attacked by a number of my elders, who came and brought up my sins against my arduous episcopate, certainly that day I was struck a heavy blow so that I might fall here and for ever; but the Lord graciously spared me, who was a stranger in a foreign land for His name's sake, and He helped me greatly when I was trampled under foot in this way. I pray God that it may not be reckoned to them as a sin that I well and truly fell into disgrace and scandal.

27 After thirty years they found a pretext for their allegations against me in a confession which I had made before I was a deacon. In a

depressed and worried state of mind I mentioned to a close friend what I had done as a boy one day, indeed in the space of one hour, because I was not yet proof against temptation. I do not know, God knows, whether I was fifteen years old at the time, and I did not believe in the living God, nor had I done since earliest childhood; but I remained in death and unbelief till I was severely chastened and in truth humiliated by hunger and nakedness, and every day too.

28 On the other hand I did not go to Ireland of my own accord, until I was nearly at the end of my strength; but this was really rather to my own good, since as a result I was reformed by the Lord, and He fitted me to be today what was once far from me, that I should be concerned and busily active for the salvation of others, whereas at that time I took no thought even for myself.

35 But it would be tedious to relate all my labours in detail or even partially. I shall briefly tell how God in His great mercy on many occasions freed me from slavery and from the twelve dangers in which my life was threatened, quite apart from many traps and things which I cannot put into words. I should not like to cause offence to my readers; but God is my witness, who knows all things even before they happen, that He frequently gave me a warning in a divine prophecy, despite my being a poor waif and uneducated.

41 And how has it lately come about in Ireland that those who never had any knowledge of God but up till now always worshipped idols and abominations are now called the people of the Lord and the sons of God, and sons and daughters of Irish underkings are seen to be monks and virgins of Christ?

42 And there was also a blessed lady of native Irish birth and high rank, very beautiful and grown up, whom I baptised; and a few days later she found some reason to come to us and indicated that she had received a message from an angel of God, and the angel had urged her too to become a virgin of Christ and to draw near to God. Thanks be to God, six days later she most commendably and enthusiastically took up that same course that all virgins of God also do—not with their fathers' consent; no, they endure persecution and their own parents' unfair reproaches, and yet their number grows larger and larger (and we do not know the numbers of our family of faith who have been reborn there), not to mention widows and the self-denying. But it is the women kept in slavery who suffer especially; they even have to endure constant threats and terrorisation; but the Lord has given grace to many of

His handmaidens, for though they are forbidden to do so, they resolutely follow His example.

43 And so even if I wanted to part with them and head for Britain— and I would have been only too glad to do so, to see my homeland and family; and not only that, but to go on to Gaul to visit the brethren and to see the face of my Lord's holy men; God knows that I longed to, but I am bound by the Spirit who testifies to me that if I do so He will mark me out as guilty, and I am afraid of wasting the labour which I have begun—and not I, but Christ the Lord who commanded me to come to be with them for the rest of my life, if the Lord so desire and shield me from every evil way, so that I may not sin before Him.

"I had the fear of God as my guide for my journey through Gaul and Italy, and also on the islands in the Tyrrhenian Sea."

—Saint Patrick

"I had the fear of God as my guide."

49   For though I am entirely untalented, I have done my best to safeguard myself, even in my dealings with Christian brethren and virgins of Christ and with pious women, who would give me unsolicited gifts and throw some of their jewellery on the altar, and I would return it to them, and they would take offence at my doing so; but I did so for the hope of eternity, to safeguard myself carefully in everything so that they would not catch me out or the ministry of my service under some pretext of my dishonesty and so that I would not give unbelievers the slightest opportunity for denigration or disparagement.

50   But perhaps when I baptised so many thousands I hoped for even a halfpenny from any of them? Tell me, and I will give it back. Or when the Lord everywhere ordained clergy through someone as ordinary as me and I conferred on each of them his function free, if I asked any of them for even so much as the price of my shoe, tell it against me, and I shall give it back to you.

51   No, rather I spent money on your behalf so that they would accept me, and I travelled amongst you and everywhere for your sake, beset by many dangers, even to the remote districts beyond which there was no-one and where no-one had ever penetrated to baptise or ordain clergy or confirm the people. With God's favour I have produced all these results tirelessly and most gladly for your salvation.

56   See now I commend my soul to my God in whom we trust absolutely, for whom I am an ambassador despite my obscurity, because He is no respecter of persons and He chose me for this task, to be just one among the least of His servants.

58   And so may God never allow me to be separated from His people which He has won in the ends of the earth. I pray to God to give me perseverance and to deign to grant that I prove a faithful witness to Him until I pass on, for my God's sake.

PATRICK, who had no taste for ecclesiastical politics, struggled against enormous difficulties. He had first to convince Roman churchmen that the conversion of heathen foreigners was in itself desirable, he was suspect to his fellow clergy in Britain, and in Ireland he appeared in the guise of an enemy agent. He overcame the obstacles because his devotion defeated suspicion and his resolution prevailed against threats and hostility.

—John Morris

62   But I beg those who believe in and fear God, whoever deigns to look at or receive this document which the unlearned sinner Patrick

drew up in Ireland, that no-one should ever say that if I have achieved anything, however trivial, or may have shown the way according to God's good pleasure, it was my ignorance at work, but consider and accept as the undeniable truth that it would have been God's gift. And this is my declaration before I die.

The shorter *Epistola* is an indignant protest against the outrages committed on Irish Christians in a raid by soldiers of the British king, Coroticus; some had been butchered, others taken prisoner. It is a second appeal for their release and is addressed to the soldiers of Coroticus, to be read out before the king and his people. But it is very much of an open letter; besides the direct address to Coroticus and to his soldiers, and the emotional apostrophe to those martyred in the raid, Patrick appeals to all right-minded Christians to have nothing to do with those involved in the atrocity. He calls down divine vengeance on the culprits and again emphasises his vocation as apostle to the Irish, despite critics in his home country.

Letter (Epistola)
(Selected Paragraphs)

1 I, Patrick, a sinner, yes, and unlearned, established in Ireland, put on record that I am bishop. I am strongly convinced that what I am I have received from God. And so I live among barbarian peoples, a stranger and an exile for the love of God; He is my witness if it is so. Not that I wanted to utter anything from my lips so harshly and bluntly, but I am compelled by my zeal for God, and Christ's truth has roused me to do so, for the love of my neighbour and my children, for whose sakes I gave up homeland and family and my life even to the point of death. If I so deserve, I live for my God, to teach the heathen, even if I am despised by some.

2 With my own hand I have written and composed these words to be given, delivered and sent to the soldiers of Coroticus—I do not say to my fellow-citizens nor to fellow-citizens of the holy Romans, but to fellow-citizens of the demons, because of their evil actions. Like the enemy they live in death, as allies of Irish and of Picts and apostates. These blood-thirsty men are bloody with the blood of innocent Christians, whom I have begotten for God in countless numbers and have confirmed in Christ!

3 On the day after the neophytes, clothed in white, had received the chrism (its fragrance was on their brows as they were butchered and put to the sword by those I have mentioned), I sent a letter with a holy priest whom I had taught from early childhood, and

No one knows the history of this ancient stone tablet of Saint Patrick in Patrickswell, Co. Limerick. One thing is certain, though: The artist who laboriously carved the figure in stone had heard the story of the snakes.

he was accompanied by some clerics; the letter requested that they should grant us some of the booty and baptised prisoners that they had captured; they roared with laughter at them.

4 And so I do not know what to lament more, those who were killed or those they took prisoner or those whom Satan has sorely ensnared. They shall be delivered up to hell along with him in eternal punishment because undoubtedly he who commits a sin is a slave and is called the son of Satan.

10 Did I come to Ireland without God's favour or according to the flesh? Who forced me? I am obliged by the Spirit not to see any of my kinsfolk. Does it come from me that I show devout mercy towards the very people which once took me captive and harried the slaves of my father's house, male and female? I was free-born

according to the flesh; my father was a decurion. I sold my good birth (not that I am ashamed or regret it) in the interest of others. In short, I am a slave in Christ to a foreign people for the ineffable glory of the everlasting life which is in Christ Jesus our Lord.

12 I am resented. What should I do, Lord? I am very much despised. See, Your sheep are torn to pieces around me and are carried off, and by the raiders I have mentioned, on the aggressive orders of Coroticus. Far from God's love is the man who delivers Christians into the hands of Irish and Picts. Ravening wolves have devoured the Lord's flock, which was in fact increasing excellently and most actively, and sons of the Irish and daughters of their under-kings were monks and virgins of Christ—I cannot count their number. Therefore be not pleased at the wrong done to the righteous; even as far as hell it shall not be pleasing.

20 I testify before God and His angels that it will be just as He has indicated to me in my ignorance. These are not my words but those of God and His apostles and prophets, which I have set out in Latin and they have never lied. "He who believes will be saved, but he who does not believe will be damned" (Mark 16.16). God has spoken.

21 I earnestly beg that whichever servant of God is ready and willing should be the bearer of this letter, so that it may not be suppressed or hidden on any account by anyone, but rather be read out in front of all the people and in the presence of Coroticus himself. But if only God may inspire them to come to their senses eventually and return to God, so that, however late, they repent of acting so sacrilegiously (murderer that he is of the Lord's brethren!) and free the baptised women whom they previously took captive, so that they may be found worthy to live for God and may be made whole here and for ever! Peace to Father, Son and Holy Ghost. Amen.

Sayings

1 I had the fear of God as my guide for my journey through Gaul and Italy, and also on the islands in the Tyrrhenian Sea.

2 You have departed from this world to go to Paradise. Thanks be to God.

3 The church of the Irish, or rather of the Romans; in order to be Christians like the Romans, you should chant among yourselves at every hour of prayer that praiseworthy cry, *Kyrie eleison, Christe eleison.* Let every church which follows me chant *Kyrie eleison, Christe eleison.* Thanks be to God.

PATRICK'S EARLY BIOGRAPHER

THE earliest and most reliable extant Latin biography of Patrick was written by Muirchu in the later 7th century. The establishment of a text bristles with difficulties; as with so many medieval compositions the tradition is more fluid than in the case of hallowed classical or patristic works. The text here is again based on the *Book of Armagh* (A) and reproduces Book 1 as defined in that manuscript (folios 2-7); this takes the story of Patrick from his infancy through to the beginning of his mission in Ireland, his clash with King Loegaire at Tara and his foundation of Armagh. The narrative is expanded in Book 2 (A) by additional miracles and information and by the death of Patrick.

Muirchu is not uneducated, and he slips in a quotation from Vergil and from Sedulius in Book 2 (A). But even if we make allowances for the poor state of the text, in, for example, ch. 27-28, it is clear that Muirchu has not achieved an homogeneous narrative style. At times his striving after what he regards as fine writing becomes apparent, particularly in the preface, which carefully observes the niceties of humility and deference to one's superior in a series of ablative phrases. The preface also exploits the metaphor of embarking upon the work as though upon a stormy sea—a well-worn rhetorical image used also by the 7th-century biographer of St. Samson of Dol and by Cogitosus, perhaps Muirchu's father, in his *Life of St. Brigit*; but Muirchu over-elaborates it to the point of bombast. Muirchu has a good grasp of the Latin language, but his style lacks elegance and consistency.

—Allan Hood

Muirchu's *Life of St. Patrick*

PREFACE

Many, my lord Aed, have attempted to organise this particular narrative in accordance with the tradition handed down to them by their fathers and by those who have been storytellers from the beginning, but because of the grave difficulties involved in recounting it and of differing opinions and numerous persons' numerous conjectures they have never succeeded in reaching the one sure path of historical fact; and so, if I am not mistaken, as our people's saying here goes, just as boys are brought into the meeting-place, so I have brought the child's rowing boat of my poor intellect onto this deep and dangerous ocean of hagiography, with the waves surging in wildly swirling walls of water, among whirlpools and jagged rocks in uncharted seas—an ocean never yet attempted or embarked on by any barque except only that of my father Cogitosus. However, to avoid giving the impression that I am exaggerating, I shall, with some reluctance, set about expounding this small and piecemeal selection from St. Patrick's numerous acts. I have little talent, dubious authorities, and am subject to lapses of memory; I have only feeble insight and a poor style; but I am

"The church of the Irish, or rather of the Romans; in order to be Christians like the Romans, you should chant among yourselves at every hour of prayer that praiseworthy cry, Kyrie eleison, Christe eleison. *Let every church which follows me chant* Kyrie eleison, Christe eleison. *Thanks be to God."*

—*Saint Patrick*

prompted by dutiful and loving affection and am obedient to the command of your holiness and dignity.

THE CHRONOLOGY OF MUIRCHU'S *LIFE OF ST. PATRICK*

1. Patrick's origins and first captivity.
2. His voyage with the pagans, their sufferings in the wilderness, and the food brought by divine agency to him and the pagans.

3. The second captivity, which he endured for sixty days at the hands of his enemies.

4. His reception by his kinsfolk when they recognised him.

5. His age when he resolved to learn wisdom, going to visit the apostolic see.

6. How he found St. Germanus in Gaul and therefore went no further.

7. His age when an angel visited him, telling him to come over here.

8. His return from Gaul, and the consecration of Palladius and his death soon after.

9. His consecration by bishop Amator on the death of Palladius.

10. The pagan king who lived in Tara when St. Patrick came bringing baptism.

11. His first journey in this island, to redeem himself from Miliucc before retrieving others from the devil.

12. Miliucc's death, and Patrick's saying about his descendants.

13. St. Patrick's plan when a problem arose about the celebration of the first Easter.

14. The first paschal sacrifice in this island.

15. The pagan festival at Tara on the same night as St. Patrick celebrated Easter.

16. King Loegaire goes from Tara to Patrick on Easter night.

17. Patrick is summoned before the king; the faith of Ercc, son of Daeg, and the death of the wizard that night.

18. The anger of the king and his followers against Patrick, and the blow God struck upon them, and Patrick's transformation before the heathen.

19. Patrick's arrival at Tara on Easter day and the faith of Dubthach maccu Lugir.

20. Patrick's contest with the wizard that day, and his amazing miracles.

21. King Loegaire's conversion, and Patrick's saying about his kingdom after him.

22. St. Patrick's teaching and baptising and signs, following Christ's example.

23. Macuil and his conversion at Patrick's words.

24. The pagans working on Sunday against Patrick's command.

25. The story of Daire, and the horse and the grant of Armagh to Patrick.

26. The fertile land turned into a salt-marsh.

27. The death of Monesan, the Saxon woman.

28. How St. Patrick saw the heavens open and the Son of God and his angels.

29. St. Patrick's conflict with Coroticus, king of Ail.

Muirchu gives a chapter to each of these subjects. He begins:

These few items concerning St. Patrick's experience and miraculous powers were written down by Muirchu maccu Machtheni under the direction of Aed, bishop of the town of Sletty.

1 Patrick, who was also called Sochet, was of British nationality, born in Britain, the son of the deacon Calpurnius, whose father, as Patrick himself says, was the priest Potitus, who came from the town of Bannavem Taburniae, not far from our sea; we have discovered for certain and beyond any doubt that this township is Ventre; and the mother who bore him was named Concessa.

and ends:

29 I shall not pass over in silence an amazing feat of Patrick. News came to him of the quite iniquitous action of a certain British king called Coroticus, an ill-starred and cruel tyrant. He was a very great persecutor and murderer of Christians. Now Patrick tried to recall him to the way of truth by means of a letter; but he scoffed at its salutary warnings. When this was reported to Patrick, he prayed to the Lord and said: "God, if it be possible, cast this traitor out from this present world and the world to come." After only a short time had elapsed, Coroticus heard someone give a musical performance and sing that he would soon pass from his royal throne; and all his dearest friends took up the cry. Then, when he was in open court, he suddenly had the misfortune to take on the appearance of a little fox; he made off before his followers' eyes, and from that day and that hour, like a passing stream of water, he was never seen anywhere again.

7 The Flowering of Monasticism

THE AWAKENING OF IRELAND

The seed was planted. The flowering would follow. But for a hundred years there was little palpable change in the life of Ireland. Cows were milked, dogs coursed, kings and peasants hunted deer and boar, pirates raided, slaves were sold, brown bulls and white bulls were rustled, and in the evening romancers told the great legends of the past, according to their rank and company. Borders changed from time to time, depending on the mood of a king and the strength of his soldiers. Christianity advanced, and priests held mass, chanting mystical formulae to a god who was invisible yet manifest in all the variety of nature, and telling good stories of the precursors of a far-off race. There was more ·gusto in the new religion, and young people felt a call to it, even giving up the comforts of ordinary life for a rigorous existence in the confines of cells. But there was not much change from old to new. The past was still rich and important, made more so, if anything, by the new faith. Druids were being ousted, not without protest, but they were a run-down class and their influence had long waned.

Gallarus Oratory, Co. Kerry. Date uncertain (eighth to twelfth century A.D.).
Built of unmortared stone, it is the only intact example of a number of
similar structures in Co. Kerry.

There is nothing to say that Christianity changed the habits of the
Irish people except in the culture of the educated classes and in ritual,
which was the outward form of a theology most of them, most of any
nation, could never understand. It was Christianity itself that changed,
as it did in most places to which it came, adapting to the customs of
its hosts. After a long incubation it would begin to affect those who
claimed it, but even then only in superficials. After hundreds of years
slavery would be abolished, and women exempted from service as
soldiers. But if the women were spared war, still their husbands went
on fighting.

The changes came in culture, among the individuals who were
alive to cultural things. Christianity fed the minds of those whose minds
hungered. There had always been such people in Ireland, the privileged,
revered classes of thinking men, and it was these whose imagination
was caught. They came in the main from the high classes of their
society, because they were the classes with time to spare for the mind. A

series of historical chances, the lottery of events, had brought them fare that stimulated their enthusiasm for everything. Part we have seen. It came from Byzantium, Sinai, the monasteries of Provence and Aquitaine, from the harsh mountains of Wales and the hampered plains of Britain; Roman dominion had spread it, Roman decline left it to take firm root. Balkan battles and the tidal rush of men from the central plains of Asia; hermits languishing in desert drought, Levantine merchants plying a far-flung trade, clerics copying manuscripts in Rome, and the seething confusion of oriental politics; all these were planks in the ship that brought a cultural revolution to Ireland. And just as important were the factors of Ireland herself; the high place of letters, the scrupulous love of scheme, priority and place, the love of facts, the closeness to nature, the values and virtues of the pagan Celt, the streak of whimsy and the unforced vein of poetry in him.

These were the ingredients, mixed by Patrick and the first order of saints. Then there was a long silence in Ireland. For fifty years there are no records of the maturing of the new spirit. And then the mind woke, and wanted to break out of its confines. For two hundred years the cultural story of Ireland is full of event and expansion and the searching for something transcendent, something that might or might not exist. Communities of saints sprang up over the country, and provided the base from which this expansion could take place. The pioneering was left to individuals, and others followed in their wake. The story must be told through these individuals. In Brendan, Columba and Columbanus is seen the insatiable questing that was the core of the character of the new Ireland. Though life went on, and there was little change for the ordinary man and woman, reflections from these archetypes were glanced down through the strata of society. People heard of the doings of the individuals, and approved them and where there was a chance they helped them. Only Drake and a ship's crew could circle the world and trounce the king of Spain, but they made the character of the England of their day.

—Brendan Lehane

Irish Isolation

IRELAND had always been outside the Empire. Towns were unknown, and the whole country was split into hundreds of tiny units based on family ties. No Roman soldier ever landed on Irish shores to enforce the civil framework on which the Church had been constructed. The basic theology percolated into the character of the nation; some of its ideals did too, the love of scholarship and the idea of material renunciation. But the centralised authority was not to find roots for hundreds of years. Ireland remained a country of scattered clusters, and took monasticism to itself like an heirloom.

—Sean O'Faolain

A SIXTH-CENTURY IRISH MONASTERY

sixth-century Irish monastery must not be pictured like one of the great medieval monasteries on the continent. It was much closer in appearance to the monastic settlements of the Nile valley or the island of Lérins than to later Monte Cassino or Clairvaux. Even the Latin word *monasterium,* when borrowed into Irish under the form *muintir,* was applied not to the buildings but to the community. For a modern equivalent one could think of the army camps to be found in various parts of the country during the 1940s, each a collection of wooden huts for sleeping in, grouped around a few larger buildings used by the whole community. A modern holiday-camp with rows of wooden chalets grouped around a few central halls would be closer to it in appearance than a modern Mount Melleray.

From Adamnán's *Life of Colum Cille,* written in Iona in the seventh century, when some of those who had entered the monastery under the founder were still alive, we can reconstruct the authentic picture in great detail. Instead of a communal residence the monks lived in individual cells constructed of wood or wattles, the abbot's cell slightly apart from the rest. In the west of Ireland, where wood was even then scarce, the cells were more likely to be constructed of stone and those are the only ones which have stood the test of time. Besides the cells of the monks the monastic enclosure included within it the *church,* usually built of oak, with a stone altar, sacred vessels, relics, and handbells for summoning the congregation (on the rare occasions when the church was of stone, this was of sufficient interest to be given a special name, the *damliag,* from which St. Cianán's foundation at Duleek, county Meath, took its name); the *refectory* with its long table, and adjoining it the *kitchen* containing an open fire, cooking utensils and a large cauldron of drinking water; the *library* and *scriptorium* with manuscripts suspended in satchels by leather straps from the walls and an ample supply of writing materials—waxed tablets, parchment, quills and stylos, ink-horns and the rest. A workshop and forge were situated nearby, while outside the rampart came the cultivated lands and pastures belonging to the monastery, furnished with farm buildings and in addition a mill and limekiln.

PRAY DAILY, FAST DAILY, STUDY DAILY, WORK DAILY

"Pray daily, fast daily, study daily, work daily," wrote Columbanus in his rule, and the monastic life became a round of divine worship, mortification, study and manual labour. With the exception of those brethren who worked on the farm the monks assembled daily in the church for the various canonical hours. Sundays and saints' feastdays were solemnized by rest from labour and the celebration of the eucharist in addition to the divine office. Easter was the chief feast of the liturgical year, a time of joy after the austerities of Lent. Christmas was also a festival of joy, preceded by a period of preparation.

While the whole life of the monk and his retirement from the world was meant to be one great act of self-denial, additional mortification was imposed at fixed intervals. Every Wednesday and Friday throughout the year, except during the period from Easter to Pentecost, was observed as a fast day, when no food was taken till the late afternoon, unless when hospitality to a guest demanded relaxation of the rule. During Lent the fast was prolonged every day except Sunday till evening when a light meal was allowed. The ordinary diet consisted of bread, milk, eggs and fish, but on Sundays and festivals and on the arrival of a guest meat was probably permitted. The monks wore a white tunic underneath and above it a cape and hood of coarse, undyed wool. When working or travelling they wore sandals. At night they

The early monastery of Sceilg Mhichil, off the coast of Co. Kerry, viewed from the peak of Great Skellig Rock. The cluster of beehive cells may be seen in the center foreground.

slept in their habits. Their tonsure, unlike the Roman shaving of the crown of the head, took the peculiar Irish form of shaving the hair to the front of the head and allowing the hair at the back to grow long.

The principal subject of study was the sacred scriptures, much of which was committed to memory, especially the psalms. Columbanus, a pupil of sixth-century Bangor, and Adamnán, a pupil of seventh-century Iona, show an extensive knowledge of Latin classical authors in their writings, especially of Virgil and Horace, and pagan authors must be included among the liberal writings studied in Irish monasteries as mentioned by the Venerable Bede. Lives of the fourth- and fifth-century continental saints such as Sulpicius Severus' *Life of St. Martin of Tours* and Constantine's *Life of St. Germanus* found their way into the Irish monasteries at an early date and were used for reading to the community. Recent research has pointed to close cultural connexions between Ireland and Spain in the sixth and seventh centuries and the writings of Isidore of Seville reached Ireland before being brought by Irish monks to Central Europe.

The manual labour in which the early Irish monks engaged was primarily agricultural. Ploughing, sowing, harvesting, threshing are all mentioned as occupations of the sixth-century Iona monks. Others were engaged in making the various articles required for domestic use, and the need for sacred vessels of all kinds inspired an artistic approach to metalwork. Since fish formed such an important element in the diet, it is not surprising that the monks of Iona, as of all monasteries situated near the sea or the larger rivers, spent long hours in their boats. Like all true fishermen they liked to tell later of the "big ones" which did not get away, and so Adamnán heard of the two huge salmon which Colum Cille's companions netted on the River Boyle in Roscommon more than a century before.

Some of the Irish monasteries seem to have had very large communities. Medieval sources refer to 3,000 monks of both Clonard and Bangor, but if this is not simply an exaggeration, it must be taken to include all their daughter-houses as well. Upwards of a hundred would probably be the normal number during the sixth century in the larger monasteries—for instance Columbanus had two hundred monks divided among his three foundations in Gaul. By the early seventh century, when many English students flocked to Ireland, the numbers in some monasteries reached a few hundred. The great majority of the monks in each foundation were laymen and remained so, but a small number of the officeholders were in sacred orders. At the head of the community stood the abbot, who often nominated his own successor. He was assisted by the vice-abbot or prior, who looked after the material resources of the house, and by a group of the older brethren called the *seniores*. One of these was usually in bishop's orders and one or two were ordained to the priesthood to celebrate mass and administer the sacraments. Other posts in the monastery were those of scribe, cellarer, cook, guestmaster, miller, baker, smith, gardener, porter and so on. Many monasteries had one or more anchorites who secluded themselves from the rest of the community and lived lives of silence and prayer.

MONASTIC DISCIPLINE

It is well known that Irish monastic discipline was strict but a few instances from the rule of Columbanus will show just how severe it sometimes was. The smallest penalty, imposed for minor infringements of the rule, was the recitation of three psalms. Corporal punishment, inflicted on the hand with a leather strap could vary from six to one hundred strokes. Periods of extra silence, fasting on bread and water, expulsion and exile were other penalties. The most severe, imposed by Columbanus for murder, was ten years exile, of which some at least were to be spent on bread and water. Corporal punishment was nowhere prescribed in the Irish civil law and its introduction as a form of monastic chastisement is therefore all the more surprising. When the Irish monks went to the continent, however, they found it, together with the more extreme fasts and vigils, opposed by their continental recruits and ultimately abandoned it.

—Cardinal Tomás Ó Fiaich*

PRAYER TO SAINT PATRICK

We invoke holy Patrick, Ireland's chief apostle.
Glorious is his wondrous name, a flame that baptized heathen;
He warred against hard-hearted wizards.
He thrust down the proud with the help of our Lord of fair
    heaven.
He purified Ireland's meadow-lands, a mighty birth.
We pray to Patrick chief apostle; his judgment hath delivered us
    in Doom from the malevolence of dark devils.
God be with us, together with the prayer of Patrick, chief apostle.

—*Ninine (eighth century),*
Translated by Whitley Stokes
and John Strachan

ROUND TOWERS

Round towers were a striking feature within a monastic enclosure. Not only did they summon travelers from miles around, as do church spires, but they provided safe refuge for persons and strongrooms for church valuables.

* Now Cardinal Archbishop of Armagh and Primate of All Ireland.

An average tower is about 95 feet high and tapers from base to top. The doorway is always a considerable height, about 16 feet aboveground, and access was gained by means of a ladder which was then drawn up by persons seeking safety within.

When were round towers first built? The antiquary, George Petrie, wrote in 1845 that some of the towers belonged to the time of the great monastic founders in the sixth and seventh centuries, and some scholars argue for an even earlier date. The majority of towers, however, are believed to have been built during the ninth and tenth centuries. Although their erection has been correlated to the need for strongholds during the Viking incursions, their *raison d'être* may have been less practical.

The Old Irish name for a tower of this kind, *cloigtheach,* or "bell house," suggests that the people of the time thought of them as belfries. Since there is no evidence for the existence of large hanging bells, we might visualize small bells of the type associated with Saint Patrick being rung by hand from the upper windows of the towers.

Over a hundred round towers in various states of preservation remain in Ireland, including a number which have, surprisingly, survived virtually unscathed.

—Alice-Boyd Proudfoot

Ardmore Round Tower, Co. Waterford. That Saint Declan built the Ard-more Round Tower in one night in the early fifth century seems the height of Irish romanticism. However, since—according to the ninth-century Calen-dar of Aengus—*he introduced rye into Ireland, maybe it only seemed* like *one night!*

ST. DECLAN (DEAGLAN)

The story of St. Declan is interesting not only for itself, but because of its bearing on the theory that there were Christians in Ireland before the coming of St. Patrick. Declan has been placed by some historians as late as the seventh century, but he undoubtedly belongs to the fifth and was a contemporary of St. Patrick. As a young boy he was sent to fosterage with a certain Dimma, who is said to have been a foreigner and a Christian. After leaving Dimma he went to Rome, where he studied for the priesthood and was later consecrated a bishop.

On his return to Ireland, he founded a monastery at Ardmore, near Waterford, the ruins of which are still to be seen. He was also the first Bishop of Ardmore, and was confirmed in this office by St. Patrick.

The site of Declan's church on the headland of Ardmore is marked by a round tower, which is in an excellent state of preservation, and by the ruins of an oratory which is said to cover his grave.

In one night Declan is supposed to have built the famous Round Tower—the most perfect of its kind in Ireland—and the nearby church, of which the ruins remain. Declan's patron day, the 24th of July, was for a long time the occasion of a considerable pilgrimage to Ardmore, and his Oratory, a rude hut, is still standing. The Round Tower, originally used as a belfry and refuge, differs from other Irish towers in that it is divided by four beltings, or string courses, into as many stories, with window opening to each. It is built of cut stone, is ninety-seven feet high, with a diameter at the base of fifteen feet; the round-headed entrance door is thirteen feet from the ground. The conical cap still stands, but the crutch-like cross which once surmounted it was long ago destroyed by soldiers who used it as a mark for musket shots.

In 1841, excavations in the base of the Tower revealed the remains of two skeletons, laid in a bed of sifted earth. Above this was a floor of concrete, over which were four successive layers of large stones, closely fitted, and overlaid in turn by a floor of smoothed concrete.

Declan is credited with many miracles, and is said to have arrested a serious plague by his prayers and fasting. Among his minor achievements—this is recorded in the *Calendar of Aengus*—is that of being the first to introduce rye into Ireland.

THE CHURCH BELL IN THE NIGHT

> Sweet little bell
> That is struck in the windy night,
> I liefer go to a tryst with thee
> Than to a tryst with a foolish woman.

—Translated by Whitley Stokes

St. Brigid

ST. Brigid, the pioneer of the conventual life for women in Ireland, was born at Faughart, near Dundalk. She founded her famous monastery at Kildare about the year 500 and died there a quarter of a century later.

Many lovely stories are told of her princely hospitality, her way with animals, her sanctity and wisdom, and how, when a surly chieftain offered her, as a site for her convent, as much ground as her cloak would cover, the cloak billowed and spread miraculously until it took in as much ground as she needed; and somewhere beneath this wealth of myth and legend is the real Brigid.

Brigid was one of the greatest of Ireland's saints, and her name has always been linked with those of Patrick and Colmcille.

—Aer Lingus

THE HEAVENLY BANQUET

I would like to have the men of Heaven
in my own house;
with vats of good cheer
laid out for them.

I would like to have the three Marys,
their fame is so great.
I would like people
from every corner of Heaven.

I would like them to be cheerful
in their drinking.
I would like to have Jesus, too,
here amongst them.

I would like a great lake of beer
for the King of Kings.
I would like to be watching Heaven's family
drinking it through all eternity.

—*Ascribed to Saint Brigid*
Translated by Sean O'Faolain

The early Irish Church differed in many ways from the rest of the Christian world. The early religious poetry gives an interesting insight into many aspects of this religious life: The hermit in his cell; the monk at his devotion, or copying under the open sky; the ascetic, alone or with twelve chosen companions, living on an island, or in the solitude of the woods or mountains.

THE HERMIT'S DIET

Bee-keeping (an art possibly introduced, like the water-mill, from Roman Britain) is frequently mentioned in the texts; and honey seems to have been a favourite food and may have been used in the manu-facture of mead. Apples and nuts were plentiful, and wild berries and herbs were eaten. From the well-known ninth-century poem wherein the hermit praises his hermitage we have some idea of the possibilities of his meatless diet:

> Produce of mountain ash, black sloes from a
> dark blackthorn, berry foods bare fruits of a bare . . .

> A clutch of eggs, honey, mast and heath pease
> (sent by God), sweet apples, red cranberries, whortleberries.

> Beer and herbs, a patch of strawberries (good to taste
> in their plenty), haws, yew berries, nut kernels.

> A cup of excellent hazel mead, swiftly served;
> brown acorns, manes of bramble with good blackberries.

The literature mentions beer and mead frequently, wine less often; in the lives of the saints there are references to brewing. In a late twelfth-century poem from the Finn cycle, we find the mouth-watering description:

> There is a vat there of princely enamel
> into which flows the juices of pleasant malt,
> and an apple tree above the vat with
> abundance of heavy fruit.

> —*Maire and Liam de Paor*

OATEN HONEYCOMB

Oatmeal, milk and milk products have been used since the earliest days as food in Ireland, in both sweet and savoury ways. Many monastic settlements lived entirely on these foods.

½ lb. (2 cups) flake oatmeal
2 oz. (½ cup) ground almonds
1 pt. (2 cups) milk
3 heaped tablesp. sugar
a pinch of ground cinnamon

3 eggs, separated
2 tablesp. honey
2 heaped tablesp. raisins or the grated rind of 1 lemon
3 tablesp. melted butter

Bring the milk to the boil, sprinkle the flakemeal in, and cook slowly for about 15 minutes, stirring all the time. Leave to cool, then beat in one at a time the ground almonds, honey, sugar, raisins or lemon peel, cinnamon, melted butter and beaten egg yolks. Mix it all well and finally add the stiffly beaten egg whites. Put into a buttered bowl or basin, cover and steam over hot water for 1½ hours. Turn out and serve hot with warm melted honey or cream. It is more delicate in flavour if made with lemon peel.

—Theodora FitzGibbon

WINES OF SAINT PATRICK

As the early Irish monks brought the Christian light to a darkened Europe, they also brought the accompanying skills. In monastery garden, kitchen and sickroom they enlightened the benighted. Not least, they cultivated the vine.

Saint Patrick has been honoured in that two wines are called after him. One is the red Rhone wine, Chateauneuf-du-Pape Saint Patrick, which is made from the grapes of a famous vineyard in the Rhone valley of southern France. This vineyard has been owned for many generations by the Establet family. Local tradition says that Saint Patrick, when on his way to Rome, rested at this vineyard, thus giving his name to it ever since. The wine is full-bodied and very fragrant and it is recommended that it should accompany red meats and game at table.

At the end of the eighteenth century, an Irishman named William Garvey from Annagh Castle, County Waterford, settled in Jerez, about 100 miles north of Gibraltar, in Spain. And since this is the traditional home of sherry, he began shipping the local sherries. This was in 1780.

His most famous sherry is Fino San Patricio, a dry sherry which is accounted the most valued in Spain.

His son, Patrick Garvey, born in Spain in 1796, attained the highest rank among sherry shippers and their firm has been maintained by following generations of the family, of which the fourth and fifth generation are the present owners.

The Irish flag flies to-day over their main buildings in Jerez. And there are statues of Saint Patrick over the entrance to three of their *bodegas* (cellars).

—Anonymous

SCATTERING THE SEEDS—THE MISSIONARIES

The great era of Irish monastic expansion abroad falls later than our period but already during the sixth century the pioneers of it had left Ireland. In its initial stages it had nothing of the character of the modern foreign missionary movement; in fact it was not an organised movement at all. The motive uppermost in the minds of the *peregrini* was that of mortification and self-sacrifice—to renounce home and family like Abraham and seek a secluded spot where the ties of the world would not interfere with their pursuit of sanctity. Colum Cille's journey to Iona in 563 did not differ essentially, therefore, from Enda's journey to Aran a generation before. But once in Scotland he found unlimited scope for his missionary zeal in the conversion of the Picts. Thus he became the prototype to later generations of the patriotic exile, thinking longingly in a foreign land of the little places at home he knew so well:

Colum Cille's mission inspired his namesake Columbanus to go further afield a generation later and England, France, Belgium, Germany, Switzerland, Austria and Italy would soon re-echo to the tramp of Irish monks. Luxeuil, the greatest of Columbanus's foundations in France, was destined to influence directly or indirectly nearly one hundred other houses before the year 700. His journey from Luxeuil to Italy like another Patrick or another Paul was surely one of the great missionary voyages of history—twice across France, up the Rhine to Switzerland, across Lake Constance to Bregenz in Austria, southward through the Alps and Northern Italy till he founded his last monastery at Bobbio in 613.

To stand by his tomb in Bobbio is therefore to realise what the advent of Christianity meant to the Irish people. He was still proud of that people: "We Irish, living at the edge of the world, followers of Saints Peter and Paul—there has never been a heretic or a schismatic among us." He still retained his individuality, that independence of spirit which had hurled anathemas at kings and queens and requested a pope not to allow "the head of the church to be turned into its tail. . . for in Ireland it is not a man's position but his principles that count." He was still reluctant to give up his Irish method of calculating Easter or the episcopal exemption which the Irish monasteries enjoyed. To this native inheritance he added a mastery of Latin learning which few of his contemporaries could emulate, fashioning the new language into letters and sermons, poems and songs, even into a rowing chorus:

> The tempests howl, the storms dismay,
> But skill and strength can win the day,
>   Heave, lads, and let the echoes ring;
> For clouds and squalls will soon pass on
> And victory lie with work well done
>   Heave, lads, and let the echoes ring.

The original Latin of this song is a far cry from the stumbling prose of Saint Patrick. It is a clear indication that the native and foreign elements in the Irish heritage are being welded into a new Christian culture and that Ireland which received much from Europe since the arrival of Saint Patrick has now also much to offer in return.

—Cardinal Tomás Ó Fiaich*

THE HOLY SEED

Cromlechs crumble by the sea,
Ruined shells lie scarred and scattered—

* See note page 128.

A dolmen prone upon a lea,
A monastery strewn and shattered
By the war-cry of the Norse,
A lonely crozier lapped in gorse.

Now a relic draped in moss,
The tower reflected in the river;
Massive mounds of ivy gloss
A chapel arch with verdant cover
Where echoes of the pagan Vikings
Startled kneeling monks and High Kings.

Sunk beneath these ancient walls
The grains of Christianity
Spread their roots through Eire's hills,
Flowering for humanity.
And from grey pods, the priests, like birds,
Carry the seed of the Holy Words.

—*Alice B. Stockdale*

Wherever they went, the Christian Celts planted active colonies of religion
and culture. Indeed, their homelands—Ireland, Britain, and Brittany—
were together only a small part of the area of their influence. From the
sixth to the tenth centuries both monastic missionaries and scholars
settled in large numbers on the continent, and their presence ameliorated
the culturally destructive invasions of Europe by unlettered pagan peoples.

8 Early Christian Art

BELL SHRINES

By far the most splendid of the bell shrines is that commissioned for Saint Patrick's Bell between 1094 and 1105 A.D. It is made of bronze plates and its shape conforms closely to that of the bell. The front of the body is covered with an openwork silver frame of thirty-one panels, the smaller ones in the centre following a cruciform arrangement. Four are empty, and in ten of the remaining panels ovals of rock crystal and coloured glass have been inserted which detract considerably from the appearance of the shrine. The remaining insets are interlacements in imitation gold filigree made from gold-plated bronze or copper wires, no two patterns being alike. The front of the top of the shrine is elaborately ornamented with gilt silver interlacing and elongated silver scrolls, between which are panels of gold zoomorphic interlace on a gilt background. The back of the body is covered with a sheet of silver pierced by equal-armed crosses to form a diaper pattern and has an Irish inscription on the margin recording the names of the maker and of his patrons. On top there is an openwork design in cast silver composed of two confronted birds, the wings, tail, neck and beak of each

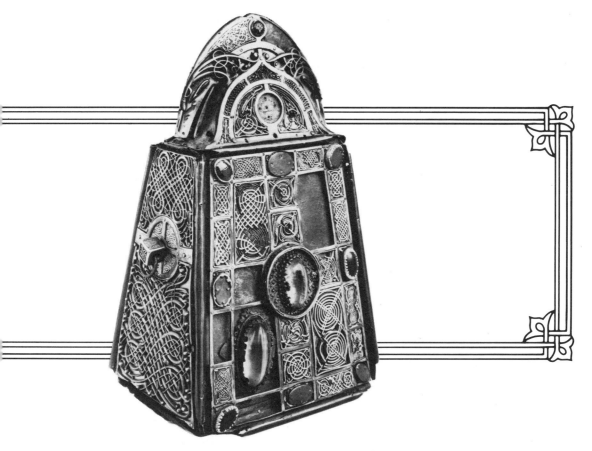

Shrine of Saint Patrick's Bell. A.D. 1094–1105.

being enmeshed in the spiral turns of a snake-like creature with long slender jaws which fuses with its fellow to give an impression of a stylised vine with two symmetrically wreathed tendrils.

In many respects the sides of the shrine are its most impressive features, the greater part of their surfaces being covered by a bold open-work interlace in sweeping curves. This is of cast silver, originally gilt, and is set off against a brightly gilt background. At about two-thirds of the height is a circular silver frame, with four embossed panels of gold-plated interlace, from the centre of which projects a decorated square knob, pierced to take a carrying ring.

—A. T. Lucas

SAINT PATRICK'S BELL

The veneration of bells as relics seems to have been peculiar to the Celtic Church. The bell of an Irish saint, like his gospel-book and his pastoral staff, was normally preserved and enshrined in a portable reliquary. Most precious of all these bells, by reason of its traditional association with

Saint Patrick himself, is the Clog an Edachta, or Bell of Saint Patrick's Well. Like all Irish bells of pre-Norman date it resembles a cow-bell in shape. It is more or less rectangular, the height being a little over 6 inches, and was presumably intended to be rung by hand. It is absolutely plain and indeed rather rough in appearance, being made of two sheets of iron, fastened together by large rivets, and subsequently dipped in bronze. By comparison with other Irish bells, such as those of Clogher, Armagh and Lough Lene, which may be seen, like the Bell of Saint Patrick's Well, in the National Museum of Ireland, but are of cast bronze and much more regular in shape, it will be understood that, though there is no proof that this is a bell of fifth-century date, yet it is undoubtedly of primitive type and it may be said that there is nothing to contradict the traditional attribution to Saint Patrick.

—H. A. Wheeler

EARLY CHRISTIAN ART

To the monastic communities, flourishing under the patronage of local dynastic families, the development of Early Christian art is, in large measure, due. They had to meet out of their own resources the demand for books for study and recitation of the monastic office and divine service; this ultimately entailed the establishment in, at least, the larger monasteries of scriptoria, where trained scribes devoted themselves to the multiplication of the required texts. It is probable, too, that the monasteries had to make provision for supplying the vessels and other articles necessary for church and altar use and that some members of the community specialised in metalwork, although they may also have employed lay craftsmen for this purpose. As a result of the closer contacts with Europe made through the agency of the Irish missionary monks of the sixth and seventh centuries, scribe and craftsman became acquainted with new artistic styles and motifs, which they adopted, developed and made their own, blending them with the surviving Iron Age artistic tradition to produce an art which, in all its essential features, continued to be characteristic of the country till the twelfth century. It remains to us in a few manuscripts and a very considerable amount of stone sculpture and metalwork but there is evidence to show that it also found expression in such more perishable media as wood, leather and textiles. The real preoccupation of the artists of the Early Christian period is the vast repertoire of abstract patterns which, in unlimited variation and combination, they exploited to the uttermost.

—A. T. Lucas

THE monks, for the most part, were neither theologians nor men of genius. Their lives were austere, devoted mainly to prayer and studies of the Bible.

Yet their creativity cannot be overemphasized: They were poets, artists, and craftsmen, whose manuscript illuminations, metalwork, and stone crosses reached the zenith of artistic expression.

CROZIERS

Perhaps to a greater extent even than his bell, the saint's staff is the emblem of his status and the vehicle of his supernatural power. As a shepherd boy, with instructions to keep the calves and cows apart, he draws a line on the ground with it between them which neither calf nor cow dare cross; if he forgetfully leaves it sticking in the ground, it grows into a huge and venerated tree; if he needs water to baptise a convert, he strikes the earth with it to cause a well to appear; if he is fording an icy stream, he signs the current with it and it becomes warm; if he wishes to inscribe a cross on a rock, the point of the staff cuts the stone as if it were soft clay. He curses with it, he blesses with it, he heals with it, and he uses it to quell his enemies, human, bestial and demonic. A blow of it on the ground, and things long buried will suddenly

Lismore Crozier, Lismore, Co. Waterford.
A.D. 1090–1113.

emerge or the earth will open to swallow a sinner or an adversary. If he stands in such favour with God that he is permitted to bring the dead to life, he works the miracle by a touch of his staff. When he dies, it becomes one of the most treasured possessions of his community.

So much we learn from pious legend but there is also ample historical evidence to show that the cult of the saint's staff was a very old and widespread one. A penitential which is not later in date than the end of the eighth century prescribed forty years on bread and water for the theft of a crozier; the rigour of this sentence contrasts with the mere seven years' penance which the same text lays down for the theft of a gospel book. The annals contain many references to staffs attributed to certain saints: their enshrining, their theft, their profanation, their destruction, their use as talismans in battle or for swearing oaths and affirming agreements. The Irish name for such a staff was *bachall,* a loan-word from the Latin *baculus,* and the most famous of all was the *Bachall Iosa* or "Staff of Jesus" which, legend said, Saint Patrick had received directly from heaven. It is repeatedly mentioned down the centuries but it was burned in Dublin as an object of superstition during the religious troubles of the sixteenth century.

The Lismore Crozier serves as a typical example of those belonging to the last phase of the Early Christian period. That from Lismore, one of the most lavishly decorated, contains a yew wood staff which may, conceivably, have been associated in tradition with Saint Carthach or Carthage of Lismore who died in 638 A.D. At the base of the crook the crozier bears an inscription in Irish asking prayers for Niall Mac Aeducáin, Bishop of Lismore from 1090 to 1113, who commissioned it, and for Nechtan, the artificer who made it.

—A. T. Lucas

AN IRISH CROZIER-HEAD IN SWEDEN

In Stockholm's Museum of Antiquities, in a gallery which contains much pirated material, there are three glass cases displaying, to quote the guidebook, the most notable treasure of all. In one of these there is an Irish crozier-head of the year 700 A.D.

Blond stares are all some give
the refugee from Christian lustre;
shufflers most, unfeelingly they mock
the sandaled thinking of an Irish cloister.
In the tuneless skirmish of a fountain's play
nearby, it is a splinter of a lakeful age
where it bowed like a Glory in a psalmody of waters.
When the raiders shipped their slaughter crop of skulls
did this come trunkless too? What axeman dared

to savage symbol, to embattle care?
What longship's gullet, or what monster's hull
scaly with bucklered brilliance cast it on a heaving mull?
Or was it when the Viking died
his hatchet kin armed passion to divide
the staff that coralled herds of water?
Who knows what fickle smithies brooched the head
for valour's cloak and April's daughter?
Now for the scanner of walls it hangs exposed
scalped of its skin of radiance and stalked like the head of a
    traitor.
Traitor? No. Not gauntlet-running through the twist of seas,
not exile's tarnish nor the armed heel's rack,
not the corroding kiss of time,
the dungeon of a hoarder's sack
nor company of maggots wried its loyalty.
The blossom of its message never hawed.
Its figures, bird and dog and man and serpent, speak
in the uncorrupted native tongue of God.
The bird nests in the eaves of the moon:
beauty is a winged thing and blessed are the meek:
'God is to be praised' spires the swallow's beak.
The dog embosses the sharp muzzle of hell;
his mouth of sin a craggy citadel
he snarls of wickedness to souls he spanieled.
The serpent buckles his belt of truth—
living proceeds from death to youth—
and he convolutes through eternity's golden tunnel.
The man has carvel eyes,
his brow they colonise,
one is awareness and the other wonder;
his ears are sealed by hands;
what is their clenched command?
'Heed not the world's cries
but listen to the inner whisper.'
It is the gospel molten in its humble size:
not big with rule
not proud with bigness,
not coarsely decorative with pride
its head is as small
as the hand of an infant
and the heart that ruled the hand that held it was a gentle heart
    and kind.

—Jerome Kiely

Cross of Patrick and Columba in Kells, Co. Meath. Early ninth century A.D. One of the strangest phenomena of the Irish art of this time is the translation of the fine patterns of the goldsmiths and bronzesmiths into carved sandstone.

HIGH CROSSES

At Kells, Co. Meath, the monastic remains consist of a round tower, a small stone-roofed building and five high crosses. One of these, which stands beside the tower, is inscribed: *Patricii et Columbae Crux*, "The Cross of Patrick and Columba." Its surface is far less rigidly divided into formal panels than in the Monasterboice examples, and areas of abstract ornament and figure sculpture are freely intermingled. The cap which crowned the top is missing but the tenon which held it in place remains. The figure panels on the east face of the lower shaft show, at the bottom, Adam and Eve, and Cain killing Abel, and, above them, the children in the furnace and Daniel and the lions. On one arm Abraham sacrifices Isaac; on the other the raven feeds the hermits Paul and Anthony. The panel on the upper shaft combines two subjects: David playing the harp and the miracle of the loaves and fishes. Christ and David are seated opposite each other, the former blessing the loaves before him and the crossed fishes beneath his feet, the hungry multitude being symbolised by two rows of heads. The west face is unusual in having two subjects which are normally on opposite faces: the crucifixion on the shaft and Christ in glory above.

—A. T. Lucas

THE CELTIC CROSS*

Through storm and fire and gloom, I see it stand
    Firm, broad, and tall,
The Celtic Cross that marks our Fatherland,
    Amid them all!
Druids and Danes and Saxons vainly rage
    Around its base;
It standeth shock on shock, and age on age,
    Star of our scatter'd race.

Holy Saint Patrick, father of our faith,
    Beloved of God!
Shield thy dear Church from the impending scaith,
    Or, if the rod
Must scourge it yet again, inspire and raise
    To emprise high
Men like the heroic race of other days,
    Who joyed to die.

Fear! wherefore should the Celtic people fear
    Their Church's fate?
The day is not—the day was never near—
    Could desolate
The Destined Island, all whose clay
    Is holy ground:

Its Cross shall stand till that predestin'd day
    When Erin's self is drowned.

—*Thomas D'Arcy McGee*

* Selected verses.

Manuscripts

SCRIPTORIA

AMONG the simple structures of each Celtic monastery stood a hut that was used as a scriptorium, a busy place where manuscripts were written and made into codices. Before the era of monasticism the codex had replaced the more clumsy roll in Christian bookmaking; the more conservative pagans, to their own disadvantage, kept the old style longer. The writing surface was a laboriously prepared vellum, the skins for which came from flocks and herds owned by the monastery or otherwise available. Quill pens were made by the monks from the feathers of large birds such as geese, swans, and crows. The conception of writing as an art and not merely a utility for preserving valued compositions seems to have been dominant. The earliest extant writings by Irishmen are in a majuscule script with some elementary decoration of selected initial letters, or other illumination, a style apparently imitated from Gallic or Italian models. Many books now lost must have been used—and many written—by Patrick and his contemporaries, and their influence on later calligraphy must be assumed. But Irish monastic

144

"Alas, my hand!"

scribes soon went on to develop their artistic manuscript styles independently and with amazing skill. The Ogham script found on about 350 memorial stones in Ireland and Wales, using an alphabet of straight lines at right angles or in diagonal juncture with a basic line, is an ingeniously contrived device suitable for short inscriptions in a narrow vocabulary. But Ogham has nothing to do with books. Most of the Latin manuscripts painstakingly written and embellished were portions of the Scriptures, and no effort was spared in making the revered text a thing of beauty to the eye. Brilliant and durable colors were obtained by the use of seashells and plant juices, and patterns of great complexity were introduced. These were in many instances geometrically designed for a space, or a page, and made use of crosses, medallions, trumpet shapes, symbolic animal forms, and human figures, with much interlacing of flowing ribbons and elongated reptilian creatures. Appropriation, with variations, of elements from Syrian, Coptic, and other Eastern Christian art has been recognized in certain details, and this, together with the constant use of authentic Christian symbolism, indicates that scholarly and theologically sophisticated minds controlled the illuminator's hand.

As the scriptoria multiplied and became veritable factories for the reproduction of books, no doubt the need of economy in the use of vellum asserted itself, and was a factor in the adoption of the Irish half-uncial or reduced majuscule script, as well as the still more economical minuscule which more directly contributed to what became the dominant continental cursive, a practical script for speed of writing and economy of space. In Ireland countless manuscripts were doomed to destruction in the violence and pillage often inflicted on monasteries in local wars; and from about 800, ruthless Norsemen in their incursions burned or otherwise destroyed monastic libraries, first ripping off the rich metal ornamentation of the finest volumes. We have evidence enough that the precious codices left, by which Irish calligraphy and illumination must be judged, form only a minute portion of the actual production; and the known fortunes of some of the extant manuscripts read like adventure fiction.

—John T. McNeill

THE BOOK OF KELLS

The finest product of Irish art in this period was not the famous Ardagh chalice (c. 1000) —an astonishing union of 354 pieces of bronze, silver, gold, amber, crystal, cloisonné enamel, and glass; it was the *Book of Kells*—the Four Gospels in vellum, done by Irish monks at Kells in Meath, or on the isle of Iona, in the ninth century, and now the prize possession of Trinity College, Dublin. Through the slow intercommunication of monks across frontiers, Byzantine and Islamic styles of illumination entered Ireland, and for a moment reached perfection there. Here, as in Moslem miniatures, human or animal figures played an insignificant role; none was worth half an initial. The spirit of this art lay in taking a letter, or a single ornamental motive, out of a background of blue or gold, and drawing it out with fanciful humor and delight till it almost covered the page with its labyrinthine web. Nothing in Christian illuminated manuscripts surpasses the *Book of Kells*. Gerald of Wales, though always jealous of Ireland, called it the work of angels masquerading as men.

—Will Durant

A NATIONAL OBSESSION

The genius of the Irish is that of language. Now they had offered to them not only salvation for the soul but sustenance for the mind in the shape of the classics and the Latin alphabet. We are not sure of

Patrick's scholarship since we have from his pen only his *Confessions,* but like any self-respecting churchman of his day he must have traveled with books in his luggage—and those books, both sacred and profane, became the treasures of the island. It is as if the people had been starving for a religion superior to their former belief in sea gods and wood spirits, had been famished for reading. They could not get enough of either. Books began to count as part of the country's wealth like gold and cattle. Students spent their lives copying them or writing others. For them kings waged war and whole monasteries sprang up around a set of volumes.

By the end of the fifth century the land pulsed like a beehive with piety and learning. Tales say that there were three hundred universities in the country. Even if we discount Irish exaggeration and realize, also, that these "universities" were probably nothing more than a group of wattled huts built near a church, where the studious prayed, chanted, illuminated manuscripts, and wrote out their lessons, it does seem as if learning had become a national obsession. Roaming scholars even began drifting in from other countries to sit at the feet of Saint Finnian or Saint Sechnall or Saint Ita—for women as well as men took part in the educational blossoming. And all this went on while Rome was disintegrating under the attacks of Alaric, Gaiseric, and finally Attila. By 476, when Odoacer deposed the last emperor, it was scarcely even a city and Mediterranean culture lay dying. Only in tiny Ireland flourished the seeds of exuberance and hope.

—Phyllis McGinley

ST. COLMCILLE

St. Colmcille (the name means the "Dove of the Church") , or Columba, as he is often called, was of royal blood, being descended from Niall of the Nine Hostages, and was born at Gartan, near Kilmacrenan, in Co. Donegal, in 521. He was a man of striking appearance, being described as well-formed and strong, and with large, luminous, grey eyes. He was also a scholar and a poet, with a dynamic character and an intense love of God.

Montalembert described him as lacking in gentleness, but Adamnan, the biographer of Colmcille, paints the saint as a lover of men and beasts and books. Colmcille studied at the monasteries of Moville, Clonard, Aran and Glasnevin, and afterwards himself founded many monasteries, of which the chief were Derry, Durrow, and Kells.

In 563, Colmcille set out with twelve companions and sailed to the barren island of Iona, off the coast of Scotland, where he founded the famous monastery which was ever afterwards associated with his name. Adamnan says that Colmcille left Ireland of his own free will, but the tradition is that after he had quarrelled with St. Finian over a translation of the Gospels which he had made without Finian's permission, Colmcille incited his relatives, the Northern Uí Néill, to war, and that exile was the penance imposed upon him by St. Molaise after the Battle of Cul Dreimhne, in which three thousand men were slain.

Colmcille's monastery of Iona was a centre of remarkable missionary activity. He began by converting the people of Dal Riada, an Irish colony on the mainland near Iona, and then he preached to the pagan Picts, whose territory stretched northwards beyond the Grampians. By the time of his death, in 597, all Britain north of the Clyde, as well as the Hebrides and the Orkneys, had been converted.

Shortly before his death, Colmcille wrote on a copy of the Psalms which he was transcribing: "Here I must stop. Let Baithen write the rest." The remark had the quality of a prophecy, for though Colmcille's life was ending, his work was destined to go on. It was monks from Iona who began the conversion of Northumbria, Mercia, Essex and Sussex, and long after Colmcille's death his tradition dominated the Church in Ireland, whilst his rule was followed in many monasteries of western Europe until it was replaced by the milder dispensation of St. Benedict.

—Aer Lingus

BROTCHÁN FOLTCHEP*

Traditional leek and oatmeal soup. For many centuries oatmeal, milk and leeks were the staple diet of the Irish. Here they are combined to make a substantial soup. Legend has it that Saint Patrick tended a dying woman, who said that she had seen a herb in the air, and would die unless she ate it. Saint Patrick said to her: "What is the semblance of the herb?" "Like rushes," saith the woman. Patrick blessed the rushes so that they became a leek. The woman ate it afterwards, and was whole at once.

6 leeks (large)	2 pts. (4 cups) milk or
1 heaped tablesp. butter	stock
1 tablesp. chopped parsley	salt and pepper
2 tablesp. flake oatmeal	

Wash the leeks thoroughly to remove grit. Leave on the green part and cut them into chunks about 1 in. long. Heat up the liquid with the butter and when boiling add the oatmeal. Let it boil, then add the chopped leeks and season to taste. Put the lid on and simmer gently for 45 minutes. Add the parsley and boil again for a few minutes.

For nettle brotchán use 4 cups young nettle tops, packed tightly. Wear gloves when picking them and cut with scissors. A little cream can be added if liked.

—Theodora FitzGibbon

The "Cathach" of Saint Columba (Colmcille) is a late sixth-century fragmentary copy of the psalms, traditionally looked upon as the copy made by the saint himself. A monastic scholar and scribe *par excellence*, Saint Columba laid the foundation of a scribal art which, with its later

---

* Brotchán is the Irish for broth, and this soup made with young nettle tops was a favourite dish of the great Saint Colmcille.

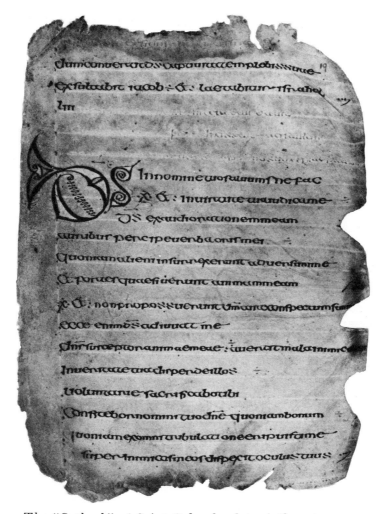

The "Cathach" of Saint Columba, late sixth-century

illuminative elements, formed one of the greatest glories of Irish monasticism.

It is in a damaged condition, more than half of its original nine-by-six-inch leaves having been lost. Already thus mutilated, in the eleventh century it was encased in a wooden box, which was much later enclosed within a silver case. When it was opened for inspection in 1813, its leaves were stuck together; but it was made legible and deposited in the Royal Irish Academy in Dublin. It now consists of fifty-eight pages of the Psalter written in Latin in Irish majuscule script, with a few large initials illuminated in red and yellow. While it shows none of the brilliant illumination of Irish manuscripts of a century or two later, it is a precious relic from the dawn of Irish Christianity. Only a handful of surviving manuscripts go back to the sixth century.

The name "Cathach," meaning "Battler" has reference to its use as protective talisman by the O'Donnell chiefs in their battles.

COLUMCILLE THE SCRIBE

My hand is weary with writing,
My sharp quill is not steady.
My slender beaked pen pours forth
A black draught of shining dark-blue ink.

A stream of the wisdom of blessed God
Springs from my fair brown shapely hand:
On the page it squirts its draught
Of ink of the green skinned holly.

My little dripping pen travels
Across the plain of shining books,
Without ceasing for the wealth of the great—
Whence my hand is weary with writing.

—Translated by Kuno Meyer

LITERARY DOODLES

Though they came from the hermit traditions, stories were written, and a lot invented, in the monasteries. Like the artistic designs they became in time more involved, and a literary doodle grows up to match the artistic one. Sometimes these whimsical comments develop into poetry. They grace the margins of many weighty manuscripts, and have sometimes commanded greater attention than the central matter. "Wondrous is the robin there singing to us, and our cat has escaped us" a scribe informs the world in his margin; while another, before laying down his pen, allows himself the groan: "Alas! my hand"; and another: "Let no reader blame this writing, for my arm is cramped through excess of labour." But it was nature that brought solace to the busy monk, as it did to the hermit.

The awareness of nature, starting with the musings of the exiled ascetic, gradually grew to the beautiful finesse of mature Irish poetry:

THE SCRIBE*

Found on the margin of *St. Gall, Ms.* The Irish St. Gall, who died in 635 at the age of ninety-five, founded a monastery on Lake Constance, Switzerland.

> A hedge of trees surrounds me:
> A blackbird sings to me
> Above my booklet, the lined one,
> The thrilling birds sing to me

* A new arrangement, by Kathleen Hoagland, combining the Whitley Stokes and John Strachan translations.

In a grey mantle, from the tops of bushes,
The cuckoo chants to me
May the Lord protect me from Doom!
I write well under the greenwood.

> —*Anonymous (probably ninth century)*

Poem on the parting of summer, often quoted:

My tidings for you: the stag bells,
Winter snows, summer is gone.

Wind high and cold, low the sun,
Short his course, sea running high.

Deep-red the bracken, its shape all gone—
The wild-goose has raised his wonted cry.

Cold has caught the wings of birds;
Season of ice—these are my tidings.

> —*Anonymous (probably ninth century)*

These were the poet's thoughts; his words were Irish. Part of Ireland's luck in escaping the Romans was in being able to keep her own tongue and develop it in a literary way. The Irish kept their spontaneity in their vernacular literature, though they took willingly to Latin for scriptural and scholastic purposes.

> —Brendan Lehane

THE BLACKBIRD

Found on a margin in the *Leabhar Breac,* or *Speckled Book.*

Ah, blackbird, thou art satisfied
Where thy nest is in the bush:
Hermit that clinkest no bell,
Sweet, soft, peaceful is thy note.

> —*Anonymous (twelfth century)*
> *Translated by Kuno Meyer*

The following fragment from "The Devil's Tribute to Moling" is found on the margin of *Codex S. Pauli* of the Monastery of Carinthia.

The Devil appears to Saint Moling as he is at prayer, and asks him to bestow either a blessing or a curse on him, which the saint refuses to do. Then the Devil wonders how he can earn a blessing, and Moling tells him to fast. "I have been fasting since the beginning of the world, and not the better thereof am I," replies the Devil. "Make genuflexions," says Moling. "I cannot bend forward," says the Devil, "for backwards are my knees." "Go forth," says Moling; "I cannot teach thee, nor help thee." Then the Devil says, thoughtfully:

THE HOLY MAN

He is a bird round which a trap closes,
He is a leaky ship to which peril is dangerous,
He is an empty vessel, he is a withered tree,
Whoso doth not the will of the King above.
He is pure gold, he is the radiance round the sun,
He is a vessel of silver with wine,
He is happy, is beautiful, is holy,
Whoso doth the will of the King.

—Anonymous (eighth century)
Translated by Whitley Stokes
and John Strachan

MY LITTLE LODGE

On the margin of *Codex S. Pauli*

My little lodge in Tuaim Inbir,—
There's no great house of statelier timber;
With its stars at evening bright,
Sun by day and moon by night.

Gobban's was the hand that planned it—
Listen, would you understand it—
And God of heaven, my heart's beloved,
The roofer that built the roof above it.

A house in which the rain-storm falls not,
A spot where spear-point sharp appalls not;
A very garden, full of light,—
And no forbidding fence in sight!

—Anonymous (eighth century)
Translated by F. N. Robinson

SPONTANEITY

Nature was no longer menacing, and the Irish monks looked on creation with the enchantment of children emerging from a dark room. The brilliant, spontaneous little lyrics we begin to find, scribbled in commonplace books or jotted down in the margins of more orthodox texts, are not the productions of cowed and dispirited men. Sometimes there is only, as it were, a note for a poem: "Pleasant is the sun upon the margin of this book, because it flickers so"; sometimes there is a finished jewel of several verses. The language is Irish; the metres are distinctively Irish forms of the Latin hymn metres. There may be elements in them of the old pagan seasonal rites, but the intensely personal and individual approach is of the new dispensation.

—Maire and Connor Cruise O'Brien

The End of the Golden Age

AS this golden age of Ireland had been made possible by freedom from the Germanic invasions that threw the rest of Latin Europe back by many centuries, so it was ended by such Norse raids as in the ninth and tenth centuries annulled in France and England the progress so laboriously made by Charlemagne and Alfred. Perhaps the news had reached Norway and Denmark—both still pagan—that the Irish monasteries were rich in gold, silver, and jewelry, and that the political fragmentation of Ireland forestalled united resistance. An experimental raid came in 795, did little damage, but confirmed the rumor of this unguarded prey. In 823 greater invasions plundered Cork and Cloyne, destroyed the monasteries of Bangor and Moville, and massacred the clergy. Thereafter raids came almost every year. Sometimes brave little armies drove them back, but they returned, and sacked monasteries everywhere. Bands of Norse invaders settled near the coast, founded Dublin, Limerick, and Waterford, and levied tribute from the northern half of the island. Their King Thorgest made Saint Patrick's Armagh his pagan capital, and enthroned his heathen wife on the altar of Saint Kieran's Church at Clonmacnois. The Irish kings fought the invaders separately, but at the same time they fought one another. Malachi, King of Meath, captured Thorgest and drowned him (845); but in 851 Olaf the White, a Norwegian prince, established the kingdom of Dublin, which remained Norse till the twelfth century. An age of learning and poetry gave way to an era of ruthless war, in which Christian as well as pagan soldiers pillaged and fired monasteries, destroyed ancient manuscripts, and scattered the art of centuries. "Neither bard nor philosopher nor musician," says an old Irish historian, "pursued his wonted profession in the land."

—Will Durant

HAS THE EXTENT OF THE DECLINE BEEN EXAGGERATED?

The favourable conditions created at home by the growth of the monasteries and the fertile contacts made abroad combined to produce a great outburst of artistic production in the service of the church which manifested itself in manuscript illumination, metalwork and sculpture and reached its highest development in the eighth century.

It has been customary to ascribe the supposed decline in standards during the ensuing centuries to the havoc wrought on church and society

It is unfortunate that here, as in so many portrayals, Saint Patrick is depicted in late medieval vestments of the fifteenth and sixteenth centuries. It gives no more idea of the appearance of a Celtic bishop a thousand years earlier than a stained-glass window of the saint in a Brooks Brothers suit and Gucci shoes. Although we do not know exactly what garments Patrick wore, those depicted by Sister Aloysius McVeigh in her painting, "*I am Patrick*" (see page 157), are simple and utilitarian, more in keeping with the needs of a missionary bishop and consistent with the character of Saint Patrick as we know him.

Stained-glass window of Saint Patrick in Saint Patrick's Cathedral, New York. This window is set into the west wall of the cathedral's south transept. Created by Nicholas Lorin in 1879, it was a gift to the cathedral from John Renwick, the Episcopalian architect.

by the Viking invaders, the earliest recorded appearance of whom off the Irish coast dates to 796. It may be, however, that the extent of the decline has been exaggerated by the acceptance of such outstanding objects as the Tara Brooch and Ardagh Chalice as the norm of eighth-century achievement when, in fact, they are so wholly exceptional that they occupy a position all to themselves. The opinion is also gaining ground that the effects of the Viking raids were not as catastrophic for Irish society or Irish art as the formerly prevailing interpretation of the ancient evidence implied. It has been overlooked that in early (as in medieval) times the more valuable personal possessions of the inhabitants of the surrounding district were placed for safekeeping in the local church where they enjoyed the privilege of sanctuary under the protection of God and the patron saint and that it was this cache of lay property and not the church treasures which was the real quarry of the Viking raiders. It has also been overlooked that the early chroniclers were almost exclusively churchmen who were, understandably, assiduous in reporting Viking depredations involving church property and that later historians were all too prone to invoke the Vikings as a *diabolus ex machina* to whose intervention might be attributed anything in Irish society which seemed less than ideal. The instances of intermarriage between Norse and Irish at the highest social level, the frequent alliances between them in raiding and war and the many words borrowed from Old Norse into the Irish language all suggest the existence of a closer relationship between the two peoples than has hitherto been supposed. Indeed, recent excavations on the site of the old city of Dublin seem to indicate that the Viking settlement there and, by inference, those at Wexford, Waterford, Cork and Limerick, which evolved into the first real urban communities the country had ever known, may well have made an important contribution to the art of the Early Christian period in its latest phase. Certainly many of the surviving examples of Irish decorative art of the eleventh and twelfth centuries show Irish adaptations of Scandinavian style. We may take the Anglo-Norman invasion from Britain towards the end of the twelfth century as marking the close of the long independent Irish artistic tradition.

—A. T. Lucas

10 The Proliferation of Patrick

PATRICIAN ART

HE painter or sculptor in search of what we might call the true face of Saint Patrick has a long and difficult road to travel. We know the saint best from his writings and in the end it is from these that we get the most life-like portrait.

In a village I know, some kind people wanted to donate a statue of the local Saint Brendan to the church. A statue duly arrived but, though the saint held no shamrock and no serpent lay beneath his foot, everyone recognised not St. Brendan but St. Patrick. The end of the story is worth recording for the benefit of those who aspire to the making of saints' portraits: the statue was sent back and after months was returned from the makers with a new head—beardless—truly St. Brendan.

Our idea of St. Patrick comes from the nineteenth century when the bearded bishop driving away serpents and teaching the doctrine of the Trinity with the help of a leaf of shamrock became the conventional representation of our National Apostle.

I am Patrick. *The storm-tossed cornfield and trees, the dark mountains, and sky depict the turmoil and troubles of our time. But Patrick is with us, offering faith, strength, and compassion.*

It has been said that tradition is like a flat picture which shows no perspective. Events perhaps a thousand years apart are in the folk memory, contemporary or nearly so. But despite this and other short-comings it is hardly ever wholly wrong.

It is really on the folk memory that we depend for our information about this likeness of St. Patrick. And even back to the earliest repre-sentations, though we get gaps of a hundred years between these, there is a striking uniformity which gives us faith in our modern versions of what the saint looked like.

The material to be drawn on is surprisingly small. Though devotion to the saint was strong from the earliest times, as is seen in the pride with which places all over the country associate themselves with the name of Patrick, this pride did not show itself very strongly in images of the saint—or if it did these must be lost to us.

The beginning of the nineteenth century gives us the immediate background to the modern St. Patrick. Here and there in the country there are locally made carved statues of the saint—as at St. Patrick's Well in Singland or at Patrickswell in Co. Limerick.

Towards the end of the eighteenth and early nineteenth centuries we find two interesting illustrations of St. Patrick. One is a frontispiece to Patrick Lynch's *Life of St. Patrick.*

There are at least three editions of this work and the earliest I have seen has no picture and is printed before 1800.

The second edition has a drawing of the saint. He carries a crosslike crozier and wears a mitre and pallium—which is not very probable as the pallium was first brought to Ireland at the Synod of Kells in 1152.

The saint stands on a winged dragon which he pierces with his crozier very much like Saint George. The work is signed "T. Kelly."

The picture in the 1828 edition is obviously based on the earlier one but the saint is a much more nineteenth-century personage, and while in the first picture the background contains a fruit tree with a dead serpent hanging from it in what seems to be a Rhineland landscape, with hills, lake and mountain fir trees, the second one had the more rounded hills of Ireland and a very typical example of a late eighteenth-century Catholic church.

It is a pity that there is no illustration in the first edition which appeared about 1788 and which perhaps contained the original drawing on which both these are based.

On the seal of the dean of St. Patrick's in Dublin, dated 1794, there is a St. Patrick figure wearing cope and mitre and holding a staff-like crozier.

Our next source of information is in the chiselled headstones of County Wexford and adjoining counties.

In the churchyard of St. Mullins in Co. Carlow on a headstone erected by E. Moriarty and carved by Kehoe are the figures of Patrick, Brigid and Colmcille. It is a typical piece of folk art. St. Patrick is rather splendid if slightly rotund in a full-length cope. He is apparently beardless.

This question of whether St. Patrick wore a beard or not has been much debated.

The picture which appeared in a few copies of the first Catholic book published in the Irish language—*Teagasc Criosdaidhe* or *Christian*

Doctrine—composed by the friar Bonaventure O hEodhasa in 1611, probably gave rise to this controversy. It shows a beardless bishop and is a better drawing than the Kelly one.

In the sixteenth-century poem in the Book of Hy Maine we are told that a true saint has hair but no beard. But to balance this statement O'Grady in his *Catalogue to the Irish Manuscripts* in the British Museum issues the grave warning: "Woe betide anyone who gets into a saint's beard!"

Perhaps the answer lies in the fact that shaving with a bronze razor was not always easy, especially when Patrick made his constant and sometimes dangerous journeys. So that the saint may from time to time have possessed a beard and even a flowing one.

On the Continent, especially in Italy, where our saint was and still is venerated, there must be many early images of the saint. I have not had the chance of seeing these, though in places like Genoa, Pavia, Orvieto and Vertova his cult still lives.

In an early French manuscript there is a miniature of St. Patrick revealing Purgatory. The saint (without beard) shows a companion a giant lion's mouth in whose flaming interior are seen suffering souls.

Again in Peter de Navalibus's *Catalogue of the Saints* there is a woodcut showing St. Patrick, who paces the cave at Lough Derg with a staff. Here the saint has a long beard and is dressed like a friar with cowl and rosary beads.

In Ireland the late fifteenth century gives us some carvings.

There is a very precise work over the north doorway at Clonmacnois. The saint gives his blessing and wears a chasuble with the high neckline of the period. His mitre is rather like a modern fez, and he wears sandals. The saint's name is written on the narrow cornice above the figure.

At Clontuskert Priory in Co. Roscommon there is a rather similar but freer carving which is usually said to be St. Patrick. It is notable for the very ornate crozier head and for the fact that he shares the crushing of the devil with Saint Catherine, who stands beside him.

Again about the same period there is the well-preserved smiling figure of the saint on the frontal of the tomb niche at Straid Friary in Co. Mayo. The saint lifts his hand in blessing and carries a short crozier.

In the late twelfth century we find a small bust of St. Patrick—with "Patricius" inscribed—on a silver halfpenny minted by John de Courcy and discovered at Lismahon Motte, County Down.

It is strange that we do not find St. Patrick in the illuminated manuscripts or indeed on the many fine carved crosses throughout the country.

There is one exception, our earliest representation of him: on the east side of the unique and wonderful "Patrick's Cross" on the Rock of Cashel.

Here we find a full-length figure which tradition has it is St. Patrick. It is much worn and partially disfigured, but even as it is, the elongated body, with its hand raised, gives us a feeling of great dignity.

Here we have our earliest St. Patrick fittingly enough on this great cross—fitted into a base which was used for the coronation of the Kings of Cashel.

These, then, are some signposts on the way which leads back to the real St. Patrick. For his full likeness we must search his life and his words. We must try to know the Patrick who spent whole nights in prayer under frost and rain. The Patrick without any personal ambition, but with an unshakable devotion to the cause of salvation of souls. The Patrick whose love of God was coupled with a sincere and profound love for the people of Ireland.

—The Rev. Jack Hanlon, the Priest Artist

"Saint Patrick's Money": halfpenny (left) *and farthing. Late twelfth century.*

THE OLDEST LEGEND

Saint Patrick on a day as he preached a sermon of the patience and sufferance of the passion of our Lord Jesu Christ to the king of the country, he leaned upon his crook or cross, and it happened by adventure that he set the end of the crook, or his staff, upon the king's foot and pierced his foot with the pike, which was sharp beneath. The king had supposed that Saint Patrick had done it wittingly, for to move him the sooner to patience and to the faith of God, but when Saint Patrick perceived it he was much abashed, and by his prayers he healed the king. And furthermore he impetred and gat grace of our Lord that no venomous beast might live in all the country, and yet unto this day is no venomous beast in all Ireland.

America can be proud that it is the home of the oldest known painting* of Saint Patrick, dating from around 1300. In fact it is not only the oldest known painting but the oldest identified representation in any

---

* The Saint Patrick picture illustrates a legend [above] still well known in Ireland. The text is William Caxton's translation, itself published before Columbus discovered America.

The oldest known painting of Saint Patrick, a miniature from a late thirteenth-century French manuscript

form of the saint. For, while figures on stone High Crosses of an earlier date may represent Saint Patrick, none of these can definitely be identified as the saint himself.

The painting is in the Huntington Library & Art Gallery in San Marino, California. It is in a manuscript of the *Legenda Aurea*—the *Golden Legend*—by Jacobus de Voragine (c. 1229-1298). Jacobus was an Italian Dominican who became Archbishop of Genoa and was later beatified. The *Golden Legend* is his best-known work and he wrote it in the last quarter of the 13th century. It contains incidents from the lives of the saints and information about holy days and the seasons, the whole being arranged as readings *(legenda)* for each day in the church's Calendar—Saint Patrick, of course, coming in under March 17th.

The *Golden Legend* was one of the most popular works of the later Middle Ages. Although written originally in Latin, it was swiftly translated into a number of European languages, and it was one of the first books to be printed in English—Caxton's edition appearing in 1483.

The San Marino manuscript was illuminated, probably in a Paris workshop, around or shortly after 1300—and thus only a few decades after Jacobus had written the work. The manuscript, which was in England for many years before the Huntington Library bought it in the 1920s, is beautifully illustrated.

—Peter Harbison

THE SAGA OF THE SHRINE OF SAINT PATRICK'S HAND

This beautiful relic of the Shrine of Saint Patrick's hand consists of a silver case in the shape of a hand and arm, from fingers to elbow. The fingers are bent in the attitude of blessing. The shrine represents an ecclesiastic of rank wearing a jewelled glove and having embroidered drapery on the sleeve, and was formerly set both around the wrist and also at the termination of the elbow with a large number of gems and precious stones. The only inscription which it bears is the sacred monogram, I.H.S., engraved on the plate at the base.

The history of the shrine in brief is as follows: At the time of the Translation of the relics of SS. Patrick, Brigid and Columcille, in 1186, under the supervision of Cardinal Vivian, the hand of Saint Patrick was enshrined and placed on the high altar of the Abbey church of Downpatrick. When Edward Bruce plundered the church in 1315 this relic was carried off, and we next find it in possession of the Magennis and Russell families of Co. Down. Through intermarriage, the relic became located with the Savage family of Portaferry. One of the Savages, having become Protestant, handed over the relic to Father James Teggart, P.P., of the Ards, with instructions that after Father Teggart's death it was to be delivered to Mr. McHenry of Carrstown, whose mother was Russell and who was nearest of kin to the Magennis family. It was next handed over to Dr. Denvir, bishop of the diocese in 1847, and has remained in the possession of the diocese ever since. The reliquary was opened by Dr. Denvir, and it contained a piece of wood nine inches long with a hole or socket for the insertion of a wristbone. The bone had been dissolved by water which persons were accustomed to pour through the shrine for the curing of sores and ailments. The bishop caused the shrine to be renovated, and new stones were inset to replace the lost Irish diamonds which formerly decorated the wrist and elbow. When Cardinal Vivian returned to Rome from Down in 1186, he brought back with him some of the relics of our National Apostle, which were carefully preserved and honoured in the Church of Saint Mark in Rome. One of these relics was obtained by the bishop of the diocese and inserted in the shrine at its proper place, under the crystal at the back of the hand. A record of this fact is made on an inscription on the outside of the shrine, with the seal of the Cardinal of Saint Mark's Church and the signature of the bishop.

The shrine is at present in the custody of the bishop of Down and Connor. It was exhibited at Downpatrick during the Patrician celebrations in June 1961.

—The Rev. L. McKeown, P.P.

MAYNOOTH COLLEGE

"The most important ecclesiastical seminary in Christendom" is what John Cardinal Newman—a former Anglican who was given a red hat without ever becoming a bishop—called Maynooth College when it was founded in Co. Kildare in 1795. Since that prophetic statement, Maynooth has trained over ten thousand priests, touching the lives of not only the Irish, but people the world over. Many American bishops and theological scholars have been Maynooth priests.

In the true pioneering spirit of Saint Patrick, Maynooth priests have founded three Irish missionary movements to pagan lands.

The College, also a Pontifical University, confers all higher degrees in theology in Ireland. Accepting lay students since 1966, it expects its ever-expanding programs and buildings to accommodate three thousand students by the mid-eighties. Affiliated with Maynooth is Saint Patrick's College in Thurles.

—Alice-Boyd Proudfoot

THE SOCIETY OF SAINT PATRICK'S MISSION

One might say it really began in 432 with the coming of Patrick himself; the missionary tradition has not faltered.

When young Pat Whitney was ordained at Maynooth in 1920, he heard an appeal for priests to go to Southern Nigeria. He accepted the challenge, surely not knowing what a fruitful seed he was planting. Others followed in a steady, if trickling, stream from Maynooth and in a decade the idea of a permanent society, named Saint Patrick's Mission, began to take shape in Kiltegan, Co. Wicklow.

Adapting the liturgy to tribes which never knew it, four hundred volunteers are now teaching a variety of skills: irrigation, mechanics, carpentry, sharing in the care of the sick and the total development of peoples, and bringing Christ to them or, as Bishop Fulton J. Sheen would have said, "bringing Christ *out* of them."

The society has spread to other parts of Nigeria, to Kenya, Malawi, Zambia, the Caribbean, and Brazil. Recently four newly ordained priests set out for Nigeria, where Pat Whitney had planted the seed sixty years before.

—Alice-Boyd Proudfoot

CHURCHES DEDICATED TO SAINT PATRICK

Saint Patrick's Cathedral, Dublin (Anglican)

JUST outside the walls of the old city of Dublin, to the south, stands the Collegiate and Cathedral Church of Saint Patrick on a site of great antiquity. According to ancient writings, Saint Patrick baptised a number of his converts at a well on one of his visits to Dublin and some time later a small wooden church was erected close by. Certainly local tradition in the twelfth century associated the name of Saint Patrick with a church built beside a sacred well. The site was most unsuitable, as it was between two branches of the River Poddle, a small river which flows from the Dublin hills northeastwards to join the Liffey. The well of Saint Patrick appears to have flourished until the late sixteenth century. In 1901, however, the site of the well was rediscovered during excavations when the old houses were demolished and the present park, beside the cathedral, was being laid out. A stone slab was unearthed, covering the remains of the ancient well and this slab, probably of the late ninth century, is now preserved in the northwest end of the cathedral.

In the old Irish settlement of Dublin were four churches of Celtic foundation: Saint Bride's, Saint Michael-le-Pole, Saint Kevin's and Saint Patrick's; but following the Danish influence, more and more churches were established as the population grew and the city developed. When Archbishop Laurence O'Toole died in 1180, the Anglo-Norman invasion was already well under way and the foreigners were firmly established in Dublin. Henry II was very anxious to exert his influence over the Irish Church so the rather untimely death of O'Toole was an opportunity for him to appoint one of his most trusted followers. John Comyn was a Benedictine monk from Evesham and had a wide reputation as a learned judge, an able diplomat and a brilliant administrator. Although enthroned as archbishop in England in 1181, he did not in fact land in Ireland until 1184, when his first duty was to make plans for the forthcoming visit of Prince John in the following year.

Saint Patrick's Cathedral (Anglican), Dublin

While John's visit was hardly a success, he did make a number of important grants to John Comyn in order to enlarge and enrich the See of Dublin. When Prince John had departed, Comyn lost no time in imposing his influence and in carrying out the king's wishes to re-organise, where possible, the Irish Church but he was disturbed by the Priory of Christ Church and the fact that he had to reside in a palace beside it. However, he was loathe to displease the local people by altering the monastic character of Christ Church but he refused to live in a palace where he was subject to the jurisdiction of the City Provosts. He solved the two problems by erecting a palace and a church outside the city walls, on his own domain, where he could exercise complete control. He selected the site of the old church of Saint Patrick, beside the well with the sacred association, and rebuilt the church "in hewn stone, in the form of a cross, right goodly to be seen with fair embowed works, fine pavements and an arched roof overhead with stonework." The old name, so much venerated, he retained. The church was dedicated on Saint Patrick's Day, 1192, to "God, Our Blessed Lady Mary and Saint Patrick" and about the same time his new palace was completed, close to the church. This palace, known as St. Sepulchre's, remained the seat of the archbishops of Dublin until 1806 when it was sold to the Crown as a police barracks, which it is still today.

JONATHAN Swift was appointed dean of Saint Patrick's Cathedral in 1713 and his name is indissolubly connected with the history of Saint Patrick's and, indeed, of Dublin.

A tower at the northwest end of the cathedral was part of the thirteenth-century building, but this, including part of the west nave, was destroyed by fire in 1362. Through the energies of Archbishop Minot, the damage was made good and the tower was rebuilt in 1370, still standing supreme on Dublin's skyline after 600 years.

The reason why Dublin possesses two cathedrals of the Church of Ireland may now be apparent, and for many hundreds of years each possessed jointly the rights of the Cathedral of the Diocese of Dublin and Glendalough (Kildare later) and it is not difficult to imagine the arguments which ensued. In 1872, however, the General Synod enacted that Saint Patrick's should become the National Cathedral, having a common relation with all the dioceses of the Church of Ireland with canonical representation in the chapter from each diocese.

The cathedral suffered much over the centuries due to desecration, fire, neglect and wear, and numerous efforts were made towards repair and restoration, although sadly limited by monies available. In the 1850s, Dean Pakenham carried out an excellent restoration of the Lady Chapel but the main cathedral was in a state of decay. But for the re-markable generosity of Sir Benjamin Guinness, who completely restored the fabric between 1860 and 1864, at a cost of about £160,000, the cathedral might not be standing today. Two of Sir Benjamin's sons, Lord Iveagh and Lord Ardilaun, continued the restoration of the interior at the end of the last century, but due to pollution over the years, another major restoration was necessary in recent years and in 1972 work commenced on structural repairs, windows, lighting, heating and further modernisation. Little remains of the old fabric but, in the north choir aisle, two of the ancient capitals can be seen and most of the vaulting of the north and south choir aisles is original thirteenth-century work.

—Victor Jackson

Saint Patrick's Crosses

A custom particular to March 17th in Ireland is the wearing of Saint Patrick's crosses. Nowadays the custom only survives in the badges and ribbons worn by children, but in the past the practice was a common one. The crosses were worn on the right shoulder and consisted of a single or double cross formed of pieces of narrow silk ribbon stitched to a circular disk of white paper, nicked at the edge and measuring from 3 to 4½″ in diameter. At the ends of the arms of the cross a very small bow or rosette was stitched and one a trifle larger at the junction of the arms; the more and the brighter the colours of the silk, the more handsome the crosses were considered.

Jonathan Swift referred to the practice in his *Journal to Stella* on 17 March 1712—"The Irish folks were disappointed that the Parliament did not meet today because it was Saint Patrick's Day, and the Mall was so full of crosses that I thought all the world was Irish."

—Anonymous

A Swift Kick at Jonathan

WHEN Jonathan Swift was appointed dean of Saint Patrick's Cathedral in Dublin in 1713, a contemporary and countryman, Dean Smedley, said that he was "always in jest, but most so in prayer"; but that is an exaggeration, for Swift was mostly in grim earnest. The charge implies that many of his contemporaries had difficulty in satisfying themselves as to when he joked and when he was serious.

Smedley is responsible for a poem directed against Swift, which was posted upon the door of Saint Patrick's when the great writer was appointed its dean. One verse read:

> This place he got by wit and rhyme,
> And many ways most odd,
> And might a bishop be in time,
> Did he believe in God.

IN the Minot Tower, the uppermost chamber is the belfry. The bells are rung on Sundays and other special occasions by the Saint Patrick's Cathedral Amateur Society of Change Ringers, continuing a tradition extending over seven hundred years.

Within the stone image:

THIS STONE
WAS FOUND IS [JUNE] 1901 SIX FEET
BELOW THE SURFACE ON THE TRADITIONAL SITE OF
S⁺ PATRICK'S WELL,
[C.9] FEET DUE NORTH FROM THE NORTH WEST
ANGLE OF THE TOWER

*Saint Patrick's Well stone at Saint Patrick's Cathedral,
Dublin. This stone slab was unearthed in 1901 during excavations beside the cathedral. Probably of the ninth century,
it covered the remains of Saint Patrick's Well, where the
saint reputedly baptized a number of his converts.*

The Glory of Saint Patrick's in Rome

Though Irish communities had existed in Rome for centuries, it
was not until the close of the last century that any move was made to
have a church in honour of the National Apostle, Saint Patrick, erected
in the Eternal City.

The church is designed in fourteenth-century Lombardo-Gothic
style. Its bright interior, with high altar, altar rails and floor of white
marble, has a beauty and dignity that immediately impress themselves
on all who enter it.

Its most striking feature, however, is the mosaic apse depicting
Saint Patrick on the Hill of Tara explaining the mystery of the Blessed
Trinity to King Laoghaire and his court.

This is a work which, because of its scale, its blended colours, its sense of movement combined with unity, excites the admiration of the experts. Its beauty is further emphasised by the green marble that stretches from the mosaic to the floor; hanging like a curtain it serves as a beautiful background to the high altar.

—The Rev. J. F. Madden

Saint Patrick on the Hill of Tara explaining the mystery of the Blessed Trinity to King Laoghaire and his court. Apse mosaic over the high altar, Saint Patrick's Church, Rome.

Six-Hundred-Year Devotion in a German Village

Saint Patrick's Church and shrine at Hohenstade is in the heart of Germany, and it merits a foremost place in any account of Patrician devotion abroad for two simple reasons: (1) It is one of the few places which claim to possess a relic of the Irish saint; (2) it is the centre of a living devotion to the saint which can be traced back for nearly six centuries and is still manifested in an annual pilgrimage which draws thousands of worshippers from the surrounding districts to pray before Saint Patrick's Shrine.

Why a strong devotion to Saint Patrick should have captured the hearts of generations in this part of Germany has never been satisfactorily explained. Undoubtedly it must owe its origin to some long-forgotten Irish missionary who laboured in these parts, but whether he came in the wake of Saint Killian to Würzburg in the seventh century or belonged to the Irish Benedictine houses, the *Schottenklöster,* of which about a dozen were scattered about Central Europe from the 12th to the 15th centuries, is difficult to decide.

—Cardinal Tomás Ó Fiaich*

How Many Saint Patrick's Churches Are There?

Veneration for the saints of the homeland has ever marked the path taken by Irish missionary endeavour down the ages. During the expansion to continental Europe in the early Middle Ages devotion to the saints of Ireland and especially to the three national patrons followed in the wake of monk and scholar and left its mark in church dedications and in manuscripts, some of which have survived till our own time.

The Feast of Saint Patrick was celebrated at Luxeuil and Péronne, both founded by Irish monks in modern France, as early as the seventh century, and the saint had become a popular saint with the country people in Brittany and Southern Germany by the later Middle Ages.

In similar fashion, the second great expansion of the Irish Church in the nineteenth and twentieth centuries to Great Britain, U.S.A., Canada, Australia, New Zealand, South Africa and the Argentine, followed by the missionary movements to the unconverted millions in the Far East and in Africa, dotted these new territories with churches, chapels, parishes and schools dedicated to Saints Patrick, Brigid, Colmcille, Columban, Malachy, Lorcan O Tuathail and a dozen other Irish saints from Saint Patrick's Cathedral, New York, in the north, to Saint Patrick's Cathedral, Melbourne, in the south.

An incomplete list of churches dedicated to Saint Patrick throughout the world compiled in 1932 revealed the enormous total of 461 in the U.S.A., 166 in Ireland, 164 in Australia, 73 in Great Britain, 65 in Canada, besides numerous others in New Zealand, Africa, India, China, South America and the Pacific islands.

The compiler of this list took little account of the European mainland. When to these figures are added those churches which eluded his enthusiastic researches in 1932 and those which have since been erected, the number of churches alone dedicated to Ireland's national apostle must now be close to the two-thousand mark. Add to that the countless shrines, side chapels, altars, schools, hospitals, monasteries, convents [and the twenty-two Episcopal churches named after Saint Patrick in the United States alone],† and one has some idea of the worldwide spiritual empire which Patrick has made his own.

—Cardinal Tomás Ó Fiaich*

* See note page 128.
† Editor's addition.

11 | Patrick in Modern Ireland

PILGRIMAGES

Croagh Patrick

O N the bleak summit of Croagh Patrick, Patrick's Holy Mountain, the saint spent the forty days of Lent in the year 441 in penance and passionate prayer for the people of Ireland. Every year, on the last Sunday of July, pilgrims from all corners of Ireland come to Co. Mayo to follow, often barefoot, the stony path which Patrick himself trod. Close by is the little harbor of Westport from which the emigrant ships left during the Great Famine of the mid-1850s. As the ships pulled out for America, the exile's last glimpse of his native land was this hallowed mountain.

The late Dr. Healy, Archbishop of Tuam, wrote in his history of Croagh Patrick:

> When the skies are clear and the soaring cone can be seen in its own solitary grandeur, no eye will turn to gaze upon it without delight. Even when the rain clouds shroud its brow, we know that it is still

Croagh Patrick, Co. Mayo. Jocelyn, in the twelfth century, wrote: "Crowds of people watched and prayed on Croagh Patrick, believing confidently that by so doing they would never enter the gates of hell, for that privilege was obtained from God by the prayers and merits of Saint Patrick."

there, and that when the storms have swept over it, it will reveal itself once more in all its calm beauty and majestic strength. It is, therefore, the fitting type of Ireland's faith, and of all Ireland's nationhood, which nothing has ever shaken, and with God's blessing, nothing can ever destroy.

—Alice-Boyd Proudfoot

YOUNG FOLLOW NEW STYLE
PILGRIMAGE IN STRENGTH

Croagh Patrick pilgrimages are not what they used to be. Once upon a time the majority of pilgrims started climbing in darkness, eager to be at the summit of Ireland's 2,500-foot holy mountain for the first Mass of the day at 4 a.m.

Yesterday was like the last few "easy" years. Masses were celebrated continuously in the Oratory on the summit from 9 a.m. to 3 p.m., a dozen priests were on hand and there was Confession too.

Even the possibility that some might make it to the Reek and not get religious attention was considered; for those deprived souls, there was a special Croagh Patrick Mass at 6 p.m. in St. Mary's Church, Westport, six miles away.

Croagh Patrick may be softer now but it is still one of our best religious crowd-pullers. No one could quite estimate the crowd yesterday.

The gardai thought 45,000 and some of the priests thought it might be 70,000. Certainly they came from all parts of the country, the strong nasal tones of Antrim and Derry mixing with the soft lilts of Cork and Kerry.

They were in the main young folk and they were outfitted by Mr. Wrangler and Mr. Levi Strauss. St. Patrick, who was there in the year 441, must definitely have loved the young people of Ireland from his even greater vantage point.

Archbishop Joseph Cunnane came along in the afternoon to welcome the pilgrims back from the summit. He says Croagh Patrick year after year is a sure indication that the young retain a strong identification with the Church. He has been noticing the growth in the numbers of younger pilgrims in the past five or six years.

Croagh Patrick also brings out the entrepreneurs, the mineral, chip and hamburger stands and those pushing cheap religious objects.

Predictably the minerals, chips and hamburgers were not cheap. The stiff path up from Murrisk was well-populated with these mobile traders and there were, too, the ubiquitous H-Block protesters with collecting-boxes.

Archbishop Cunnane has a certain pragmatic approach about the commercial activities. "If you get thousands of people and they need food and drink and that food and drink has to be dragged to the top of a mountain by a donkey, then maybe they're entitled to charge a little extra."

The "easy" pilgrimage has been going on at Croagh Patrick for about six years now. Until then the climb at midnight or before was the norm rather than the exception, it was done by a majority rather than a minority.

The piety of former years had a festive accompaniment because there were licensing exemptions in Murrisk. Croagh Patrick, to the old-fashioned purist, may be less rigorous now, but everybody agrees that it is also a quieter, less alcoholic affair. There were not too many bare-footed yesterday.

Father Anthony King, the Administrator in Westport, who was with Archbishop Cunnane, said they counted 15 barefooted people in about an hour.

Yesterday for a few hours, against the magnificent backdrop of Clew Bay, the people of Ireland, mainly young, walked, knelt and prayed where Patrick, their saint, spent 40 days in prayer and fasting.

The pilgrimage yesterday, on a misty and sunless day, was still a spectacular sight. Croagh Patrick deserves the tribute of a former Archbishop of Tuam, Dr. Healy, who said: "It is the proudest and most beautiful of the everlasting hills that are the crown and glory of this Western land of ours."

—Andrew Hamilton, *The Irish Times, Monday, July 27, 1981*

Lough Derg

The Cross of Saint Patrick, recovered from Lough Derg many years ago, is the starting point of the pilgrim's spiritual exercises on the island.

"I am from California," said a flaxen-haired girl of about sixteen years (as I was bandaging the sole of my foot). "Will you countersign these cards, and write the address, Lough Derg, Ireland."

I wrote as directed. When words speak for themselves, do not interrupt.

She naïvely continued: "My Dad made this pilgrimage many times before he left Ireland. Since I was a kid he constantly related stories of it. If I grumbled at my food, clothes or shoes, he always said: 'You would be glad to have these in Lough Derg.' He promised me a holiday in Ireland provided that I came immediately and performed the pilgrimage. So I have to convince him that I am really here at last."

Recently Bob Flint, John Callanan and Ron Flannery, chemists, of Sydney, Australia, purchased a car for £60 in England, came to Ireland; did the pilgrimage and felt terrific physically and spiritually after it. They had worthwhile stories to tell when they arrive "down under" in November.

Similar stories could be told of Irish exiles and their descendants wherever they have settled. They come back to tread this holy ground, to recapture the penitential spirit of their forefathers.

In one recent year 33,269 pilgrims, 435 priests, two Bishops—Dr. Manning of Los Angeles and Dr. Neligan of Ontario—performed it, 1,500 being the largest number there during Whit weekend.

Pius IX, I think, said: "It is the last great virile example of the ancient canonical penances of the Church."

Lough Derg—or the Red Lake—so called from the legend that a monster inhabited the island. Saint Patrick slew it, and its blood reddened the waters.

It is situated in a remote, barren corner of County Donegal, surrounded by heather-clad hills, monotonous and dull—a lonely place, even today, completely cut off from the rest of the world. The pilgrimage opens on the first of June and continues till the 15th of August.

As the boat approaches the island, the pilgrim sees a cluster of five private houses. Four are used by the caretakers and boatmen (but these are to be taken down to make way for a new hostel). The Prior's house; Saint Mary's Church; two existing hostels; and rising supreme like a brooding guardian is the Basilica.

Lough Derg, Co. Donegal

It looks like a floating temple or a giant lantern, octagonal in shape, built solidly of native stone. Hiberno-Romanesque, the style which began with Cormac's Chapel in Cashel. Here begin the Stations.

The first pilgrimage is the easiest. In a hazy way something is known of the various exercises. But to really know and understand, it must be performed.

It is of three full days' duration, beginning with the fast from midnight at home, ending after midnight the third day at home. The journey is made fasting. Pilgrims must be on the island before three o'clock on the first day.

On landing one meets a dishevelled and somewhat windswept crowd in bare feet, walking tenderly: a programme is bought; directions to the hostel obtained; a bed procured; shoes removed.

The walk to the Basilica is the test. If it is raining, the cold gives a kind of electric shock to the system. If dry, the many and numerous pebbles cleave and bore into the feet, and make one walk as sensitively as if walking on eggs. Perhaps the nomenclature "tenderfoot," originated here.

After the visit to the Basilica the stations begin at Saint Patrick's Cross. The rough cement acts like emery paper on the feet, while the dull thud of lake water lapping underneath enhances the impression of being afloat.

Now to the Beds! These were once small, round, beehive oratories. Only the foundations survive. There are six, dedicated to Saint Brigid, patroness of Ireland; to Saint Brendan, the navigator, who, tradition holds, first discovered America; to Saint Catherine; to Saint Columba, Abbot of Iona; to Saint Molaise, a local saint; to Saint Dabheoc, the First Abbot.

Three times walking round each, reciting three Paters, Aves and one Creed. The same recital while kneeling at the entrance of each and similarly while walking around inside and while kneeling at the Cross at the centre.

Remember that these are sloping, serrated flags with pebbles everywhere; that hundreds of people are constantly moving; that you slip and slide, are pushed, and you push; that now your feet and legs and knees and mind cry out!

The Penitential Beds follow, with the same procedure of prayers. Here, probably, was the famous cave where pilgrims descended to make the vigil of old, were locked in at night, and where they allegedly obtained a vision of Purgatory.

Here Saint Patrick had a vision of the torments of Purgatory. Legend tells that the imprint of his knees are on a flagstone there.

Then to Saint Patrick's Cross and back to the Basilica.

Some follow the same procedure of the outside Stations by walking around inside, standing and kneeling while reciting the prayers. At short intervals all go out into the night air to keep the senses fresh. Smelling salts are freely used.

Dawn is watched rising behind Kinnagoe streaking the waves weirdly. Reveille is tolled about 6 a.m. Mass at about 6.30 a.m.

Others, like myself, seek a favourite niche to read or watch the colours change on the hills, watch the endless movement of the water and listen to its ripple against the shore, or contemplate the procession of pilgrims who walked this way before me. The Europeans who came and made such noise of their visions:

In 1147, the Knight Owen, whose account is in the Chronicle of Henry of Saltrey.

In 1275, Jacobus de Voragine, an Italian, includes this in his *Golden Legend.*

In 1397, Raymond de Perelhos, a grandee of Spain, attached to the Court of Benedict XII, and with whose permission he came.

In 1353, Georgius Crissaphen came from Hungary.

In 1358, Louis d'Auxerre arrived from France, and many others. Their accounts survive.

Briefly, they made their vigil in a cave. Here they obtained a vision of Purgatory—a heaving, sulphurous mass, emitting flames day and night, where they were tortured by evil spirits, full of fantasy, made more macabre still in the telling.

To the more practical Irish it is a cure for the seven deadly sins. No one could be proud in old clothes and bare feet. No one could be gluttonous or slothful on an empty stomach. Anger, sloth, envy are unknown.

Here one feels that none may presume on God. Here one knows that no one may despair.

Feet are washed; shoes are worn again, almost awkwardly. Those who looked shabby and poor now look respectable.

It is the final day. And soon we are in the boats. The sun is strong. The fast is hard on the traveller. But there is a special joy in coming home to break it.

And Lough Derg in retrospect? Why, man, once there and you want to go back again next year . . . and the year after . . . and the year after that.

—The Rev. George Quinn

There is the island of Lough Derg in Donegal, where Saint Patrick had his vision of purgatory. An incorrigibly enduring story surrounds this place. It's said that in the twelfth century, a knight in the service of King Stephen of England, crawled through a cave on the island, crossed a bridge and found himself in purgatory. The word spread, and soon pilgrims from many lands were searching for the cave. Finally, Pope Alexander VI ordered the pilgrimage abandoned and the cave filled in. This was done on Saint Patrick's Day in 1497. But soon another cave appeared nearby, and the pilgrims resumed their journeys. Other attempts were made to ban what were thought to be heathen superstition, but it took an act of the English Parliament in the eighteenth century to close the second cave. A chapel named for Saint Patrick was built there, and the island now has a church and hostels for tourists. Still they come.

—Bob Considine

Co. Down: One Day's Visit to Patrick's Holy Sites

John Betjemen says, "When our Lord was on earth He was associated with particular places, and people had to journey to reach Him. The journey itself was in the nature of a prayer, going to see God Incarnate."

And so it is with pilgrims who travel on March 17, as have the faithful for centuries, to those holy places most dear to Patrick. In one day the pilgrim may attend celebrations in Saint Patrick's Church in Saul, where he founded his first church and where he died; in the Cathedral Church of the Holy Trinity in Downpatrick, the site of his burial; and in the Cathedral Church of Saint Patrick in Armagh, where Patrick built a church and decreed it to be his chief church in all Ireland. Nearby are two ruins, one of which is closely associated with him. Up Saint Patrick's Road, a mile from Down, is Struel Wells. The wells are Saint Patrick's Wells, and there is a chair-like rock formation on the side of Struel Hill called "Saint Patrick's Chair."

Stations of the Cross and penitential exercises were performed at Struel for centuries on June 23 and August 1, which would indicate that visits were made to Struel long before Patrick. Those dates are feasts in the Celtic pagan calendar, and the probability is that Patrick found, on his visit to Struel, a ready-made audience to whom he preached and for whom he blessed the wells. Pilgrims came to Struel from all parts of Ireland, and even from England and Scotland in medieval times.

The route of the modern-day pilgrimage would start at:

SAUL

The Church of Saul takes its name from the barn (sabhal) given to Saint Patrick for worship in 432 by a local chieftain, Dichu, the saint's first convert in Ulster. Here he built a church and a monastery was founded; here he died on March 17, 461. It was at Saul that Patrick spent his first winter in Ireland, acquiring a considerable knowledge of the political and social conditions of the country. He was, we might say, getting "the lay of the land" before journeying to Tara to secure the approval of the highest civil authority there and to begin his apostolic campaign for Ireland.

In the ninth and tenth centuries the Danes burned the church at Saul, which was refounded by Malachy in 1130 as an Augustinian priory, a wall of which is still to be seen to the northwest of the present building.

From 1316 until 1788 the church was in ruins, but in the latter year it was rebuilt. The eighteenth-century structure remained until 1933, when it was replaced by the present church.

At Raholp, about a mile from Saul Church on the road to Strang-

Saint Patrick National Memorial, Saul, Co. Down

ford, are the ruins of the Church of Saint Tassach, probably one of the oldest existing stone churches in Northern Ireland. Bishop Tassach, it is said, was Saint Patrick's favorite disciple, and from his hands the saint received the Holy Communion for the last time, shortly before his death.

DOWNPATRICK

Two miles from Saul is the Cathedral of the Holy Trinity of Down. The tradition that Saint Patrick founded it as the Church of Dendalethglass, and that there he is buried, is, according to one Bishop Reeves, so ancient that "he who doubts it may well doubt the very existence of the saint." The large granite slab bearing Patrick's name is a reminder that somewhere in the cathedral precincts he is buried, as were, tradition also claims, Saint Brigid and Saint Columcille.

The Church of Down, like many other Celtic settlements, has its varied history of fame and decay. In the ninth century its school was one of the four great schools of Ireland, but in the next three hundred years it was frequently plundered.

In 1183 John de Courcy, having expelled the Augustinian canons settled there by Malachy, brought from Chester, England, monks of the Order of Saint Benedict for the great cathedral church he built. He changed the dedication of the cathedral to Saint Patrick, and thus it remained until the dedication to the Holy Trinity was restored in the Charter of James I. It was this same John de Courcy who minted silver halfpennies featuring a small bust of Saint Patrick—with "Patricius" inscribed—one of which was discovered at Lismahon Motte, Co. Down.

From its destruction in 1538 the cathedral lay in ruins, and for two centuries the Bishop of Down was enthroned within the naked walls. The work of restoration was begun in 1790 when the former chancel became the cathedral we know today.

"JUST as on some beaches the waves crash louder, so, in some places God's Word rings more clearly."

—Father Marius at the 1976
annual Saul pilgrimage

Armagh

In the year 444 or 445 Saint Patrick, having founded many churches and established many religious communities throughout Ireland during twelve years of missionary effort, came to Armagh. He sought ground for a church from the local chieftain, Daire, and at first had to be content with a low-lying site. Later the chieftain gave him the hilltop Ard Macha, and there Patrick built a church. Two years afterward he decreed that Armagh should have pre-eminence over all the churches in Ireland, and that his church there should be the chief church in the land.

Saint Patrick's simple edifice, built most probably of wattle, must have soon decayed, and the many calamities, through fire and war, from which the city suffered during the next seven centuries—especially during the Danish incursions—made necessary the building of successive churches on the hilltop. The "great church" of Armagh, afterward the cathedral, is first mentioned in the Irish Annals of 839. In 995 it was burned and remained in a ruinous condition until Archbishop Celsus had it re-roofed in 1125. Archbishop O'Scannell rebuilt the cathedral in 1268 with transepts, aisles, choir, and crypt, to its present plan. This building was burned again by Shane O'Neill in 1566; was restored, and burned again in 1642 by Sir Phelim O'Neill. While the ground plan remains unaltered, the only parts of the thirteenth-century cathedral which can now be said with certainty to remain are the crypt, the masonry at the base of the tower, and the lower courses of some parts of the walls.

The cathedral remains the seat of the Primate of the Church of Ireland, Archbishop John Ward Armstrong. His counterpart in the United States is John Maury Allin, Presiding Bishop of the Episcopal Church.

—Alice-Boyd Proudfoot

Saint Patrick's reputed gravesite in Downpatrick, Co. Down, in Northern Ireland. This great slab of Mourne granite, put down in 1899, bears the one word Patric. On it is incised an ancient Celtic grave cross.

ET PERREXIT PATRICIUS (AND PATRICK TRAVELLED ON)

Et perrexit Patricius . . . And Patrick travelled on. . . . One outstanding feature of Saint Patrick's missionary work in Ireland is his extensive journeying through the country. North, south, east, and west, Ulster, Munster, Leinster, and Connacht—history and tradition can follow his footsteps until we must wonder at the zeal that drove him on and the enduring spirit that kept his feet on the road. He was, indeed, no stranger to travel or to hardship. His six years as a slave herdboy on Slemish Mountain in County Antrim was an apprenticeship to wind and weather and want, and his escape from slavery, with its two-hundred-mile tramp to an unnamed port (Wexford, maybe, or Waterford?) where he shipped to France with a roughneck crew and a cargo

of dogs, is material for an epic. Then there were long journeys in
Europe before he returned to face Irish roads (which have improved
quite a lot since his time). Still, there were roads on which one might
make good speed with a chariot and a pair of horses; indeed, the Brehon
Laws then in vogue made mention of furious driving of chariots and
the penalties therefor. Charioteering was not without its risks and dis-
comforts. The saint's horses were stolen in Roscommon and again in
Tipperary. Some people in Kildare went further and dug pits in the
roads, which they camouflaged with branches and sods, but to no purpose, for his equipage passed safely over. On a journey through Laois,
his faithful charioteer, Odhran, induced him to change places in the
chariot and took in his own body the flung spear meant for Patrick.

Often, too, he walked at the head of his little company, as he did
from the Paschal fire at Slane to Royal Tara to face the anger of the
High King and the malice of the Druids and overcome both, as he did
through the ambushed ranks of his enemies (who saw only a herd of deer
passing by) reciting the "Breastplate":

> I arise to-day
> In the power of God for my support,
> In the wisdom of God for my guidance,
> In the hand of God for my security,
> In the shield of God for my protection.

Today we may follow his wanderings into the four corners of Ireland. Killala, where he founded a church. Cashel, where he thrust, by
accident, the point of his staff through the foot of King Aengus, which
the monarch bore without flinching, believing it to be part of the rite
of baptism. Magh Sleacht in County Cavan, where he overthrew the
idols. Aileach in County Donegal, where he stood on the rampart of
the great stone fort to bless Inishowen. We may join the pilgrim thousands at the holy places of his prayer and fasting, Croagh Patrick above
Clew Bay or the island in Lough Derg or walk alone where he walked
on green hillsides like Ardpatrick above the Golden Vale. Or we may
drink water from one of the wells where he baptized his converts, at
Tubberpatrick beside Sligo Bay, at Dunseverick in County Antrim
within sight of Scotland, at Finglas in the suburbs of Dublin or
Singland on the outskirts of Limerick, at Ballyshannon or Ballyelan or
Clonmel or Naas or any of a hundred other places.

He crossed bogs and climbed over mountain passes and forded
rivers. At Bundrowes the fisher-boys were kind to him and he blessed
the Drowes River and gave it abundance of salmon. The same blessing
he gave to the Suir and the Boyne, although it was near the Boyne that
some miscreants stole the goat which was trained to carry his water
jars. Tradition is, however, strangely divided as to the exact place where

this was done. Dwellers on the northern bank are unswerving in their belief that it was on the south side, while among the inhabitants of areas south of the river there is an equally persistent opinion that such an outrage could only occur on the northern side.

We may follow him through place name and legend. Patrickswell near Rathvilly and Patrickswell near Lough Gur, Donaghpatrick near Tuam and Downpatrick where his grave is. At Mullaghatinny, **near** Clogher, a wicked king set savage hounds on him, but the hounds, turning about, ran down and devoured the king. At Armagh he got a gift of a fine bronze cauldron. . . .

And so he travelled about Ireland and so we may follow him, from Saul, where he made his first convert, back again to Saul where, at last, he died.

Et perrexit Patricius . . . et baptizavit . . . et perrexit . . . et aedificavit ecclesiam . . . et perrexit. . . .

—Caoimhín Ó Danachaír

. . . AND TRAVELS ON

From time immemorial maritime craft have been placed under the protection of God through the intermediacy of His saints, so the naming of aerial craft after saints is a natural progression of a custom that has continuing relevance in the era of jet travel.

In the case of Aer Lingus, the national airline of Ireland, the practice has a special appropriateness. Many of the Irish saints after

His Holiness Pope John Paul II arriving at Dublin Airport aboard the Aer Lingus flagship St. Patrick *on September 29, 1979*

whom their aircraft are named were themselves mighty voyagers, crossing dangerous lands and seas on God's business, with little armour beyond His grace and their own zeal. The litany of these saints is a long one, and some names in it glow like stars—Patrick and Colmcille, Killian and Malachy. And because of their teaching not only their names, but the names of saints who never left Ireland are remembered and honoured from the Loire to the Danube and from the Pennines to the Pyreenees. Ireland enjoyed a special place in Europe long before distant travel became commonplace.

The flagship of Aer Lingus—starting with a Douglas DC-3, and now a giant Boeing 747—has always been named after Saint Patrick, the patron saint of Ireland.

—Aer Lingus

SAINT PATRICK THE BULLFIGHTER
(AND THE TALES GO ON)

Very few saints anywhere have so many legends and lore adding to their fame as Saint Patrick, as I was vividly reminded by a fine blind old man I met in Strandhill, a few miles out the sea road from Sligo.

He was probably in his seventies, and sipping his pint in the corner, he could tell you all about the battles he had helped to fight in the First World War, of the great cities and countries he had seen before his eyesight failed. But always his talk would turn eventually to Saint Patrick and to the tales overheard and memorized by the fireside sixty years ago.

"Have you been to Coney?" he asked me. Coney Island is a mile-long grass and sand-dune island in Sligo Bay. When I said I was afraid to risk the journey across the sands at low tide, the old man shook his head in disapproval. "That didn't stop Saint Patrick," he told me. "Do you know that the saint built a road to Coney when he was bringing a mission to the people out there? Four days it took him."

And when Patrick reached the island, continued my friend, he went to a certain woman for his midday meal and asked for a rabbit.

"And do you know what she did?" queried the old man. "She caught a cat and cooked it, and put it down before the saint. Well, now, Saint Patrick always blessed his meat, and when he had finished his blessing, didn't the cat get up and walk away, and that made the saint very angry. He was raging! 'Well, now I have a chance to complete the miracle I was going to work out here,' he said to the woman in a terrible voice. 'And the miracle is that there's never going to be another person with your name on this island for all time.' And there wasn't!"

I asked where Saint Patrick has built his road. "Just near the markers," he told me. "Never a tide would touch it, and there's a little

". . . and that made the saint very angry."

piece of it left, Dún na Pádraig, and no tide can touch that either, even though it's only a couple feet high."

There is, indeed, a tiny grassy hummock, the size of a large carpet, to the seaward side of the line of markers lining the low-water track out to Coney.

"A man still living here can tell you that no waves fly over Dún na Pádraig," the old man continued. "He was coming back from Coney with his horse one night when the waters rose against him, and he just managed to reach Dún na Pádraig, and then he stayed there all night. And no waves came near him!"

Another story the old man told me dealt with a missionary visit by the saint to a village a mile or two from Sligo town. "At that time there were no clocks, of course, and the people depended on the crowing of cocks to wake them up in the morning. Saint Patrick stayed at this house, and asked the woman there to wake him up at cockcrow. Well, didn't the woman let the saint sleep it out, and he was furious. 'To mark this day no cock will crow in this village ever again,' he said in his rage. And no cock has crowed there since. They tried everything. They even brought cocks from India. But it was no use. No cock has crowed there since the morning Saint Patrick slept it out."

Consider this little item and it seems to give a glimpse of a strange pre-Christian Ireland:

"When Saint Patrick first went to Croagh Patrick to begin his work there he found the people all slaves, and the tyrants had a great white bull that they used to cower everybody. Well, Saint Patrick couldn't do anything at all, in spite of all his preaching. The people just wouldn't turn Christian because they knew that the tyrants would send the bull among them. So Saint Patrick went down the hill and right up to the white bull, caught it by the bob and brought it like that to the people. 'Now there's no need to be afraid anymore,' he said, and when the people saw what had happened, and the bull caught by the bob by Saint Patrick, they were delighted and became Christians that very day."

Strandhill, of course, is a part of a district that is rich in prehistoric sites and stones. Almost every skyline brings you reminders of the distant. On top of nearby Knocknarea, for instance, is a huge cairn, eighty feet high, which has been crowning the hill for several thousands of years. A few miles down the road is one of the largest concentrations of ancient tombs in Europe. It's no wonder, in such an area, that Saint Patrick seems like the man who was knocking at the cottage door only yesterday.

It was cold and ghostly with shreds of mist when I finally summoned enough energy to climb Knocknarea. As I struggled across the heather toward the huge cairn I thought I saw a bearded figure in flowing robes sitting on a slab of rock ahead and waiting for me. He turned out to be a friendly archeologist in a plastic mack, but by then I wouldn't have been surprised at anything.

—Jim Edwards

". . . I thought I saw a bearded figure."

Poking Fun

THE treatment of sacred subjects by Irish wits differs from that of most Catholic countries. Saint Patrick is hardly regarded as a conventional saint by Irish humorists, and it is curious that even Saint Peter is accepted as a legitimate object of pleasantry. If, however, Irish humorists occasionally seem to lack reverence for things that are holy in their eyes, "it is only for fun," as Charles Lamb suggested. Only those who are in the closest intimacy with objects venture to treat them familiarly, and the Irish find it easy to joke, without disrespect, of that which is dearest to them. However, only an Irish-*American* could ever have conceived the idea of Saint Patrick as an editor of *Prayboy* magazine.

—Henry D. Spalding

12 The Americanization of Patrick

STRIKE UP THE BAND

Too bad, for the sake of alliteration, that it wasn't March 17, 1717. Actually, it was twenty years later, in 1737, that the Boston Irish jumped the gun on the other American cities that had large numbers of immigrants from the auld sod, and held the first Saint Patrick's Day parade in America. The celebration was inspired that year by the formation of the Charitable Irish Society.

In Philadelphia, the Friendly Sons of Saint Patrick took to the streets in 1780.

Although the first New York parade was in 1762, the laggards were the Friendly Sons of Saint Patrick, who didn't skirl the bagpipes until 1784. An oddity of the New York society was that it was jointly sponsored by Irish Roman Catholics and Presbyterians. The society's first president was a Presbyterian.

—Alice-Boyd Proudfoot

100,000 STEP UP FIFTH IN SALUTE TO ST. PATRICK

Fifth Avenue resounded to the joyful noises of the annual St. Patrick's Day parade yesterday, becoming a wintry canyon awash in green as New York's Irish celebrated their patron saint and themselves.

Saint Patrick's Day parade, 1871. Although there had been Saint Patrick's Day parades in New York as far back as colonial times, they did not begin to take on the nature of a civic holiday until the mass immigrations of the 1840s and '50s. By 1871 New York's annual March 17 parade had been transformed into a lavish extravaganze of floats and banners, without parallel in other cities' parades or, indeed, in recent New York celebrations. Here, passing through Union Square, is a float adorned with maids of Erin and a bust of Daniel O'Connell.

More than 100,000 marchers drove the traffic from the elegant avenue, a fleeting 20th-century parallel to St. Patrick's routing of the snakes from Ireland. For more than five hours, the avenue was filled with marching bands, the primal wail of skirling bagpipes, banners, flags and cheers.

The cheers came from a crowd, estimated by the police at upward of a million, although there was really no way to tell. People stood behind barricades from 44th to 86th Street in weather as changeable as a bagpipe's erratic pitch.

'The 219th Consecutive Year'

It was gray. It was sunny. It was windy. It was calm. Then snow flurries dappled the marchers, disappeared into tubas and chilled the knees of unflappable drum majorettes.

A huge green official program, published by parade sponsors, described the event with an admirable absence of hyperbole.

"Now marching for the 219th consecutive year on the business streets of New York," the program said. "Marched for the first time on March 17, 1762—14 years before the Declaration of Independence was adopted."

There was every sort of green but the green of spring. But somehow, even in the chill, the parade was a harbinger of nature's coming green. There were green hats and canes, green-tinted hair and mustaches. Carnations were dipped in green dye and worn on green lapels and some of the many platoons of soused teen-agers looked a bit green from the excesses of their self-centered debauches.

In the morning, while the traffic still flowed along the avenue, there were preparade parties such as the one at Charley O's on West 48th Street. Here politicians gathered over Irish coffee and huge plates of corned beef hash and eggs, drifting moth-like toward the occasional bursts of television camera lights.

Their shop talk ceased when the St. Columcille United Gaelic Pipe Band from Kearny, N.J., stifled the babble with the sounds of pipers.

"Today's my 45th parade up Fifth Avenue," said Morgan Geoghan, one of the St. Columcille musicians. He is the last of a breed, he said, because the Irish immigration has tapered off and the young are not struggling with the catlike wails a beginner with a bagpipe must face.

"That's the long and the short of it," he said, downing a big Irish coffee. "I came here in the Depression and I married Bridget Bonner from Donegal. Of course she's now Mrs. Geoghan."

Koch's Theory of Irish Origins

For some, the day began with 10 A.M. mass at St. Patrick's Cathedral, its huge Gothic vault jammed with people standing 30-deep in the back. During the service, one could hear a sound like a wave as the vast congregation rose to its feet or moved forward from their seats to kneel.

Outside the merrymakers and the hustlers mingled. One enterprising woman with the Hare Krishna sect wore a green sari and was selling an inedible-looking green cracker to the gullible for $5.

The line of march began at 44th Street and Fifth Avenue, and early arrivals drank coffee at the Thames coffee shop while the bands rehearsed. Mayor Koch, swaddled in a huge green, white and gold scarf on top of a bulky Irish sweater, arrived as members of the St. Gerard Majella drum corps of Hollis, Queens, warmed up, giving it everything they had, which was considerable.

The Mayor held forth on his theory that the lost tribes of Israel settled a long time ago in Ireland and that therefore he was Irish. The crowd loved it, and Mr. Koch's procession up the avenue was greeted with cheers.

Mr. Koch, a politician in the envious position of facing re-election without serious competition to date, walked the avenue with his thumbs up, relishing this early acknowledgment of his hammerlock on City Hall.

Walking with the marchers up the avenue provided a glimpse of another parade, a stationary procession of city faces from every conceivable part of the globe lined up behind the barricades to watch the Irish strut by.

At the cathedral a mighty carillon was drowned out by a surge of drums and bugles. Terence Cardinal Cooke, seated on the cathedral steps, waved to the marchers led by an elegantly turned out band from Bishop McDevitt High School in Wyncote, Pa.

Everyone showed their stuff at the 64th Street reviewing stand, where Governor Carey, wearing several shades of green, sang "Danny Boy" as a band played the lachrymose air.

There was special zest to the contingent from Monaghan in Ireland as it paraded, thanks in large measure to the efforts of Pat McGrory, a Manhattan doorman, who raised much of the money needed to bring the 25-piece Monaghan Community Brass Band to New York for the big do. "I'm a life member of the band," he said. "Isn't it grand."

This evening, the band will serenade the tenants of 77 Seventh Avenue since some of the tenants there helped in making arrangements for the band's stay.

John Duffy, an elderly smiling man, stood at 45th Street, wearing a splendid silk sash and clutching a clipboard. "I'm the one that puts it together," he said, giving the high sign to a contingent to pull out of the side street and get moving. "Sure there's delays, what with the TV and the different paces. But I'll close the gaps." When last seen he was still issuing marching orders.

The tread of feet was to continue for a long, long time up the elite boulevard in a city where at one point in the day Gene Yee's Canton Restaurant was serenading the luncheon crowd with "I'll Take You Home Again, Kathleen," and where hours later, standing under the Hebrew lettering that adorns the facade of Temple Emanu-El, a happy knot of celebrants sang "Come Back to Erin, Mavourneen, Mavourneen."

—By William E. Farrell, *The New York Times,* March 18, 1981
Copyright © 1981 The New York Times.

One enterprising woman with the Hare Krishna sect wore a green sari and was selling an inedible-looking green cracker to the gullible for $5.

"The Lost Tribes of Israel settled a long time ago in Ireland and therefore I'm Irish."

> —*Ed Koch, mayor of New York City, marching in the 1981 Saint Patrick's Day parade, wearing an Irish sweater and green scarf.*

BROUHAHA OVER PARADE DATE

Whoever heard of staging the world's largest Saint Patrick's Day parade on March 14? Faith and begorra! Such a calamitous fate almost befell the 1982 parade in New York City.

The parade committee announced late in 1981 that due to commerical disruptions caused by weekday parades, the biggest and most raucous parade of the year would be changed to the Sunday before Saint Patrick's Day. The decision was made for the "welfare of New York City." It may also have been aimed at discouraging rowdy teeenagers from flocking to Fifth Avenue with their six packs; their annual Rite of Spring has become a source of embarrassment to the Archdiocese of New York and a vexation to the police, many of whom are Irish.

Six days after the jolting story broke on the front page of *The New York Times,* James J. Comerford, the retired criminal court judge who has run the parade for many years, arrived at a meeting of the United Irish Counties. After nearly a week of recriminations "he marched in," according to a spectator, "made one announcement—'The parade will be on March 17'—and marched out again."

Who, after all, could respond otherwise to the outcries of over 350 Irish organizations in New York?

"Don't rain on my parade" is obviously Mr. Comerford's theme song but rain it did, on the 1982 parade. Among those seemingly oblivious to it were musicians and dancers, known as the Patricians, who flew in from Saint Patrick's High School in Singapore to add a new slant to the festivities. Alternating Chinese dances to the bong of gongs and Irish reels to the thump of drums, they were accompanied up Fifth Avenue by a marching band of Christian, Buddhist, Moslem, and Hindu classmates.

Showers aside, the spirits of exuberant young wayfarers were dampened by the presence of a thousand extra policemen who helped deter the youths' anticipated hijinks. Their acceptable, if forced, behavior may make it unnecessary to consider future Saint Patrick's Day parades on any date other than good old March 17.

> —Alice-Boyd Proudfoot

An oval painting, Saint Patrick and the Angel, *on the ceiling of the State Apartments in Dublin Castle*

PATRICK, THE TWO-FISTED
SAINT OF IRELAND

I sometimes fantasize that St. Patrick, surely by mistake, gets invited to a White House prayer breakfast.

There he is in his hair shirt, smelling of wet sheep, peat moss and Irish whiskey, which he is said to have invented, perhaps giving President Reagan a playful poke with his iron-shod bishop's staff or asking the First Lady if she'd like him to clear the garter snakes out of the Rose Garden.

Perhaps he would show the Reagans an old trick he used to dazzle the heathens with—setting snowballs on fire.

In these days of TV preachers with slick suits, lizard boots and $20 hairdos, we need a man like St. Patrick around. He was a Hall of Fame holy man back when it really meant something.

Back in the 4th century, a kid growing up with a name like Magonus Sucatus had to be tough. That stood Patrick in good stead when he was kidnapped by Irish raiders, who, overlooking any early signs that he might be saint material, set him to herding swine.

After six years in slavery, God came to Patrick in a dream. God's advice: "Make a break for it, Patrick."

Patrick escaped and was back in England minding his own business when God came to him again in a dream. God's message: "Go back to Ireland, Patrick."

No fool he, Patrick promptly went to the French Riviera, specifically Cannes. The town was then known for its monks. The topless starlets and film festival came much later.

Patrick became a priest, was promoted to missionary bishop, and given his first assignment—Ireland, where, Patrick wrote, his mission was "to preach the gospel and bear insults from the unbelievers."

The Irish of the day were serious barbarians and dedicated to remaining that way. It was every bit as bad as Patrick remembered—heresy, idolatry, paganism, elf worshipping, and worst of all, the Druids, who up until then had held the local religious franchise.

Patrick set to work, bashing druids, baptizing the heathen, running snakes off the island and, in general, cleaning up Ireland's act.

Saints are generally pictured as thin, wimpy guys with Cocker Spaniel eyes. Patrick, it seems, was more like a one-man motorcycle gang. When Patrick decided to drop in on Miliucc, the slave owner who had put him in with the pigs for six years, Miliucc locked himself in his house and put a torch to it rather than face Patrick.

Patrick could never be invited to the White House because he would make the Secret Service very, very nervous. He was risky to be around. A lot of people close to him seemed to come to bad ends.

One day Patrick got the urge to drive his own chariot so he changed places with his chauffeur, Odhran. Odhran was killed in an ambush because the Druids figured the guy sitting in the back of the chariot had to be Patrick.

One of his followers, Colman the Thirsty, died of thirst because Patrick told him to lay off the hard stuff until dusk. While baptizing a local chieftain, Patrick inadvertently crushed the convert's foot with his crozier. The poor man limped off, bleeding but a Christian.

A hapless Druid challenged Patrick to a trial by fire. The magician ended up getting incinerated while Patrick passed among the congregation signing up new Christians.

We honor this two-fisted saint tomorrow, a day he shares with St. Gertrude of Nivelles, who, Englebert's "Lives of The Saints" tells us, is "invoked against rats, mice, fever, and madness as well as finding good lodging when traveling."

So while you're celebrating hoist one for St. Gert too.

Happy St. Patrick's Day.

—Dale McFeatters, *The Chicago Tribune*, March 16, 1981

SONS OF IRELAND

If there was ever a paradigm for the emergence of the Irish in America, it is in the names of the four people injured Monday by the bullets of a would-be assassin. Reagan, Brady, McCarthy, Delahanty— it sounds like the guest list for the annual dinner of the Friendly Sons of St. Patrick.

McCarthy and Delahanty are in police work. Reagan and Brady are in politics. All four, then, have their feet set on the two ladders that traditionally led the descendants of Irish immigrants out of poverty. And one of them has climbed his to the very top.

Too bad another Irishman, William Butler Yeats, isn't here to comment on the sometimes terrible price of political success in the United States; that same Yeats who often celebrated what he called "the indomitable Irishry."

—*The New York Times,* editorial, April 1, 1981,
after assassination attempt on President Reagan

SAINT PATRICK'S CATHEDRAL, NEW YORK

Saint Patrick's Cathedral was called "Hughes' Folly" when construction started over 120 years ago, a comment on Archbishop John Hughes' decision to locate the church on the rural outskirts of the city. Building it cost twice as much and took four times as long as estimates had predicted, and some critics didn't like it when it was finished. The largest Roman Catholic cathedral in the United States has, however, become firmly established over the past century as a magnetic attraction for visitors, a beloved neighborhood church to thousands of New Yorkers, a building of immense dignity and spectacular beauty, a landmark worthy of the name. Its development over the years echoes and reflects that of its home city.

Certainly, the windows of Saint Patrick's are a stellar attraction.

Saint Patrick's Cathedral, New York

There are seventy in all, most made in France near the cathedral town of Chartres. At varying levels, with the light of early morning or of the evening sun shining through, the stained-glass panels set in the walls of the church are alternately glittering and jewel-like or softly glowing in dusky shades of blue and rose.

Over the south transept door is the storied window dedicated to Saint Patrick, filling the space to the very top of the gable. It is twenty-eight-feet wide by fifty-eight-feet high, and divided into six lancet divisions, in which a series of scenes tell the story of Patrick's life, a sort of epic in stained glass.

The titular window of the cathedral, Saint Patrick's window over the Fiftieth Street entrance, gives his history in eighteen scenes. Beginning at the base of the lefthand bay and reading the scenes upward in lines of three each, the story unfolds.

Ten decades have worked extraordinary changes on Saint Patrick's. Designed as a splendid tribute from man to God, the cathedral was to have been first and foremost a working church. It remains so, but is in addition a stellar tourist attraction as well as a symbol of permanence in a particularly dynamic setting.

—Leland Cook

Of the nineteen bells which greet New Yorkers at eight o'clock each morning, sound the Angelus at noon, and speed city workers from their offices at five o'clock, the largest is named after Saint Patrick. On it is inscribed: *Your Patrick, I; As your sires, so also ye; Ever be, Emulators, imitators of me.*

ALL THIS, HE STARTED

Watch a little girl, face aglow, every ribbon in place, trip off to her First Communion. Walk the hushed corridors of a great Catholic university. Look on while nursing sisters go silently about their tasks in the honeycomb of a big hospital. Step off Fifth Avenue's noisily crowded sidewalk in New York into the silent and breathtaking vastness of Saint Patrick's Cathedral—far from a world ridden by rock-and-roll and Russia, divorce and delinquency—and let the peace of God magically infiltrate your soul. All this, Saint Patrick started, and you can readily see how his name was chosen for the cathedral on Fifth Avenue.

—Bob Considine

"GOOD MORNING AMERICA" TOASTS PATRICK

Top o' the morning, America!

Leprechauns and clover, and the wearin' of the green . . . We've asked Irish stars all over what Saint Patrick's Day can mean.

Peter O'Toole, from London, puts it simply: "I'm going to an Irish pub and I'll have a couple of Irish coffees."

One thing we've been told on very good authority—in the person of Maureen O'Hara—is that in Ireland, all the pubs are closed because it's a holy day. Well, Americans are known for changing rules. Maureen also said, "When I was a child in Ireland, it meant no school, no homework, and we'd all go into the fields and gather shamrocks."

Taking the trip from Ireland to the White House, President Reagan told us, "The Irish, like the presence of God, are to be found everywhere. Even the Reagan family, with roots in Valley Careen, County Tipperary, is rumored to have a home in Washington, D.C."

Merv Griffin flew to the Big Apple, which is green today, to be honorary Grand Marshal of the Emerald Society of New York's Fire Department contingent in today's Saint Patrick's Day Parade, on Fifth Avenue, of course.

Ed McMahon said *he* started celebrating *last Friday* and might take it right through to Saint Joseph's Day on the 19th, when the swallows come back to Capistrano.

And grand old Pat O'Brien said, "Everybody is Irish on Saint Patrick's Day—doesn't matter what race, color or creed. It belongs to the world."

On the other side of the world, in Sri Lanka, where Richard Harris is filming *Tarzan*, he told us: "We could use Saint Paddy here—there are quite a few snakes he could get rid of."

Gene Kelly said, "Saint Patrick's Day is a very *personal* holiday for me and my family. It's the gathering of the clan."

Comic and writer Pat McCormick said, "When I was a kid in the little town of Rocky River, Ohio, the annual Saint Patrick's Day Parade was me, an Irish setter, and a guy who owned five Dennis Day albums."

And, last but not least, Carroll O'Connor had two words of advice for Saint Patrick's Day. And they were: *Don't drive.*

And I wrote a little ditty myself:

> In America, we sing the songs
> And drink to the Emerald Isle
> Some will bring a tear to the eye,
> And some will bring a smile.
> But without a touch of the Blarney,
> I think we all should pray,
> For peace in every Irish home
> On this Saint Patrick's Day.

I'm Ruth—O'Batchelor.

—Ruth Batchelor, ABC-TV News

SAINT PATRICK'S RIVAL—SAINT WHO? SAINT UHRO!

Saint Patrick's Day may never be the same in the upper reaches of the United States. Not if the Finnish-Americans have anything to do with it. They're too exhausted from celebrating Saint Uhro's Day on March 16.

Richard Mattson of Virginis, Minnesota, still laughs at the repercussions of the tall tale he concocted nearly a quarter of a century ago when he created "Saint Uhro."

Finnish-Americans far outnumber the Irish in the northern tier of states and they had had "enough" of Saint Patrick's Day. So Mr. Mattson, tongue-in-cheek, dreamed up "Saint Uhro," patron saint of Finnish vineyard workers, who "drove the grasshoppers out of Finland." Since then the governors of Minnesota, North and South Dakota, Washington and Oregon, have proclaimed March 16 as "Saint Uhro's Day," to be celebrated annually as an officially special occasion. And the saint grows more popular every year.

Sporting green and purple Saint Uhro's Day ribbons, the revellers sing, dance, and imbibe in grape juice, fermented or otherwise. The result, according to James Honkanen, commander of the Knights of Saint Uhro and dean of admissions at Lake Superior State College in Sault Ste. Marie, Michigan, is high-spirited feasts accompanied by shouts of "Herring Go Braugh." He clings to the notion, though, that Saint Uhro evicted not grasshoppers, but frogs.

The late Sulo Havumaki, professor at Bemidji State Teachers College in Minnesota, wrote: "Before the last glacial period the Finnish grape crop was threatened by a plague of grasshoppers. Saint Uhro drove them out of Finland on March 16 with the banishment 'Heinasirkka, heinasirkka, mene taalta hiiten.' Translated that means, 'Grasshopper, grasshopper, go away.' " It worked, of course, and memorialized the saint.

Will the counter holiday to Saint Patrick's Day survive the test of time? Maybe, when even the Irish begin to accept it. Asked what he thought of all the Saint Uhro's Day nonsense, an Irish Catholic priest from the ould sod replied, "In these trying times we need all the saints we can muster."

—Alice-Boyd Proudfoot

Canadian Greenery

WHILE subway stations in the States have succumbed to areosol graffiti resembling a cross between Pollack and Miro, the metro station in Toronto remains as pristine as when it opened thirty years ago. The Saint Patrick metro station, so named for the area in which a large Saint Patrick's church is situated, is painted—well, what else? A strong, clean green.

—Alice-Boyd Proudfoot

Sculpture of Saint Patrick at Saint Patrick's College, Maynooth

Sculpture of Saint Patrick in Washington (Episcopal) Cathedral, Washington, D. C.

WERE HE ALIVE TODAY—
SAINT PATRICK, THE EPISCOPALIAN

Saint Patrick's theology and discipline are reflected in his documents as well as the Christian community he set up. A common but mistaken idea persists—in particular around his feast day—that Patrick was a Roman Catholic. In fact, Roman Catholicism did not evolve until long after his death, nor were its characteristics introduced into Ireland until the late Middle Ages. Were he alive today, he would recognize the Church of Ireland (as the Episcopal Church has always been known there) as his spiritual home. It was an unhappy series of later events that provoked the divisions in the saint's original foundation.

First of these occurred in Dublin in 1038. Between Patrick's death in 461 and this date, many internal changes had come over the Irish Church. Tribal Ireland had given place to organized counties, towns and villages. The old monasteries ceded their power to growing dioceses. Once upon a time the Irish themselves had been invaders; but more recently they had experienced invasion from Danes, Anglo-Saxons and the Scots, many of whom remained to dilute the old Celtic blood and to become part of the Irish Christian community.

A great many of these "foreigners" settled in and near the important town of Dublin. And when in 1038 it was decided to create a diocese for Dublin and Kildare, the Anglo-Irish urged that their new bishop-elect be consecrated by Lanfranc, currently Archbishop of Canterbury. Of course, the English archbishop appreciated this opportunity to extend his influence. But the Celtic Irish were miffed that a bishop on their soil had not given unconditional fealty to the successors of Saint Patrick at Armagh. But when a new constitution was designed for the Church of Ireland in 1152, the Irish Church found itself united to the Church of England just as the governing of Ireland had passed to the British crown. Not every Dubliner accepted Canterbury's control graciously. The Anglo-Irish organized their church life around Saint Patrick's Cathedral. In protest the Celtic or "country" Irish established Christ Church Cathedral as their focus. Interestingly enough, the situation continues to the present day! Ironically, no native Irish clergymen were appointed to the staffs of *either* cathedral until the reign of Elizabeth I—five hundred years later! Church of Ireland leadership was mainly Anglo-Irish.

The *second* major crisis coincided with the reformation of the English Church. The rebirth of learning opened many eyes to the appalling corruption and errant theology which had grown up in the medieval Church. In 1537 the British parliament began suppression of monasteries, including Irish ones. But the act that truly offended the Irish was the promulgation of the Book of Common Prayer in 1549. It has been proposed that had the prayer book been provided for Ireland in Gaelic, the religious reforms would have preserved a united Church. But with seven centuries of political and cultural indignities behind them, many Irish preferred a Latin mass to an English eucharist. In 1570, the Papacy denounced the British reforms, which split the Church of Ireland. A majority of the clergy and a minority of the lay-people remained within the Church of Ireland. But the majority of "country Irish" became instant and fertile fields for Jesuit missionaries.

The Church of Ireland continued organically linked with the Church of England until the year 1870. Thus the *third* major occurrence in Irish Church life was the "act of disestablishment" passed by parliament which had granted certain temporal privileges to the Church for two and a half centuries. In 1922, the newly formed Republic of Eire did recognize constitutionally both the Church of Ireland and the Roman Catholic Church as representation of Ireland's long Christian heritage. Fears that "dis-establishment" and a great exodus of Church of Ireland membership between 1880 and 1930 would cause the Church's disappearance never materialized. Numbers of "Anglicans" did actually decrease sharply in the southern (republican) dioceses. But a reverse trend has laid upon the urban northern dioceses the need to form new dioceses, parishes and church facilities.

Throughout sixteen hundred years the Christian community originally gathered by Saint Patrick has persisted. Our fellow Irish Episcopalians, who belong to one of the oldest national churches in the world, will be found worshipping in ancient buildings a thousand years old or in modern churches completed no more than a few months ago. Never losing its missionary character, overseas Anglican Churches owe much of their origin to adventurous Irish clergy of earlier centuries. Few parishes in the English-speaking world can fail to account for Irish names on the parish list who are emigrants or descendants of emigrants from the ancient Church of Ireland. As we celebrate another Saint Patrick's Day, Episcopalians—Irish or no—rejoice in this legacy of Patricius Magonus Sucat, ex-slave to an Irish king.

—The Rev. Canon Edmund W. Olifiers, Jr.

Epilogue

The Pope's Prayer for Peace in Ireland

I pray with you that the moral sense and Christian conviction of Irish men and women may never become obscured and blunted by the lie of violence, that nobody may ever call murder by any other name than murder, that the spiral of violence may never be given the distinction of unavoidable logic or necessary retaliation.

> —*Pope John Paul II, preaching a sermon in Drogheda, Ireland, on September 29, 1979.*

The Archbishop's Prayer for Peace in Ireland

It takes courage to make positive gestures in the present climate of harsh and sometimes historical rhetoric where appreciation of another's religious tradition without compromise of theological principle can lead to accusations of a "sellout." I should like to pay tribute to all those who are engaged in this work. The courage they show comes only to people who are looking beyond themselves to a future which we pray will be more Christlike, more like the Kingdom which cannot be moved and which Jesus Christ offers to those who follow His way. If we have our eyes on Him, then anything is possible.

> —*Robert Runcie, 102nd Archbishop of Canterbury, preaching a sermon in Saint Patrick's Cathedral, Dublin, on June 4, 1981.*

The Collect
Patrick, Bishop and Missionary of Ireland, 461

Almighty God, who in Thy providence didst choose Thy servant Patrick to be the apostle of the Irish people, to bring those who were wandering in darkness and error to the true light and knowledge of Thee: Grant us so to walk in that light, that we may come at last to the light of everlasting life; through Jesus Christ Thy Son our Lord, who liveth and reigneth with Thee and the Holy Spirit, one God, now and for ever. Amen.

—*Lesser Feasts and Fasts* 1973.

A FINAL WORD

IN reading the lives of the saints we are compelled to observe that the children of God in all ages and in all lands have a strange family likeness. To all of them there is one thing in common—a vivid and impelling sense of a clear and personal call from God Himself. Of this call—come how it may—they themselves have no doubt; and its fulfilment becomes the overmastering power and passion of their lives. In so far as they have obeyed that call, the promise made by God to Abram has been ful-

Saint Patrick overlooks Armagh, scene of Irish religious conflict

filled in them—God blessed them and made their names great. As we think of Abram, of Samuel, of Isaiah, of Paul and of Augustine we may recall in the story of each a vivid moment when God spoke to them and when they were conscious of His call. "Speak, Lord, for thy servant heareth"; "Here am I, send me"; "Lord, what wilt thou have me to do?" So it was with St. Patrick.

What is true of the great and imposing roll of the saints who shine like planets in the firmament of history is true also of the humblest saint whose light may be but that of the smallest star. What the call may be, and how it may come, is of small matter. Great calls are for great souls; small calls are for small souls. What makes the saint is that he hears his call when it comes and then bends all the powers of body, soul and spirit to do what is recognised as the will and purpose of God. It is along the path of sacrifice and of service that true greatness comes and men become a blessing.

The age of the saints has not passed, and no branch of the Church of Christ, which continues to be their spiritual home, can die. In our modern times there shine out great names who heard the call of God to some special Damien, to the lepers of Molokai; Wilberforce, to the slaves; Livingstone, to the dark Continent; Ellice Hopkins, to the prostitutes of the streets. Their lot was toil, isolation, ridicule. To them, as to Abram and to Patrick, the call came to go out into a strange land. They went out in faith. And God did not fail to bless their work and make their names great.

Not only the Church of Ireland, but every Irishman who has been baptised into the Church of Christ all the world over, pays honour to one who had once been a humble slave, but is now and for all time one of the greatest names upon the roll of God's saints. As we read over the story of that life it seems to carry with it a message down fifteen centuries to our own day. St. Patrick had been deeply wronged by the people of this land. By their hands he had been torn from his home as a child and held in slavery. But he never paused to brood over the wrongs done him or nursed the lurking grudge. He sought no revenge, save the revenge of serving those who had wronged him. In the spirit of the great Apostle, he had the grace to forget those things which are behind, and to press on to the better future. In the spirit of his Master, Christ, he set himself to love those who had despitefully treated him. If the people of this land could but catch that fine spirit, to forget and to forgive the wrongs of days gone by, and set themselves to study the task of mutual help and service, then, indeed, we should begin to prove ourselves worthy of our inheritance in the Saint who brought the Church of Christ to Ireland. For to an individual or to a nation, blessing and greatness can come by only one way. And that way is the path along which St. Patrick trod.

—G. A. Chamberlain

TEXT SOURCES
AND PERMISSIONS

Sources and permissions are expressed in their entirety only the first time they appear. Sources are listed in the order in which they appear in the text.

p. 2.   Peter Harbison, "Bronze-Age Settlements." In *Ireland before St. Patrick*. Dublin: Eason & Son Ltd., © 1978. Used with permission.

p. 2.   Will Durant, "Early Ireland." In *The Age of Faith*. The Story of Civilization, vol. 4. Copyright © 1950. Reprinted by permission of Simon & Schuster, a Division of Gulf and Western Corporation.

p. 6.   Douglas J. Gillam, "Ireland is a country . . ." In Max-Albert Wyss, *Irelande*. Neuchatel and Paris: Editions Idea at Calendes, 1954.

p. 6.   Theodora FitzGibbon, "Salmon." In *A Taste of Ireland*. London: Pan Books Ltd., 1950. Reprinted with permission.

p. 6.   Theodora FitzGibbon, "Colcannon." In *A Taste of Ireland*. Reprinted with permission.

p. 7.   Thomas D'Arcy McGee, "The Celts." In Samuel Lover and William Molyneux, *Irish Literature*. New York: P. F. Collier & Son, 1904.

p. 8.   Peter Harbison, "Gold Collar." In *Ireland Before St. Patrick*. Dublin: Eason & Son Ltd., © 1978. Used with permission.

p. 8.   James Hardiman, Esq., "The Destruction of Ancient Records." In *History of Galway*. Galway: Connacht Tribune Pub. Co., 1958.

p. 10.   Clare Boothe Luce, ed., "What Is a Saint?" In *Saints for Now*. New York: Sheed and Ward, 1952.

p. 12.   Alice-Boyd Proudfoot, "How Do You Spell It?" Adapted from *Ireland of the Welcomes*. Used with permission.

p. 13.   John Bruce, "Patrick, Were You Born Here? . . ." In *History of the Parish of West, or Old, Kilpatrick*. Glasgow, 1893.

p. 14.   I. M. M. McPhail, ". . . Or Here?" In *Dumbarton Castle*. Edinburgh: John Donald, 1979.

p. 15.   G. A. Chamberlain, *St. Patrick: His Life and Work*. Dublin: A.P.C.K., 1932

p. 19.   John Bruce, "Place of Captivity." In *History of the Parish of West, or Old, Kilpatrick*.

p. 24.   The Rev. George Quinn, "The Tree That Blooms at Christmas." In Seamus Brady, ed., *St. Patrick*. National Souvenir of the Patrician Year, Dublin, 1961. Used with permission.

p. 29.   Walter Bryan, "According to legend . . ." Reprinted by permission of Grosset & Dunlap, Inc. from *The Improbable Irish* by Walter Bryan, © 1969 by Ace Books, Inc.

p. 32.   G. A. Chamberlain, *St. Patrick: His Life and Work*.

p. 35.   Phyllis McGinley, "Patrick the Missioner." In *Times Three*. New York: Viking Press, 1960. Used with permission.

p. 45.   Walter Bryan, "The Lighting of the Fire." In *The Improbable Irish*.

p. 46.   "The Rune of St. Patrick." In *Irish Literature*.

p. 46.   "The Blessing of Saint Patrick." In Seamus McManus, *The Story of the Irish Race*. Copyright © 1921 by Seamus McManus, renewed 1949. With permission of the Devin-Adair Company, Inc., Old Greenwich, Conn.

p. 49.   "The Lorica of Saint Patrick," trans. Mrs. Cecil Frances Alexander.

p. 51.   St. Patrick, "Deer's Cry." In *Thesaurus Palaeohibernicus*. Cambridge: University Press, 1903.

p. 52.   G. A. Chamberlain, *St. Patrick: His Life and Work*.

p. 57.   H. V. Morton, "The Enchantment of Cashel." In *In Search of Ireland*. London: Methuen & Co., Ltd., 1930. Used with permission of Mrs. H. V. Morton.

p. 62.   R. L., "Cashel." In *The Kilkenny Magazine*.

p. 63.   H. V. Morton, "Climbing Croagh Patrick." In *In Search of Ireland*. Used with permission of Mrs. H. V. Morton.

p. 67.   Walter Bryan, "The early Irish church . . ." In *The Improbable Irish*.

p. 68.   The Rev. Francis C. Lightbourn, "Expulsion." In *The Living Church*, March 15, 1981. Used with permission.

p. 68.   Giraldus Cambrensis, 1187. "There are neither snakes nor adders . . ." *Topographia Hibernica*. In *The Improbable Irish*.

p. 68.   "The Wearing of the Green." Source unknown.

p. 69.   "The Shamrock for Good Luck." Source unknown.

p. 70. Walter Bryan, "Scrambled Shamrocks." In *The Improbable Irish*.

p. 74. Caelius Sedulius, "Invocation." In *Irish Literature*.

p. 80. Seamus Brady, "Patrick the Man." In *St. Patrick*. National Souvenir of the Patrician Year. Used with permission.

p. 85. The Rev. George Quinn, "St. Patrick's Household." In *St. Patrick*. National Souvenir of the Patrician Year. Used with permission.

p. 88. "St. Macartan." Reproduced by permission from Aer Lingus' booklet *The Story of an Airline's Saints*.

p. 89. John Bruce, "His Gospels." In *History of the Parish of West, or Old, Kilpatrick*.

p. 89. The Very Rev. Patrick Eaton, "A Link with St. Patrick's Sister." Used with permission.

p. 92. Patrick C. Power, "The Saint's Curse." In *The Book of Irish Curses*. Templegate Publishers, Springfield, Ill. © by Patrick C. Power, 1974. Used by permission.

p. 95. "An Even-Song." In Kuno Meyer, trans., *Ancient Irish Poetry*. London: Constable & Co., 1913.

p. 95. "Patrick's Blessing on Munster," trans. Whitley Stokes. In Whitley Stokes, trans., *Tripartite Life of Patrick*. Rolls Series. London, 1887.

p. 95. The Rev. Canon N. J. D. White, D.D., *The Teaching of Patrick*. Dublin, A.P.C.K.

p. 102. Will Durant, "Patrick's Character." In *The Age of Faith*. Used by permission.

p. 103. J. B. Bury, LL.D., "He Did Three Things." In *Life of St. Patrick*. London, 1905.

p. 103. Brendan Lehane, "Stealing the Thunder." In *The Quest of Three Abbots*. New York: Viking Press, 1968. Used with permission.

p. 107. John Morris, "Clearing Away the Rubbish." In *St. Patrick, His Writings and Muirchu's Life* (History from the Sources). Gen. Ed.: John Morris; text and translation, A. B. E. Hood. 1978. Permission of Rowman and Littlefield, Totowa, N.J.

p. 108. Allan Hood, "Introduction to Patrick's *Confessio*." In *St. Patrick, His Writings and Muirchu's Life*. Used by permission.

p. 111. Rev. C. H. H. Wright, D.D., "God and Satan, the Great Realities." In *The Writings of Patrick the Apostle of Ireland*. London, 1889.

p. 114. John Morris, "Patrick who had no taste for ecclesiastical politics . . ." In *St. Patrick, His Writings and Muirchu's Life*. Used by permission.

p. 118. Allan Hood, "Muirchu's *Life of St. Patrick*." In *St. Patrick, His Writings and Muirchu's Life*. Used with permission.

p. 122. Brendan Lehane, "The Awakening of Ireland." In *The Quest of Three Abbots*. Used with permission.

p. 124. Sean O'Faolain, "Irish Isolation." In *The Irish*. The Devin-Adair Company, Old Greenwich, Conn. © 1977. Used with permission.

p. 125.   Cardinal Tomás Ó Fiaich,* "A Sixth-Century Irish Monastery." In T. W. Moody and F. X. Martin, *The Course of Irish History.* New York: Weybright & Talley, Inc., 1967. Used with permission of RTE.

p. 128.   "Prayer to St. Patrick," trans. Whitley Stokes and John Strachan. In Kathleen Hoagland, *1000 Years of Irish Poetry.* © 1947 by the Devin-Adair Company, Old Greenwich, Conn.; renewed 1975. Used with permission.

p. 130.   "St. Declan." Reproduced by permission from Aer Lingus' booklet *The Story of an Airline's Saints.*

p. 130.   "The Church Bell in the Night," trans. Whitley Stokes. In *1000 Years of Irish Poetry.* Used with permission.

p. 130.   "St. Brigid." Reproduced by permission from Aer Lingus' booklet *The Story of an Airline's Saints.*

p. 131.   "The Heavenly Banquet," trans. Sean O'Faolain. In *1000 Years of Irish Poetry.* Used with permission.

p. 131.   Maire and Liam de Paor, "The Hermit's Diet." In *Early Christian Ireland.*

p. 132.   Theodora FitzGibbon, "Oaten Honeycomb." In *A Taste of Ireland.* Used with permission.

p. 133.   "Wines of St. Patrick." In *St. Patrick,* National Souvenir of the Patrician Year. Used with permission.

p. 133.   Cardinal Tomás Ó Fiaich,* "Scattering the Seeds—the Missionaries." In *The Course of Irish History.* Used with permission of RTE.

p. 134.   Alice B. Stockdale, "The Holy Seed." In *To Ireland, with Love.* Garden City, N.Y.: Doubleday & Co., 1964. Used with permission.

p. 136.   A. T. Lucas, "Bell Shrines." In *Treasures of Ireland: Irish Pagan and Early Christian Art.* Dublin: Gill and Macmillan, Ltd., 1973, in agreement with UNESCO. Used with permission.

p. 137.   H. A. Wheeler, "St. Patrick's Bell."

p. 138.   A. T. Lucas, "Early Christian Art." In *Treasures of Ireland.* Used with permission.

p. 139.   A. T. Lucas, "Croziers." Ibid. Used with permission.

p. 140.   Jerome Kiely, "An Irish Crozier-Head in Sweden." In *The Kilkenny Magazine,* no. 4, Summer 1961, Kilkenny, Ireland.

p. 142.   A. T. Lucas, "High Crosses." In *Treasures of Ireland.* Used with permission.

p. 143.   "The Celtic Cross," trans. Thomas D'Arcy McGee. In *1000 Years of Irish Poetry.* Used with permission.

p. 144.   John McNeill, "Scriptoria." Reprinted from *The Celtic Churches,* John McNeill, by permission of the University of Chicago Press. © 1974 by the University of Chicago.

p. 146.   Will Durant, "The Book of Kells." In *The Age of Faith.* Used with permission.

* See note page 128.

p. 146. Phyllis McGinley, "A National Obsession." In *Saint-Watching*. New York: Viking Press, 1961. Used with permission.

p. 147. "St. Colmcille." Reproduced by permission from Aer Lingus' booklet *The Story of an Airline's Saints*.

p. 148. Theodora FitzGibbon, "Brotchán Foltchep." In *A Taste of Ireland*. Used with permission.

p. 150. "Columcille the Scribe," trans. Kuno Meyer. In *1000 Years of Irish Poetry*. Used with permission.

p. 150. Brendan Lehane, "Literary Doodles." In *The Quest of Three Abbots*. Used with permission.

p. 150. "The Scribe," a new arrangement by Kathleen Hoagland. In *1000 Years of Irish Poetry*. Used with permission.

p. 151. "The Blackbird," trans. Kuno Meyer. In *1000 Years of Irish Poetry*. Used with permission.

p. 152. "The Holy Man," trans. Whitley Stokes and John Strachan. In *1000 Years of Irish Poetry*. Used with permission.

p. 152. "My Little Lodge," trans. F. N. Robinson. In *1000 Years of Irish Poetry*. Used with permission.

p. 152. Maire and Connor Cruise O'Brien, "Spontaneity." In *The Story of Ireland*. New York: Viking Press, 1972.

p. 153. Will Durant, "The End of the Golden Age." In *The Age of Faith*. Used with permission.

p. 153. A. T. Lucas, "Has the Extent of the Decline Been Exaggerated?" In *Treasures of Ireland*. Used with permission.

p. 156. The Rev. Jack Hanlon, "Patrician Art." In *St. Patrick*. National Souvenir of the Patrician Year. Used with permission.

p. 160. Peter Harbison, "The Oldest Legend." In *Ireland of the Welcomes*, vol. 28, no. 2, March/April 1979. Used with permission.

p. 162. Rev. L. McKeown, P. P., "The Saga of the Shrine of St. Patrick's Hand." In *St. Patrick, 461–1961*. Belfast: Committee for Diocesan Celebrations, June 1961. Used with permission.

p. 163. Victor Jackson, *St. Patrick's Cathedral, Dublin*. The Irish Heritage Series, vol. 9. © 1976 Eason & Son Ltd., Dublin. Used with permission.

p. 166. "St. Patrick's Crosses." Source unknown.

p. 167. The Rev. J. F. Madden, "The Glory of St. Patrick's in Rome." In *St. Patrick*. National Souvenir of the Patrician Year. Used with permission.

p. 168. Cardinal Tomás Ó Fiaich,* "Six-Hundred-Year Devotion in a German Village." In *St. Patrick*. National Souvenir of the Patrician Year. Used with permission.

p. 169. Cardinal Tomás Ó Fiaich,* "How Many Saint Patrick's Churches Are There?" In *St. Patrick*. National Souvenir of the Patrician Year. Used with permission.

* See note page 128.

p. 172.   Andrew Hamilton, "Young Follow New Style Pilgrimage in Strength." In *The Irish Times*, Monday, July 27, 1981. Used with permission.

p. 173.   The Rev. George Quinn, "Lough Derg." In *St. Patrick*. National Souvenir of the Patrician Year. Used with permission.

p. 176.   Bob Considine, "There is the island . . ." In *It's the Irish*. Garden City, N.Y.: Doubleday & Co., 1961.

p. 180.   Caoimhín O Danachair, "Et Perrexit Patricius." In *Ireland of the Welcomes*. March/April 1958. Used with permission.

p. 182.   ". . . And Travels On." Reproduced by permission from Aer Lingus' booklet *The Story of an Airline's Saints*.

p. 183.   Jim Edwards, "Saint Patrick the Bullfighter." In *Ireland of the Welcomes*. March/April 1964. Used with permission.

p. 185.   Henry D. Spalding, "Poking Fun." In *The Lilt of the Irish: An Encyclopedia of Irish Folklore and Humor*. Middle Village, N.Y.: Jonathan David Pub., 1978.

p. 186.   William E. Farrell, "100,000 Step Up Fifth Avenue in Salute to St. Patrick." *The New York Times*, March 18, 1981. © by The New York Times Company. Reprinted by permission.

p. 191.   Dale McFeatters, "Patrick, the Two-Fisted Saint of Ireland." *The Chicago Tribune*, March 17, 1981. By permission of Scripps-Howard News Service.

p. 193.   "Sons of Ireland." Editorial in *The New York Times*, April 1, 1981. © by The New York Times Company. Reprinted by permission.

p. 193.   Leland Cook, "St. Patrick's Cathedral, New York." Excerpt from *St. Patrick's Cathedral*, copyright © Leland A. Cook 1979. Copyright Quick Fox Press 1979. Used with permission.

p. 195.   Bob Considine, "All This, He Started." In *It's the Irish*.

p. 195.   Ruth Batchelor, " 'Good Morning America' Toasts St. Patrick." March 17, 1981. American Broadcasting Companies, Inc. Used with permission.

p. 199.   The Rev. Canon Edmund W. Olifiers, Jr., "Were He Alive Today— Saint Patrick, the Episcopalian." In *The Bonifacian*, March 1981. Used with permission.

p. 201.   Pope John Paul II, "Prayer for Peace in Ireland."

p. 201.   Robert Runcie, Archbishop of Canterbury, "Prayer for Peace in Ireland."

p. 202.   *The Collect:* Patrick, Bishop and Missionary of Ireland, 461. In *Lesser Feasts and Fasts*. Copyright 1973 by Charles Mortimer Guilbert as Custodian of *The Standard Book of Common Prayer*. The Church Hymnal Corporation. Used with permission.

p. 202.   G. A. Chamberlain, "A Final Word." In *St. Patrick: His Life and Work*.

ILLUSTRATION SOURCES
AND PERMISSIONS

p. 58. The Rock of Cashel. Used with permission of the Commissioners of Public Works in Ireland.

p. 65. *Saint Patrick on Croagh Patrick*. Painting by Margaret Clarke, R.H.A. (1888–1961). Courtesy, the Hugh Lane Municipal Gallery of Modern Art, Dublin. Used with permission of the artist's family.

p. 69. Saint Patrick on Wedgwood plate. Used with permission of Wedgwood.

p. 81. *Saint Patrick in the Act of Confirmation*. Sketch for a painting by The Rev. Jack Hanlon. From *St. Patrick*. National Souvenir of the Patrician Year 1961. Used with permission.

p. 89. Fragment of Saint Patrick's copy of the Gospels. In *Codices Latini Antiquiores*, Part 2, edited by E. A. Lowe. Second edition published by Oxford University Press. © Oxford University Press, 1972. Used with permission.

p. 90. Four-sided pillar. Photograph by the Very Rev. Patrick Eaton. Used with permission.

p. 91. St. Patrick's Church (Teampull Padraig). Photograph by the Very Rev. Patrick Eaton. Used with permission.

p. 95. Ogham Stone. Used with permission of the Commissioners of Public Works in Ireland.

p. 105. Marble statue of Saint Patrick in Saint Patrick's Cathedral, New York. From Leland Cook, *St. Patrick's Cathedral*, copyright © Leland A. Cook, 1979. Copyright © Quick Fox Press 1979. Used with permission.

p. 109. Opening page of Saint Patrick's *Confessio*. Used with permission of the board of Trinity College, Dublin.

p. 113. Drawing by Sally Stockdale. Used with permission.

p. 116. Ancient stone tablet of Saint Patrick. Used with permission of the Very Rev. Michael Frawley.

p. 119. Drawing by Sally Stockdale. Used with permission.

p. 123. Gallarus Oratory. Used with permission of the Commissioners of Public Works in Ireland.

p. 126. Monastery of Sceilg Mhichil. Used with permission of the Commissioners of Public Works in Ireland.

p. 129. Ardmore Round Tower. Used with permission of Bord Fáilte.

p. 137. Shrine of Saint Patrick's Bell. National Museum of Ireland. Used with permission.

p. 139. Lismore Crozier. National Museum of Ireland. Used with permission.

p. 142. Cross of Patrick and Columba. Used with permission of the Commissioners of Public Works in Ireland.

p. 145. Drawing by Sally Stockdale. Used with permission.

p. 149. The "Cathach" of Saint Columba. Royal Irish Academy. Used with permission.

p. 154. Stained-glass window of Saint Patrick. From Leland Cook, *St. Patrick's Cathedral,* copyright © Leland A. Cook 1979. Copyright © Quick Fox Press 1979. Used with permission.

p. 157. *I Am Patrick.* Painting by Sister Aloysius McVeigh in 1981. Used with permission of the artist. The original is located at Saint Patrick's Missionary Society, Kiltegan, Co. Wicklow. Copyright © Saint Patrick's Missionary Society.

p. 160. "Saint Patrick's Money." © National Museum of Ireland. Used with permission.

p. 161. Oldest known painting of Saint Patrick. The Huntington Library & Art Gallery, San Marino, California. Used with permission.

p. 164. Saint Patrick's Cathedral, Dublin. From Victor Jackson, *St. Patrick's Cathedral, Dublin.* The Irish Heritage Series, vol. 9. © 1976 Eason & Son Ltd., Dublin. Used with permission.

p. 167. Saint Patrick's Well stone. From Victor Jackson, *St. Patrick's Cathedral, Dublin.* Used with permission.

p. 168. St. Patrick on the Hill of Tara. Used with permission of Saint Patrick's Church, Rome.

p. 171. Saint Patrick statue at Croagh Patrick. Used with permission of Bord Fáilte.

p. 174. Lough Derg. Used with permission of Bord Fáilte.

p. 178. Saint Patrick National Memorial. Photograph by D. J. McNeill. Used with permission.

p. 180. Saint Patrick's reputed gravesite. Photograph by D. J. McNeill. Used with permission.

p. 182. Pope John Paul II. Photograph from Aer Lingus. Used with permission.

p. 184. Drawing. *From Ireland of the Welcomes.* Used with permission.

p. 185. Drawing. *From Ireland of the Welcomes.* Used with permission.

p. 187. Saint Patrick's Day parade, 1871. Museum of the City of New York. Used with permission.

p. 191. *St. Patrick and the Angel.* Used with permission of the Commissioners of Public Works in Ireland.

p. 194. Saint Patrick's Cathedral, New York. From Leland Cook, *St. Patrick's Cathedral.* Photograph by David Frazier. Used with permission.

p. 198. Saint Patrick statue. One of the Saints of All Nations series in the south outer aisle of Washington Cathedral, Washington, D. C., by Marion Brackenridge. Photo by H. Byron Chambers. Used with permission of Washington Cathedral.

p. 198. Sculpture of Saint Patrick. By Seamus Murphy, at Saint Patrick's College, Maynooth, Ireland. Used with permission.

p. 202. Saint Patrick overlooks Armagh. Religious News Service. Used with permission.